W9-BND-314

UNOBTRUSIVE MEASURES

Nonreactive Research in the Social Sciences

UNOBTRUSIVE MEASURES

Nonreactive Research in the Social Sciences

EUGENE J. WEBB
Stanford University

DONALD T. CAMPBELL
Northwestern University

RICHARD D. SCHWARTZ
State University of New York

LEE SECHREST
Northwestern University

Rand McNally College Publishing Company/Chicago

Rand McNally Sociology Series

Edgar F. Borgatta, *Advisory Editor*

Current printing (last digit)
15   14   13   12   11   10

Contents

We have included all of Beauvoir's footnotes, and we have added notes of our own when we felt an explanation was necessary. Among other things, they indicate errors in Beauvoir's text and discrepancies such as erroneous dates. We corrected misspellings of names without noting them. Beauvoir sometimes puts into quotes passages that she is partially or completely paraphrasing. We generally left them that way. The reader will notice that titles of the French books she cites are given in French, followed by their translation in English. The translation is in italics if it is in a published English-language edition; it is in roman if it is our translation. We supply the sources of the English translations of the authors Beauvoir cites at the end of the book.

We did not, however, facilitate the reading by explaining arcane references or difficult philosophical language. As an example of the former, in Part Three of Volume II, "Justifications," there is a reference to Cécile Sorel breaking the glass of a picture frame holding a caricature of her by an artist named Bib. The reference might have been as obscure in 1949 as it is today.

Our notes do not make for an annotated version of the translation, yet we understand the value such a guide would have for both the teacher and the individual reading it on their own. We hope one can be written now that this more precise translation exists.

These are but a few of the issues we dealt with. We had instructive discussions with generous experts about these points and listened to many (sometimes contradictory) opinions; but in the end, the final decisions as to how to treat the translation were ours.

It is generally agreed that one of the most serious absences in the first translation was Simone de Beauvoir the philosopher. Much work has been done on reclaiming, valorizing, and expanding upon her role as philosopher since the 1953 publication, thanks to the scholarship of Margaret Simons, Eva Lundgren-Gothlin, Michèle Le Doeuff, Elizabeth Fallaize, Emily Grosholz, Sonia Kruks, and Ingrid Galster, to mention only a few. We were keenly aware of the need to put the philosopher back into her text. To transpose her philosophical style and voice into English was the most crucial task we faced.

The first English-language translation did not always recognize the philosophical terminology in *The Second Sex*. Take the crucial word "authentic," meaning "to be in good faith." As Toril Moi points out, Parshley changed it into "real, genuine, and true." The distinctive existentialist term *pour-soi*, usually translated as "for-itself" (*pour-soi* referring to human consciousness), became "her true nature in itself." Thus, Parshley's "being-in-itself" (*en-soi*, lacking human consciousness) is a reversal of

Simone de Beauvoir's meaning. Margaret Simons and Toril Moi have unearthed and brought to light many other examples, such as the use of "alienation," "alterity," "subject," and the verb "to posit," which are by now well documented. One particularly striking example is the title of Volume II; "*L'expérience vécue*" ("Lived Experience") was translated as "Woman's Life Today," weakening the philosophical tenor of the French.

The Second Sex is a philosophical treatise and one of the most important books of the twentieth century, upon which much of the modern feminist movement was built. Beauvoir the philosopher is present right from the start of the book, building on the ideas of Hegel, Marx, Kant, Heidegger, Husserl, and others. She developed, shared, and appropriated these concepts alongside her equally brilliant contemporaries Sartre, Merleau-Ponty, and Lévi-Strauss, who were redefining philosophy to fit the times. Before it was published, Beauvoir read Lévi-Strauss's *Elementary Structures of Kinship* and learned from and used those ideas in *The Second Sex*. Although the ideas and concepts are challenging, the book was immediately accepted by a general readership. Our goal in this translation has been to conform to the same ideal in English: to say what Simone de Beauvoir said as close to the way she said it, in a text both readable and challenging.

Throughout our work, we were given the most generous help from the many experts we consulted. In every area Simone de Beauvoir delved into, whether in psychoanalysis, biology, anthropology, or philosophy, they helped us to produce the most authentic English version of her work. We thank them profusely.

We owe a debt of gratitude to the indomitable Anne-Solange Noble of Editions Gallimard, who for years believed in this retranslation project. Anne-Solange begged, badgered, and persuaded ("I shall never surrender!") until she found the editor who was willing to take on the monumental task. That exceptional person is Ellah Allfrey of Jonathan Cape, a patient and superb editor who astutely worked with us step-by-step for three years, strongly supported by LuAnn Walther of Knopf. Anne-Solange introduced us to Sylvie Le Bon de Beauvoir, Simone de Beauvoir's adopted daughter, and our relationship has been a very special one ever since that first lunch on the rue du Bac, where we four toasted the moment with "*Vive le point-virgule!*" ("Long live the semicolon!")

The feminist scholar Ann Shteir, our Douglass College friend and classmate, and now professor of humanities and women's studies at York University, Toronto, Canada, was always available to provide source material and to solve problematic issues, often many times a week. She, like we, felt that no task was too great to repay the debt women—and the world—

owe to Simone de Beauvoir. Michael Mosher and Daniel Hoffman-Schwartz were extremely helpful with philosophical language and concepts. Gabrielle Spiegel and her generous colleagues took on the esoteric research required for the "History" chapters, notably the passages on the French Middle Ages, on which Gaby is a leading expert. James Lawler, the distinguished professor, merits our heartfelt gratitude for retranslating, specially for this edition, the Paul Claudel extracts with such elegance and grace. Our thanks to Beverley Bie Brahic for her translations of Francis Ponge, Michel Leiris, and Cécile Sauvage; Kenneth Haltman for Gaston Bachelard; Raymond MacKenzie for François Mauriac and others; Zack Rogow and Mary Ann Caws for Breton; Gillian Spraggs for Renée Vivien. Richard Pevear and Larissa Volokhonsky allowed us the special privilege of using parts of their magnificent translation of *War and Peace* before the edition appeared in 2008; their views on translation were an inspiration to us. Donald Fanger helped us with Sophia Tolstoy's diaries.

Many writers, translators, researchers, friends, colleagues, and strangers who became friends unfailingly contributed their expertise: Eliane Lecarme-Tabone, Mireille Perche, Claire Brisset, Mathilde Ferrer, David Tepfer, Marie-Victoire Louis, Virginia Larner, Nina de Voogd Fuller, Stephanie Baumann, Jane Couchman, Catherine Legault, Robert Lerner, Richard Sieburth, Sandra Bermann, Gérard Bonal, Lia Poorvu, Leila May-Landy, Karen Offen, Sybil Pollet, Janet Bodner, our copy editors, Beth Humphries and Ingrid Sterner, and our indexer, Cohen Carruth, Inc.

Our husbands, Bill Chevallier and Dominique Borde, were among our staunchest and most reliable partners, living out the difficult passages with us, helping us overcome obstacles (and exhaustion), and also sharing the joy and elation of the life-changing discoveries the text held for us.

Very special thanks go to our expert readers. Our official reader, Mary Beth Mader, authority par excellence in French and the philosophical language of Simone de Beauvoir, enriched our text with her insights and corrections; Margaret Simons, showing no end to her boundless generosity, "tested" our texts on her students and came back to us with meticulous perceptions and corrections; Marilyn Yalom, Susan Suleiman, and Elizabeth Fallaize, with all of the discernment for which they are renowned, explored chapters with a fine-tooth comb and gave us a heightened understanding of *The Second Sex* for which we will ever be grateful.

And now it is for English readers to discover, learn, and live Simone de Beauvoir's message of freedom and independence.

| VOLUME I |

Facts and Myths

Introduction

I hesitated a long time before writing a book on woman. The subject is irritating, especially for women; and it is not new. Enough ink has flowed over the quarrel about feminism; it is now almost over: let's not talk about it anymore. Yet it is still being talked about. And the volumes of idiocies churned out over this past century do not seem to have clarified the problem. Besides, is there a problem? And what is it? Are there even women? True, the theory of the eternal feminine still has its followers; they whisper, "Even in Russia, *women* are still very much women"; but other well-informed people—and also at times those same ones—lament, "Woman is losing herself, woman is lost." It is hard to know any longer if women still exist, if they will always exist, if there should be women at all, what place they hold in this world, what place they should hold. "Where are the women?" asked a short-lived magazine recently.[1] But first, what is a woman? "*Tota mulier in utero:* she is a womb," some say. Yet speaking of certain women, the experts proclaim, "They are not women," even though they have a uterus like the others. Everyone agrees there are females in the human species; today, as in the past, they make up about half of humanity; and yet we are told that "femininity is in jeopardy"; we are urged, "Be women, stay women, become women." So not every female human being is necessarily a woman; she must take part in this mysterious and endangered reality known as femininity. Is femininity secreted by the ovaries? Is it enshrined in a Platonic heaven? Is a frilly petticoat enough to bring it down to earth? Although some women zealously strive to embody it, the model has never been patented. It is typically described in vague and shimmering terms borrowed from a clairvoyant's vocabulary. In Saint Thomas's time it was an essence defined with as much certainty as the seda-

---

1. Out of print today, titled *Franchise*.

tive quality of a poppy. But conceptualism has lost ground: biological and social sciences no longer believe there are immutably determined entities that define given characteristics like those of the woman, the Jew, or the black; science considers characteristics as secondary reactions to a *situation*. If there is no such thing today as femininity, it is because there never was. Does the word "woman," then, have no content? It is what advocates of Enlightenment philosophy, rationalism, or nominalism vigorously assert: women are, among human beings, merely those who are arbitrarily designated by the word "woman"; American women in particular are inclined to think that woman as such no longer exists. If some backward individual still takes herself for a woman, her friends advise her to undergo psychoanalysis to get rid of this obsession. Referring to a book—a very irritating one at that—*Modern Woman: The Lost Sex*, Dorothy Parker wrote: "I cannot be fair about books that treat women as women. My idea is that all of us, men as well as women, whoever we are, should be considered as human beings." But nominalism is a doctrine that falls a bit short; and it is easy for antifeminists to show that women *are* not men. Certainly woman like man is a human being; but such an assertion is abstract; the fact is that every concrete human being is always uniquely situated. To reject the notions of the eternal feminine, the black soul, or the Jewish character is not to deny that there are today Jews, blacks, or women: this denial is not a liberation for those concerned but an inauthentic flight. Clearly, no woman can claim without bad faith to be situated beyond her sex. A few years ago, a well-known woman writer refused to have her portrait appear in a series of photographs devoted specifically to women writers. She wanted to be included in the men's category; but to get this privilege, she used her husband's influence. Women who assert they are men still claim masculine consideration and respect. I also remember a young Trotskyite standing on a platform during a stormy meeting, about to come to blows in spite of her obvious fragility. She was denying her feminine frailty; but it was for the love of a militant man she wanted to be equal to. The defiant position that American women occupy proves they are haunted by the feeling of their own femininity. And the truth is that anyone can clearly see that humanity is split into two categories of individuals with manifestly different clothes, faces, bodies, smiles, movements, interests, and occupations; these differences are perhaps superficial; perhaps they are destined to disappear. What is certain is that for the moment they exist in a strikingly obvious way.

If the female function is not enough to define woman, and if we also reject the explanation of the "eternal feminine," but if we accept, even temporarily, that there are women on the earth, we then have to ask: What is a woman?

Merely stating the problem suggests an immediate answer to me. It is significant that I pose it. It would never occur to a man to write a book on the singular situation of males in humanity.[2] If I want to define myself, I first have to say, "I am a woman"; all other assertions will arise from this basic truth. A man never begins by positing himself as an individual of a certain sex: that he is a man is obvious. The categories masculine and feminine appear as symmetrical in a formal way on town hall records or identification papers. The relation of the two sexes is not that of two electrical poles: the man represents both the positive and the neuter to such an extent that in French *hommes* designates human beings, the particular meaning of the word *vir* being assimilated into the general meaning of the word "homo." Woman is the negative, to such a point that any determination is imputed to her as a limitation, without reciprocity. I used to get annoyed in abstract discussions to hear men tell me: "You think such and such a thing because you're a woman." But I know my only defense is to answer, "I think it because it is true," thereby eliminating my subjectivity; it was out of the question to answer, "And you think the contrary because you are a man," because it is understood that being a man is not a particularity; a man is in his right by virtue of being man; it is the woman who is in the wrong. In fact, just as for the ancients there was an absolute vertical that defined the oblique, there is an absolute human type that is masculine. Woman has ovaries and a uterus; such are the particular conditions that lock her in her subjectivity; some even say she thinks with her hormones. Man vainly forgets that his anatomy also includes hormones and testicles. He grasps his body as a direct and normal link with the world that he believes he apprehends in all objectivity, whereas he considers woman's body an obstacle, a prison, burdened by everything that particularizes it. "The female is female by virtue of a certain *lack* of qualities," Aristotle said. "We should regard women's nature as suffering from natural defectiveness." And Saint Thomas in his turn decreed that woman was an "incomplete man," an "incidental" being. This is what the Genesis story symbolizes, where Eve appears as if drawn from Adam's "supernumerary" bone, in Bossuet's words. Humanity is male, and man defines woman, not in herself, but in relation to himself; she is not considered an autonomous being. "Woman, the relative being," writes Michelet. Thus Monsieur Benda declares in *Le*

2. The Kinsey Report, for example, confines itself to defining the sexual characteristics of the American man, which is completely different.

rapport d'Uriel (Uriel's Report): "A man's body has meaning by itself, disregarding the body of the woman, whereas the woman's body seems devoid of meaning without reference to the male. Man thinks himself without woman. Woman does not think herself without man." And she is nothing other than what man decides; she is thus called "the sex," meaning that the male sees her essentially as a sexed being; for him she is sex, so she is it in the absolute. She is determined and differentiated in relation to man, while he is not in relation to her; she is the inessential in front of the essential. He is the Subject; he is the Absolute. She is the Other.[3]

The category of *Other* is as original as consciousness itself. The duality between Self and Other can be found in the most primitive societies, in the most ancient mythologies; this division did not always fall into the category of the division of the sexes, it was not based on any empirical given: this comes out in works like Granet's on Chinese thought, and Dumézil's on India and Rome. In couples such as Varuna–Mitra, Uranus–Zeus, Sun–Moon, Day–Night, no feminine element is involved at the outset; neither in Good–Evil, auspicious and inauspicious, left and right, God and Lucifer; alterity is the fundamental category of human thought. No group ever defines itself as One without immediately setting up the Other opposite itself. It only takes three travelers brought together by chance in the same train compartment for the rest of the travelers to become vaguely hostile "others." Village people view anyone not belonging to the village as suspicious "others." For the native of a country inhabitants of other countries are viewed as "foreigners"; Jews are the "others" for anti-Semites, blacks for racist Americans, indigenous people for colonists, proletarians for the propertied classes. After studying the diverse forms of primitive

---

3. This idea has been expressed in its most explicit form by E. Levinas in his essay *Le temps et l'autre* (*Time and the Other*). He expresses it like this: "Is there not a situation where alterity would be borne by a being in a positive sense, as essence? What is the alterity that does not purely and simply enter into the opposition of two species of the same genus? I think that the absolutely contrary contrary, whose contrariety is in no way affected by the relationship that can be established between it and its correlative, the contrariety that permits its terms to remain absolutely other, is the feminine. Sex is not some specific difference . . . Neither is the difference between the sexes a contradiction . . . Neither is the difference between the sexes the duality of two complementary terms, for two complementary terms presuppose a preexisting whole . . . [A]lterity is accomplished in the feminine. The term is on the same level as, but in meaning opposed to, consciousness." I suppose Mr. Levinas is not forgetting that woman also is consciousness for herself. But it is striking that he deliberately adopts a man's point of view, disregarding the reciprocity of the subject and the object. When he writes that woman is mystery, he assumes that she is mystery for man. So this apparently objective description is in fact an affirmation of masculine privilege.

society in depth, Lévi-Strauss could conclude: "The passage from the state of Nature to the state of Culture is defined by man's ability to think biological relations as systems of oppositions; duality, alternation, opposition, and symmetry, whether occurring in defined or less clear form, are not so much phenomena to explain as fundamental and immediate givens of social reality."[4] These phenomena could not be understood if human reality were solely a *Mitsein** based on solidarity and friendship. On the contrary, they become clear if, following Hegel, a fundamental hostility to any other consciousness is found in consciousness itself; the subject posits itself only in opposition; it asserts itself as the essential and sets up the other as inessential, as the object.

But the other consciousness has an opposing reciprocal claim: traveling, a local is shocked to realize that in neighboring countries locals view him as a foreigner; between villages, clans, nations, and classes there are wars, potlatches, agreements, treaties, and struggles that remove the absolute meaning from the idea of the *Other* and bring out its relativity; whether one likes it or not, individuals and groups have no choice but to recognize the reciprocity of their relation. How is it, then, that between the sexes this reciprocity has not been put forward, that one of the terms has been asserted as the only essential one, denying any relativity in regard to its correlative, defining the latter as pure alterity? Why do women not contest male sovereignty? No subject posits itself spontaneously and at once as the inessential from the outset; it is not the Other who, defining itself as Other, defines the One; the Other is posited as Other by the One positing itself as One. But in order for the Other not to turn into the One, the Other has to submit to this foreign point of view. Where does this submission in woman come from?

There are other cases where, for a shorter or longer time, one category has managed to dominate another absolutely. It is often numerical inequality that confers this privilege: the majority imposes its law on or persecutes the minority. But women are not a minority like American blacks, or like Jews: there are as many women as men on the earth. Often, the two opposing groups concerned were once independent of each other; either they were not aware of each other in the past, or they accepted each other's

4. See Claude Lévi-Strauss, *Les structures élémentaires de la parenté* (*The Elementary Structures of Kinship*). I thank Claude Lévi-Strauss for sharing the proofs of his thesis, which I drew on heavily, particularly in the second part, pp. 76–89.

Mitsein can be translated as "being with." The French term *réalité humaine* (human reality) has been problematically used to translate Heidegger's *Dasein*.—TRANS.

autonomy; and some historical event subordinated the weaker to the stronger: the Jewish Diaspora, slavery in America, and the colonial conquests are facts with dates. In these cases, for the oppressed there was a *before:* they share a past, a tradition, sometimes a religion, or a culture. In this sense, the parallel Bebel draws between women and the proletariat would be the best founded: proletarians are not a numerical minority either, and yet they have never formed a separate group. However, not *one* event but a whole historical development explains their existence as a class and accounts for the distribution of *these* individuals in this class. There have not always been proletarians: there have always been women; they are women by their physiological structure; as far back as history can be traced, they have always been subordinate to men; their dependence is not the consequence of an event or a becoming, it did not *happen.* Alterity here appears to be an absolute, partly because it falls outside the accidental nature of historical fact. A situation created over time can come undone at another time—blacks in Haiti for one are a good example; on the contrary, a natural condition seems to defy change. In truth, nature is no more an immutable given than is historical reality. If woman discovers herself as the inessential and never turns into the essential, it is because she does not bring about this transformation herself. Proletarians say "we." So do blacks. Positing themselves as subjects, they thus transform the bourgeois or whites into "others." Women—except in certain abstract gatherings such as conferences—do not use "we"; men say "women," and women adopt this word to refer to themselves; but they do not posit themselves authentically as Subjects. The proletarians made the revolution in Russia, the blacks in Haiti, the Indo-Chinese are fighting in Indochina. Women's actions have never been more than symbolic agitation; they have won only what men have been willing to concede to them; they have taken nothing; they have received.[5] It is that they lack the concrete means to organize themselves into a unit that could posit itself in opposition. They have no past, no history, no religion of their own; and unlike the proletariat, they have no solidarity of labor or interests; they even lack their own space that makes communities of American blacks, the Jews in ghettos, or the workers in Saint-Denis or Renault factories. They live dispersed among men, tied by homes, work, economic interests, and social conditions to certain men—fathers or husbands—more closely than to other women. As bourgeois women, they are in solidarity with bourgeois men and not with women proletarians; as white women, they are in solidarity with white men and not with black women. The proletariat could plan to massacre the

5. See second part, page 126.

whole ruling class; a fanatic Jew or black could dream of seizing the secret of the atomic bomb and turning all of humanity entirely Jewish or entirely black: but a woman could not even dream of exterminating males. The tie that binds her to her oppressors is unlike any other. The division of the sexes is a biological given, not a moment in human history. Their opposition took shape within an original *Mitsein*, and she has not broken it. The couple is a fundamental unit with the two halves riveted to each other: cleavage of society by sex is not possible. This is the fundamental characteristic of woman: she is the Other at the heart of a whole whose two components are necessary to each other.

One might think that this reciprocity would have facilitated her liberation; when Hercules spins wool at Omphale's feet, his desire enchains him. Why was Omphale unable to acquire long-lasting power? Medea, in revenge against Jason, kills her children: this brutal legend suggests that the bond attaching the woman to her child could have given her a formidable upper hand. In *Lysistrata*, Aristophanes lightheartedly imagined a group of women who, uniting together for the social good, tried to take advantage of men's need for them: but it is only a comedy. The legend that claims that the ravished Sabine women resisted their ravishers with obstinate sterility also recounts that by whipping them with leather straps, the men magically won them over into submission. Biological need—sexual desire and desire for posterity—which makes the male dependent on the female, has not liberated women socially. Master and slave are also linked by a reciprocal economic need that does not free the slave. That is, in the master-slave relation, the master does not *posit* the need he has for the other; he holds the power to satisfy this need and does not mediate it; the slave, on the other hand, out of dependence, hope, or fear, internalizes his need for the master; however equally compelling the need may be to them both, it always plays in favor of the oppressor over the oppressed: this explains the slow pace of working-class liberation, for example. Now, woman has always been, if not man's slave, at least his vassal; the two sexes have never divided the world up equally; and still today, even though her condition is changing, woman is heavily handicapped. In no country is her legal status identical to man's, and often it puts her at a considerable disadvantage. Even when her rights are recognized abstractly, long-standing habit keeps them from being concretely manifested in customs. Economically, men and women almost form two castes; all things being equal, the former have better jobs, higher wages, and greater chances to succeed than their new female competitors; they occupy many more places in industry, in politics, and so forth, and they hold the most important positions. In addition to their concrete power, they are invested with a prestige whose

tradition is reinforced by the child's whole education: the present incorpo-
rates the past, and in the past all history was made by males. At the moment
that women are beginning to share in the making of the world, this world
still belongs to men: men have no doubt about this, and women barely
doubt it. Refusing to be the Other, refusing complicity with man, would
mean renouncing all the advantages an alliance with the superior caste confers on them. Lord-man will materially protect liege-woman and will be in
charge of justifying her existence: along with the economic risk, she eludes
the metaphysical risk of a freedom that must invent its goals without help.
Indeed, beside every individual's claim to assert himself as subject—an
ethical claim—lies the temptation to flee freedom and to make himself into
a thing: it is a pernicious path because the individual, passive, alienated,
and lost, is prey to a foreign will, cut off from his transcendence, robbed of
all worth. But it is an easy path: the anguish and stress of authentically
assumed existence are thus avoided. The man who sets the woman up as an
Other will thus find in her a deep complicity. Hence woman makes no claim
for herself as subject because she lacks the concrete means, because she
senses the necessary link connecting her to man without positing its reciprocity, and because she often derives satisfaction from her role as *Other*.

But a question immediately arises: How did this whole story begin? It
is understandable that the duality of the sexes, like all duality, be expressed
in conflict. It is understandable that if one of the two succeeded in imposing its superiority, it had to establish itself as absolute. It remains to be
explained how it was that man won at the outset. It seems possible that
women might have carried off the victory, or that the battle might never be
resolved. Why is it that this world has always belonged to men and that
only today things are beginning to change? Is this change a good thing?
Will it bring about an equal sharing of the world between men and women
or not?

These questions are far from new; they have already had many
answers; but the very fact that woman is *Other* challenges all the justifications that men have ever given: these were only too clearly dictated by their
own interest. "Everything that men have written about women should be
viewed with suspicion, because they are both judge and party," wrote
Poulain de la Barre, a little-known seventeenth-century feminist. Males
have always and everywhere paraded their satisfaction of feeling they are
kings of creation. "Blessed be the Lord our God, and the Lord of all
worlds that has not made me a woman," Jews say in their morning prayers;
meanwhile, their wives resignedly murmur: "Blessed be the Lord for creating me according to his will." Among the blessings Plato thanked the gods

for was, first, being born free and not a slave and, second, a man and not a woman. But males could not have enjoyed this privilege so fully had they not considered it as founded in the absolute and in eternity: they sought to make the fact of their supremacy a right. "Those who made and compiled the laws, being men, favored their own sex, and the jurisconsults have turned the laws into principles," Poulain de la Barre continues. Lawmakers, priests, philosophers, writers, and scholars have gone to great lengths to prove that women's subordinate condition was willed in heaven and profitable on earth. Religions forged by men reflect this will for domination: they found ammunition in the legends of Eve and Pandora. They have put philosophy and theology in their service, as seen in the previously cited words of Aristotle and Saint Thomas. Since ancient times, satirists and moralists have delighted in depicting women's weaknesses. The violent indictments brought against them all through French literature are well-known: Montherlant, with less verve, picks up the tradition from Jean de Meung. This hostility seems sometimes founded but is often gratuitous; in truth, it covers up a more or less skillfully camouflaged will to self-justification. "It is much easier to accuse one sex than to excuse the other," says Montaigne. In certain cases, the process is transparent. It is striking, for example, that the Roman code limiting a wife's rights invokes "the imbecility and fragility of the sex" just when a weakening family structure makes her a threat to male heirs. It is striking that in the sixteenth century, to keep a married woman under wardship, the authority of Saint Augustine affirming "the wife is an animal neither reliable nor stable" is called on, whereas the unmarried woman is recognized as capable of managing her own affairs. Montaigne well understood the arbitrariness and injustice of the lot assigned to women: "Women are not wrong at all when they reject the rules of life that have been introduced into the world, inasmuch as it is the men who have made these without them. There is a natural plotting and scheming between them and us." But he does not go so far as to champion their cause. It is only in the eighteenth century that deeply democratic men begin to consider the issue objectively. Diderot, for one, tries to prove that, like man, woman is a human being. A bit later, John Stuart Mill ardently defends women. But these philosophers are exceptional in their impartiality. In the nineteenth century the feminist quarrel once again becomes a partisan quarrel; one of the consequences of the Industrial Revolution is that women enter the labor force: at that point, women's demands leave the realm of the theoretical and find economic grounds; their adversaries become all the more aggressive; even though landed property is partially discredited, the bourgeoisie clings to the old values where family solidity guarantees private property: it insists all the more fiercely that woman's place be in the home as her emancipation becomes a real threat; even within the working class, men tried to thwart women's liberation because women were becoming dangerous competitors—especially as women were used to working for low salaries.[6] To prove women's inferiority, antifeminists began to draw not only, as before, on religion, philosophy, and theology but also on science: biology, experimental psychology, and so forth. At most they were willing to grant "separate but equal status" to the *other* sex.* That winning formula is most significant: it is exactly that formula the Jim Crow laws put into practice with regard to black Americans; this so-called egalitarian segregation served only to introduce the most extreme forms of discrimination. This convergence is in no way pure chance: whether it is race, caste, class, or sex reduced to an inferior condition, the justification process is the same. "The eternal feminine" corresponds to "the black soul" or "the Jewish character." However, the Jewish problem on the whole is very different from the two others: for the anti-Semite, the Jew is more an enemy than an inferior, and no place on this earth is recognized as his own; it would be preferable to see him annihilated. But there are deep analogies between the situations of women and blacks: both are liberated today from the same paternalism, and the former master caste wants to keep them "in their place," that is, the place chosen for them; in both cases, they praise, more or less sincerely, the virtues of the "good black," the carefree, childlike, merry soul of the resigned black, and the woman who is a "true woman"—frivolous, infantile, irresponsible, the woman subjugated to man. In both cases, the ruling caste bases its argument on the state of affairs it created itself. The familiar line from George Bernard Shaw sums it up: The white American relegates the black to the rank of shoe-shine boy, and then concludes that blacks are only good for shining shoes. The same vicious circle can be found in all analogous circumstances: when an individual or a group of individuals is kept in a situation of inferiority, the fact is that he or they *are* inferior. But the scope of the verb *to be* must be understood; bad faith means giving it a substantive value, when in fact it has the sense of the Hegelian dynamic: *to be* is to have become, to have been made as one manifests oneself. Yes, women in general *are* today inferior to men; that is, their situation provides them

---

6. See Part Two, pp. 135–136.

* "*L'égalité dans la différence*" in the French text. Literal translation: "different but equal." —TRANS.

with fewer possibilities: the question is whether this state of affairs must be perpetuated.

Many men wish it would be: not all men have yet laid down their arms. The conservative bourgeoisie continues to view women's liberation as a danger threatening their morality and their interests. Some men feel threatened by women's competition. In *Hebdo-Latin* the other day, a student declared: "Every woman student who takes a position as a doctor or lawyer is *stealing* a place from us." That student never questioned his rights over this world. Economic interests are not the only ones in play. One of the benefits that oppression secures for the oppressor is that the humblest among them feels *superior:* in the United States a "poor white" from the South can console himself for not being a "dirty nigger"; and more prosperous whites cleverly exploit this pride. Likewise, the most mediocre of males believes himself a demigod next to women. It was easier for M. de Montherlant to think himself a hero in front of women (handpicked, by the way) than to act the man among men, a role that many women assumed better than he did. Thus, in one of his articles in *Le Figaro Littéraire* in September 1948, M. Claude Mauriac—whom everyone admires for his powerful originality—could[7] write about women: "*We* listen in a tone [*sic!*] of polite indifference . . . to the most brilliant one among them, knowing that her intelligence, in a more or less dazzling way, reflects ideas that come from *us*." Clearly his female interlocutor does not reflect M. Mauriac's own ideas, since he is known not to have any; that she reflects ideas originating with men is possible: among males themselves, more than one of them takes as his own opinions he did not invent; one might wonder if it would not be in M. Claude Mauriac's interest to converse with a good reflection of Descartes, Marx, or Gide rather than with himself; what is remarkable is that with the ambiguous "*we,*" he identifies with Saint Paul, Hegel, Lenin, and Nietzsche, and from their heights he looks down on the herd of women who dare to speak to him on an equal footing; frankly, I know of more than one woman who would not put up with M. Mauriac's "tone of polite indifference."

I have stressed this example because of its disarming masculine naïveté. Men profit in many other more subtle ways from woman's alterity. For all those suffering from an inferiority complex, this is a miraculous liniment; no one is more arrogant toward women, more aggressive or more disdainful, than a man anxious about his own virility. Those who are not threatened by their fellow men are far more likely to recognize woman as a

---

7. At least he thought he could.

counterpart; but even for them the myth of the Woman, of the Other, remains precious for many reasons;[8] they can hardly be blamed for not wanting to lightheartedly sacrifice all the benefits they derive from the myth: they know what they lose by relinquishing the woman of their dreams, but they do not know what the woman of tomorrow will bring them. It takes great abnegation to refuse to posit oneself as unique and absolute Subject. Besides, the vast majority of men do not explicitly make this position their own. They do not *posit* woman as inferior: they are too imbued today with the democratic ideal not to recognize all human beings as equals. Within the family, the male child and then the young man sees the woman as having the same social dignity as the adult male; afterward, he experiences in desire and love the resistance and independence of the desired and loved woman; married, he respects in his wife the spouse and the mother, and in the concrete experience of married life she affirms herself opposite him as a freedom. He can thus convince himself that there is no longer a social hierarchy between the sexes and that on the whole, in spite of their differences, woman is an equal. As he nevertheless recognizes some points of inferiority—professional incapacity being the predominant one—he attributes them to nature. When he has an attitude of benevolence and partnership toward a woman, he applies the principle of abstract equality; and he does not *posit* the concrete inequality he recognizes. But as soon as he clashes with her, the situation is reversed. He will apply the concrete inequality theme and will even allow himself to disavow abstract equality.[9] This is how many men affirm, with quasi good faith, that women *are* equal to men and have no demands to make, and *at the same time* that women will never be equal to men and that their demands are in vain. It is difficult for men to measure the enormous extent of social discrimination that seems insignificant from the outside and whose moral and intellectual repercussions are so deep in woman that they appear to spring from an original nature.[10] The man most sympathetic to women never knows her

---

8. The article by Michel Carrouges on this theme in *Cahiers du Sud*, no. 292, is significant. He writes with indignation: "If only there were no feminine myth but only bands of cooks, matrons, prostitutes, and bluestockings with functions of pleasure or utility!" So, according to him, woman has no existence for herself; he only takes into account her *function* in the male world. Her finality is in man; in fact, it is possible to prefer her poetic "function" to all others. The exact question is why she should be defined in relation to the man.

9. For example, man declares that he does not find his wife in any way diminished just because she does not have a profession: work in the home is just as noble and so on. Yet at the first argument he remonstrates, "You wouldn't be able to earn a living without me."

10. Describing this very process will be the object of Volume II of this study.

concrete situation fully. So there is no good reason to believe men when they try to defend privileges whose scope they cannot even fathom. We will not let ourselves be intimidated by the number and violence of attacks against women; nor be fooled by the self-serving praise showered on the "real woman"; nor be won over by men's enthusiasm for her destiny, a destiny they would not for the world want to share.

We must not, however, be any less mistrustful of feminists' arguments: very often their attempt to polemicize robs them of all value. If the "question of women" is so trivial, it is because masculine arrogance turned it into a "quarrel"; when people quarrel, they no longer reason well. What people have endlessly sought to prove is that woman is superior, inferior, or equal to man: created after Adam, she is obviously a secondary being, some say; on the contrary, say others, Adam was only a rough draft, and God perfected the human being when he created Eve; her brain is smaller, but relatively bigger; Christ was made man, but perhaps out of humility. Every argument has its opposite, and both are often misleading. To see clearly, one needs to get out of these ruts; these vague notions of superiority, inferiority, and equality that have distorted all discussions must be discarded in order to start anew.

But how, then, will we ask the question? And in the first place, who are we to ask it? Men are judge and party: so are women. Can an angel be found? In fact, an angel would be ill qualified to speak, would not understand all the givens of the problem; as for the hermaphrodite, it is a case of its own: it is not both a man and a woman, but neither man nor woman. I think certain women are still best suited to elucidate the situation of women. It is a sophism to claim that Epimenides should be enclosed within the concept of Cretan and all Cretans within the concept of liar: it is not a mysterious essence that dictates good or bad faith to men and women; it is their situation that disposes them to seek the truth to a greater or lesser extent. Many women today, fortunate to have had all the privileges of the human being restored to them, can afford the luxury of impartiality: we even feel the necessity of it. We are no longer like our militant predecessors; we have more or less won the game; in the latest discussions on women's status, the UN has not ceased to imperiously demand equality of the sexes, and indeed many of us have never felt our femaleness to be a difficulty or an obstacle; many other problems seem more essential than those that concern us uniquely: this very detachment makes it possible to hope our attitude will be objective. Yet we know the feminine world more intimately than men do because our roots are in it; we grasp more immediately what the fact of being female means for a human being, and we care more about knowing it. I said that there are more essential problems; but this one still has a certain importance from our point of view: How will the fact of being women have affected our lives? What precise opportunities have been given us, and which ones have been denied? What destiny awaits our younger sisters, and in which direction should we point them? It is striking that most feminine literature is driven today by an attempt at lucidity more than by a will to make demands; coming out of an era of muddled controversy, this book is one attempt among others to take stock of the current state.

But it is no doubt impossible to approach any human problem without partiality: even the way of asking the questions, of adopting perspectives, presupposes hierarchies of interests; all characteristics comprise values; every so-called objective description is set against an ethical background. Instead of trying to conceal those principles that are more or less explicitly implied, we would be better off stating them from the start; then it would not be necessary to specify on each page the meaning given to the words "superior," "inferior," "better," "worse," "progress," "regression," and so on. If we examine some of the books on women, we see that one of the most frequently held points of view is that of public good or general interest: in reality, this is taken to mean the interest of society as each one wishes to maintain or establish it. In our opinion, there is no public good other than one that assures the citizens' private good; we judge institutions from the point of view of the concrete opportunities they give to individuals. But neither do we confuse the idea of private interest with happiness: that is another frequently encountered point of view; are women in a harem not happier than a woman voter? Is a housewife not happier than a woman worker? We cannot really know what the word "happiness" means, and still less what authentic values it covers; there is no way to measure the happiness of others, and it is always easy to call a situation that one would like to impose on others happy: in particular, we declare happy those condemned to stagnation, under the pretext that happiness is immobility. This is a notion, then, we will not refer to. The perspective we have adopted is one of existentialist morality. Every subject posits itself as a transcendence concretely, through projects; it accomplishes its freedom only by perpetual surpassing toward other freedoms; there is no other justification for present existence than its expansion toward an indefinitely open future. Every time transcendence lapses into immanence, there is degradation of existence into "in-itself," of freedom into facticity; this fall is a moral fault if the subject consents to it; if this fall is inflicted on the subject, it takes the form of frustration and oppression; in both cases it is an absolute evil. Every individual concerned with justifying his existence experiences his existence as an indefinite need to transcend himself. But what singularly defines the situation of woman is that being, like all humans, an autonomous freedom, she discovers and chooses herself in a world where men force her to assume herself as Other: an attempt is made to freeze her as an object and doom her to immanence, since her transcendence will be forever transcended by another essential and sovereign consciousness. Woman's drama lies in this conflict between the fundamental claim of every subject, which always posits itself as essential, and the demands of a situation that constitutes her as inessential. How, in the feminine condition, can a human being accomplish herself? What paths are open to her? Which ones lead to dead ends? How can she find independence within dependence? What circumstances limit women's freedom and can she overcome them? These are the fundamental questions we would like to elucidate. This means that in focusing on the individual's possibilities, we will define these possibilities not in terms of happiness but in terms of freedom.

Clearly this problem would have no meaning if we thought that a physiological, psychological, or economic destiny weighed on woman. So we will begin by discussing woman from a biological, psychoanalytical, and historical materialist point of view. We will then attempt to positively demonstrate how "feminine reality" has been constituted, why woman has been defined as Other, and what the consequences have been from men's point of view. Then we will describe the world from the woman's point of view such as it is offered to her,[11] and we will see the difficulties women are up against just when, trying to escape the sphere they have been assigned until now, they seek to be part of the human *Mitsein*.

---

11. This will be the subject of a second volume.

| PART ONE |

DESTINY

CHAPTER 1

Biological Data

Woman? Very simple, say those who like simple answers: She is a womb, an ovary; she is a female: this word is enough to define her. From a man's mouth, the epithet "female" sounds like an insult; but he, not ashamed of his animality, is proud to hear: "He's a male!" The term "female" is pejorative not because it roots woman in nature but because it confines her in her sex, and if this sex, even in an innocent animal, seems despicable and an enemy to man, it is obviously because of the disquieting hostility woman triggers in him. Nevertheless, he wants to find a justification in biology for this feeling. The word "female" evokes a saraband of images: an enormous round egg snatching and castrating the agile sperm; monstrous and stuffed, the queen termite reigning over the servile males; the praying mantis and the spider, gorged on love, crushing their partners and gobbling them up; the dog in heat running through back alleys, leaving perverse smells in her wake; the monkey showing herself off brazenly, sneaking away with flirtatious hypocrisy. And the most splendid wildcats, the tigress, lioness, and panther, lie down slavishly under the male's imperial embrace, inert, impatient, shrewd, stupid, insensitive, lewd, fierce, and humiliated. Man projects all females at once onto woman. And the fact is that she is a female. But if one wants to stop thinking in commonplaces, two questions arise. What does the female represent in the animal kingdom? And what unique kind of female is realized in woman?

Males and females are two types of individuals who are differentiated within one species for the purposes of reproduction; they can be defined only correlatively. But it has to be pointed out first that the very meaning of *division* of the species into two sexes is not clear.

It does not occur universally in nature. In one-celled animals, infusorians, amoebas, bacilli, and so on, multiplication is fundamentally distinct from sexuality, with cells dividing and subdividing individually. For some

metazoans, reproduction occurs by schizogenesis, that is dividing the individual whose origin is also asexual, or by blastogenesis, that is dividing the
individual itself produced by a sexual phenomenon: the phenomena of
budding or segmentation observed in freshwater hydras, coelenterates,
sponges, worms, and tunicates are well-known examples. In parthenogenesis, the virgin egg develops in embryonic form without male intervention.
The male plays no role or only a secondary one: unfertilized honeybee
eggs subdivide and produce drones; in the case of aphids, males are absent
for a number of generations, and the unfertilized eggs produce females.
Parthenogenesis in the sea urchin, the starfish, and the toad has been artificially reproduced. However, sometimes in the protozoa, two cells can
merge, forming what is called a zygote; fertilization is necessary for honeybee eggs to engender females and aphid eggs, males. Some biologists have
thus concluded that even in species capable of perpetuating themselves
unilaterally, the renewal of genetic diversity through mixing of parental
chromosomes would benefit the line's rejuvenation and vigor; in this view,
then, in the more complex forms of life, sexuality is an indispensable function; only elementary organisms could multiply without sexes, and even so
they would exhaust their vitality. But today this hypothesis is most inexact;
observations have proved that asexual multiplication can occur indefinitely
without any noticeable degeneration; this is particularly striking in bacilli;
more and more—and bolder and even bolder—parthenogenetic experiments have been carried out, and in many species the male seems radically
useless. Moreover, even if the value of intercellular exchange could be
demonstrated, it would be a purely ungrounded fact. Biology attests to sexual differentiation, but even if biology were imbued with finalism, the differentiation of sexes could not be deduced from cellular structure, laws of
cellular multiplication, or any elementary phenomenon.

The existence of heterogenetic gametes alone does not necessarily
mean there are two distinct sexes;[1] the differentiation of reproductive cells
often does not bring about a division of the species into two types: both can
belong to the same individual. This is true of hermaphroditic species, so
common in plants, and also in many invertebrates, among which are the
annulates and mollusks. Reproduction takes place either by self-
fertilization or by cross-fertilization. Some biologists use this fact to claim
the justification of the established order. They consider gonochorism—
that is, the system in which the different gonads[2] belong to distinct individ-

---

1. Gametes are reproductive cells whose fusion produces an egg.
2. Gonads are glands that produce gametes.

uals—as an improvement on hermaphroditism, realized by evolution; others, by contrast, consider gonochorism primitive: for those biologists, hermaphroditism would thus be its degeneration. In any case, these notions of superiority of one system over another involve highly contestable theories concerning evolution. All that can be affirmed with certainty is that these two means of reproduction coexist in nature, that they both perpetuate species, and that the heterogeneity of both gametes and gonad-producing organisms seems to be accidental. The differentiation of individuals into males and females thus occurs as an irreducible and contingent fact.

Most philosophies have taken sexual differentiation for granted without attempting to explain it. The Platonic myth has it that in the beginning there were men, women, and androgynes; each individual had a double face, four arms, four legs, and two bodies joined together; one day they were split into two "as one would split eggs in two," and ever since then each half seeks to recover its other half: the gods decided later that new human beings would be created by the coupling of two unlike halves. This story only tries to explain love: the differentiation of sexes is taken as a given from the start. Aristotle offers no better account: for if cooperation of matter and form is necessary for any action, it is not necessary that active and passive principles be distributed into two categories of heterogenic individuals. Saint Thomas declared that woman was an "inessential" being, which, from a masculine point of view, is a way of positing the accidental character of sexuality. Hegel, however, would have been untrue to his rationalist passion had he not attempted to justify it logically. According to him, sexuality is the mediation by which the subject concretely achieves itself as a genus. "The genus is therefore present in the individual as a straining against the inadequacy of its single actuality, as the urge to obtain its self-feeling in the other of its genus, to integrate itself through union with it and through this mediation to close the genus with itself and bring it into existence—*copulation*."[3] And a little further along, "The process consists in this, that they become in reality what they are in themselves, namely, one genus, the same subjective vitality." And Hegel then declares that in order for the process of union to occur, there has to be differentiation of the two sexes. But his demonstration is not convincing: the preconceived idea of locating the three moments of the syllogism in any operation is too obvious here. The surpassing of the individual toward the species, by which individual and species accomplish themselves in their

---

3. Hegel, *The Philosophy of Nature*, Part 3, Section 369.

own truth could occur without the third element, by the simple relation of genitor to child: reproduction could be asexual. Or the relation to each other could be that of two of the same kind, with differentiation occurring in the singularity of individuals of the same type, as in hermaphroditic species. Hegel's description brings out a very important significance of sexuality: but he always makes the same error of equating significance with reason. It is through sexual activity that men define the sexes and their relations, just as they create the meaning and value of all the functions they accomplish: but sexual activity is not necessarily implied in the human being's nature. In *Phénoménologie de la perception* (*Phenomenology of Perception*), Merleau-Ponty points out that human existence calls for revision of the notions of necessity and contingency. "Existence has no fortuitous attributes, no content which does not contribute towards giving it its form; it does not give admittance to any pure fact because it is the process by which facts are drawn up." This is true. But it is also true that there are conditions without which the very fact of existence would seem to be impossible. Presence in the world vigorously implies the positing of a body that is both a thing of the world and a point of view on this world: but this body need not possess this or that particular structure. In *L'être et le néant* (*Being and Nothingness*), Sartre disputes Heidegger's affirmation that human reality is doomed to death because of its finitude; he establishes that a finite and temporally limitless existence could be conceivable; nevertheless, if human life were not inhabited by death, the relationship of human beings to the world and to themselves would be so deeply upset that the statement "man is mortal" would be anything but an empirical truth: immortal, an existent would no longer be what we call a man. One of the essential features of man's destiny is that the movement of his temporal life creates behind and ahead of him the infinity of the past and the future: the perpetuation of the species appears thus as the correlative of individual limitation, so the phenomenon of reproduction can be considered as ontologically grounded. But this is where one must stop; the perpetuation of the species does not entail sexual differentiation. That it is taken on by existents in such a way that it thereby enters into the concrete definition of existence, so be it. Nevertheless, a consciousness without a body or an immortal human being is rigorously inconceivable, whereas a society can be imagined that reproduces itself by parthenogenesis or is composed of hermaphrodites.

Opinions about the respective roles of the two sexes have varied greatly; they were initially devoid of any scientific basis and only reflected social myths. It was thought for a long time, and is still thought in some primitive societies based on matrilineal filiation, that the father has no part in the child's conception: ancestral larvae were supposed to infiltrate the womb in the form of living germs. With the advent of patriarchy, the male resolutely claimed his posterity; the mother had to be granted a role in procreation even though she merely carried and fattened the living seed: the father alone was the creator. Aristotle imagined that the fetus was produced by the meeting of the sperm and the menses: in this symbiosis, woman just provided passive material, while the male principle is strength, activity, movement, and life. Hippocrates' doctrine also recognized two types of seeds, a weak or female one, and a strong one, which was male. Aristotelian theory was perpetuated throughout the Middle Ages and down to the modern period. In the middle of the seventeenth century, Harvey, slaughtering female deer shortly after they had mated, found vesicles in the uterine horns that he thought were eggs but that were really embryos. The Danish scientist Steno coined the term "ovaries" for the female genital glands that had until then been called "feminine testicles," and he noted the existence of vesicles on their surface that Graaf, in 1672, had erroneously identified as eggs and to which he gave his name. The ovary was still regarded as a homologue of the male gland. That same year, though, "spermatic animalcules" were discovered penetrating the feminine womb. But it was thought that they went there for nourishment only, and that the individual was already prefigured in them; in 1694, the Dutchman Hartsoeker drew an image of the homunculus hidden in the sperm, and in 1699 another scientist declared he had seen the sperm cast off a kind of slough under which there was a little man, which he also drew. In these hypotheses woman merely fattened a living and active, and perfectly constituted, principle. These theories were not universally accepted, and discussion continued until the nineteenth century. The invention of the microscope led to the study of the animal egg; in 1827, Baer identified the mammal's egg: an element contained inside Graaf's follicle. Soon its structure could be studied; in 1835, the sarcode—that is, the protoplasm—and then the cell were discovered; in 1877, the sperm was observed penetrating the starfish egg. From that the symmetry of the two gametes' nuclei was established; their fusion was analyzed in detail for the first time in 1883 by a Belgian zoologist.

But Aristotle's ideas have not lost all validity. Hegel thought the two sexes must be different: one is active and the other passive, and it goes without saying that passivity will be the female's lot. "Because of this differentiation, man is thus the active principle while woman is the passive principle because she resides in her non-developed unity."[4] And even when the

wtf Hegel

4. Ibid.

ovum was recognized as an active principle, men continued to pit its inertia against the agility of the sperm. Today, there is a tendency to see the contrary: the discoveries of parthenogenesis have led some scientists to reduce the role of the male to that of a simple physicochemical agent. In some species the action of an acid or a mechanical stimulation has been shown to trigger the division of the egg and the development of the embryo; and from that it was boldly assumed that the male gamete was not necessary for generation; it would be at most a ferment; perhaps man's cooperation in procreation would one day become useless: that seems to be many women's desire. But nothing warrants such a bold expectation because nothing warrants universalizing life's specific processes. The phenomena of asexual multiplication and parthenogenesis are neither more nor less fundamental than those of sexual reproduction. And it has already been noted that this form is not a priori favored: but no fact proves it is reducible to a more elementary mechanism.

Rejecting any a priori doctrine, any implausible theory, we find ourselves before a fact that has neither ontological nor empirical basis and whose impact cannot a priori be understood. By examining it in its concrete reality, we can hope to extract its significance: thus perhaps the content of the word "female" will come to light.

The idea here is not to propose a philosophy of life or to take sides too hastily in the quarrel between finalism and mechanism. Yet it is noteworthy that physiologists and biologists all use a more or less finalistic language merely because they ascribe meaning to vital phenomena. We will use their vocabulary. Without coming to any conclusion about life and consciousness, we can affirm that any living fact indicates transcendence, and that a project is in the making in every function: these descriptions do not suggest more than this.

In most species, male and female organisms cooperate for reproduction. They are basically defined by the gametes they produce. In some algae and fungi, the cells that fuse to produce the egg are identical; these cases of isogamy are significant in that they manifest the basal equivalence of the usually differentiated gametes: but their analogy remains striking. Sperm and ova result from a basically identical cellular evolution: the development of primitive female cells into oocytes differs from that of spermatocytes by protoplasmic phenomena, but the nuclear phenomena are approximately the same. The idea the biologist Ancel expressed in 1903 is still considered valid today: "An undifferentiated progerminating cell becomes male or female depending on the conditions in the genital gland at the moment of its appearance, conditions determined by the transformation of some epithelial cells into nourishing elements, developers of a special material." This primary kinship is expressed in the structure of the two gametes that carry the same number of chromosomes inside each species. During fertilization, the two nuclei merge their substance, and the chromosomes in each are reduced to half their original number: this reduction takes place in both of them in a similar way; the last two divisions of the ovum result in the formation of polar globules equivalent to the last divisions of the sperm. It is thought today that, depending on the species, the male or female gamete determines the sex: for mammals, the sperm possesses a chromosome that is heterogenic to the others and potentially either male or female. According to Mendel's statistical laws, transmission of hereditary characteristics takes place equally from the father and the mother. What is important to see is that in this meeting neither gamete takes precedence over the other: they both sacrifice their individuality; the egg absorbs the totality of their substance. There are thus two strong current biases that—at least at this basic biological level—prove false: The first one is the female's passivity; the living spark is not enclosed within either of the two gametes. It springs forth from their meeting; the nucleus of the ovum is a vital principle perfectly symmetrical to the sperm's. The second bias contradicts the first, which does not exclude the fact that they often coexist: the permanence of the species is guaranteed by the female since the male principle has an explosive and fleeting existence. In reality, the embryo equally perpetuates the germ cells of the father and the mother and retransmits them together to its descendants, sometimes in a male and sometimes in a female form. One might say that an androgynous germ cell survives the individual metamorphoses of the soma from generation to generation.

That being said, there are highly interesting secondary differences to be observed between the ovum and the sperm; the essential singularity of the ovum is that it is supplied with material destined to nourish and protect the embryo; it stocks up on reserves from which the fetus will build its tissues, reserves that are not a living substance but an inert material; the result is a massive, relatively voluminous, spherical or ellipsoidal form. The bird's egg's dimensions are well-known. The woman's egg measures 0.13 mm, while the human sperm contains sixty thousand sperm per cubic millimeter: their mass is extremely small. The sperm has a threadlike tail, a little elongated head; no foreign substance weighs it down. It is entirely life; this structure destines it for mobility; the ovum, on the contrary, where the future of the fetus is stored, is a fixed element:

enclosed in the female organism or suspended in an exterior environment, it waits passively for fertilization. The male gamete seeks it out; the sperm is always a naked cell, while the ovum is, according to the species, protected or not by a membrane; but in any case, the sperm bumps into the ovum when it comes into contact with it, makes it waver, and infiltrates it; the male gamete loses its tail; its head swells, and, twisting, it reaches the nucleus. Meanwhile, the egg immediately forms a membrane that keeps other sperm from entering. For echinoderms where fertilization is external, it is easy to observe the rush of the sperm that surround the floating and inert egg like a halo. This competition is also another important phenomenon found in most species; much smaller than the ovum, the sperm are generally produced in considerable quantities, and each ovum has many suitors.

Thus, the ovum, active in the nucleus, its essential principle, is superficially passive; its mass, closed upon itself, compact in itself, evokes the nocturnal heaviness and repose of the in-itself: the ancients visualized the closed world in the form of a sphere or opaque atom; immobile, the ovum waits; by contrast, the open sperm, tiny and agile, embodies the impatience and worry of existence. One should not get carried away with the pleasure of allegories: the ovum has sometimes been likened to immanence and the sperm to transcendence. By giving up its transcendence and mobility, the sperm penetrates the female element: it is grabbed and castrated by the inert mass that absorbs it after cutting off its tail; like all passive actions, this one is magical and disturbing; the male gamete activity is rational, a measurable movement in terms of time and space. In truth, these are merely ramblings. Male and female gametes merge together in the egg; together they cancel each other out in their totality. It is false to claim that the egg voraciously absorbs the male gamete and just as false to say that the latter victoriously appropriates the female cell's reserves because in the act that merges them, their individuality disappears. And to a mechanistic philosophy, the movement undoubtedly looks like a rational phenomenon par excellence; but for modern physics the idea is no clearer than that of action at a distance; besides, the details of the physicochemical interactions leading to fertilization are not known. It is possible, however, to come away with a valuable indication from this meeting. There are two movements that come together in life, and life maintains itself only by surpassing itself. It does not surpass itself without maintaining itself; these two moments are always accomplished together. It is academic to claim to separate them: nevertheless, it is either one or the other that dominates. The two unified gametes go beyond and are perpetuated; but the ovum's structure anticipates future needs; it is constituted to nourish the life that will awaken in it, while the sperm is in no way equipped to ensure the development of the germ it gives rise to. In contrast, whereas the sperm moves around, the ovum is incapable of triggering the change that will bring about a new explosion of life. Without the egg's prescience, the sperm's action would be useless; but without the latter's initiative, the egg would not accomplish its vital potential. The conclusion is thus that fundamentally the role of the two gametes is identical; together they create a living being in which both of them lose and surpass themselves. But in the secondary and superficial phenomena that condition fertilization, it is through the male element that the change in situation occurs for the new eclosion of life; it is through the female element that this eclosion is established in a stable element.

It would be rash to deduce from such an observation that woman's place is in the home: but there are rash people. In his book *Tempérament et caractère selon les individus, les sexes et les races* (Nature and Character According to Individuals, Sex, and Race), Alfred Fouillée claimed he could define woman entirely from the ovum and man from the sperm; many so-called deep theories are based on this game of dubious analogies. It is never clear what philosophy of nature this pseudo-thinking refers to. If one considers laws of heredity, men and women come equally from a sperm and an ovum. I suppose that vestiges of the old medieval philosophy—that the cosmos was the exact reflection of a microcosm—are floating around in these foggy minds: it was imagined that the ovum is a female homunculus and woman a giant ovum. These reveries dismissed since the days of alchemy make a weird contrast with the scientific precision of descriptions being used at this very moment: modern biology does not mesh with medieval symbolism; but our people do not look all that closely. If one is a bit scrupulous, one has to agree that it is a long way from ovum to woman. The ovum does not yet even contain the very notion of female. Hegel rightly notes that the sexual relationship cannot be reduced to that of two gametes. Thus, the female organism has to be studied in its totality.

It has already been pointed out that for many vegetables and some primitive animals, among them mollusks, gamete specification does not lead to individual specification, as they produce both ova and sperm. Even when the sexes separate, the barriers between them are not tight like those that separate species; just as gametes are defined from an originally undifferentiated tissue, males and females develop more as variations on a common base. For certain animals—the *Bonellia viridis* is the most typical case*—the embryo is first asexual, and its eventual sexuality is determined by the incertitudes of its development. It is accepted today that in most species sex determination depends on the genotypical constitution of the egg. The virgin egg of the honeybee reproducing itself by parthenogenesis yields males exclusively; that of fruit flies in the exact same conditions yields females exclusively. When eggs are fertilized, it is to be noted that—except for some spiders—an approximately equal number of male and female individuals is procreated; differentiation comes from the heterogeneity of one of the two types of gametes: for mammals sperm possess either a male or a female potentiality. It is not really known what determines the singular character of heterogenic gametes during spermatogenesis or oogenesis; in any case, Mendel's statistical laws are sufficient to explain their regular distribution. For both sexes, fertilization and the beginning of embryonic development occur in an identical way; the epithelial tissue destined to evolve into a gonad is undifferentiated at the outset; at a certain stage of maturation testicles take shape or later the ovary takes form. This explains why there are many intermediaries between hermaphroditism and gonochorism; very often one of the sexes possesses certain organs characteristic of the complementary sex: the toad is the most striking case of that; the male has an atrophied ovary called Bidder's organ that can be made to produce eggs artificially. Mammals also have vestiges of this sexual bipotentiality: for example, the pedicled and sessile hydra, the *uterus masculinus*, mammary glands in the male, Gartner's duct in the female, and the clitoris. Even in species where sexual division is the most clear-cut, there are individuals that are both male and female simultaneously: cases of intersexuality are numerous in animals and human beings; and in butterflies and crustaceans there are examples of gynandromorphism in which male and female characteristics are juxtaposed in a kind of mosaic. Genotypically defined, the fetus is nevertheless deeply influenced by the milieu from which it draws its nourishment: for ants, honeybees, and termites, how nutrition occurs makes the larva a realized female or thwarts its sexual maturation, reducing it to the rank of worker; the influence in this case pervades the whole organism: for insects the soma is sexually defined very early and does not depend on gonads. For vertebrates, it is essentially the gonadic hormones that play a regulatory role. Many experiments have demonstrated that varying the endocrine milieu makes it possible to act on sex determination; other grafting and

---

* *Bonellia viridis* is a sandworm that has no sex chromosomes.—TRANS.

castration experiments carried out on adult animals have led to the modern theory of sexuality: in male and female vertebrates, the soma is identical and can be considered a neutral element; the action of the gonad gives it its sexual characteristics; some of the secreted hormones act as stimulants and others as inhibitors; the genital tract itself is somatic, and embryology shows that it takes shape under the influence of hormones from bisexual precursors. Intersexuality exists when hormonal balance has not been realized and when neither of the two sexual potentialities has been clearly accomplished.

Equally distributed in the species, and evolved analogously from identical roots, male and female organisms seem profoundly symmetrical once they are formed. Both are characterized by the presence of gamete-producing glands, ovaries, or testicles, with the analogous processes of spermatogenesis and ovogenesis, as was seen earlier; these glands deliver their secretion in a more or less complex canal according to the hierarchy of the species: the female drops the egg directly by the oviduct and holds it in the cloaca or in a differentiated uterus before expelling it; the male either lets go of the semen outside or is equipped with a copulating organ that allows it to penetrate the female. Statistically, the male and the female thus look like two complementary types. They have to be envisaged from a functional point of view to grasp their singularity.

It is very difficult to give a generally valid description of the notion of female; defining her as a carrier of ova and the male as a carrier of sperm is insufficient because the relation of organism to gonads is extremely variable; inversely, the differentiation of the gametes does not directly affect the organism as a whole: it was sometimes claimed that as the ovum was bigger, it consumed more living force than the sperm; but the latter is secreted in infinitely greater quantity so that in the two sexes the expenditure balances out. Spermatogenesis was taken as an example of prodigality and ovulation a model of economy: but in this phenomenon there is also an absurd profusion; the immense majority of eggs are never fertilized. In any case, gametes and gonads are not microcosms of the whole organism. This is what has to be studied directly.

One of the most noteworthy features when surveying the steps of the animal ladder is that, from bottom to top, life becomes more individual; at the bottom it concentrates on the maintenance of the species, and at the top it puts its energies into single individuals. In lower species, the organism is reduced to barely more than the reproductive apparatus; in this case, the ovum—and therefore the female—takes precedence over everything else, since it is above all the ovum that is dedicated to the sheer repetition of life;

but it is barely more than an abdomen, and its existence is entirely devoured by the work of a monstrous ovulation. It reaches gigantic dimensions compared with the male; but its members are often just stumps, its body a formless bag; all the organs have degenerated to nourish the eggs. In truth, although they constitute two distinct organisms, males and females can hardly be thought of as individuals; they form one whole with elements that are inextricably linked: these are intermediary cases between hermaphroditism and gonochorism. For the entoniscid, parasites that live off the crab, the female is a kind of whitish sausage surrounded by incubating slivers harboring thousands of eggs; in their midst are minuscule males as well as larvae destined to provide replacement males. The enslavement of the dwarf male is even more total in the edriolydnus: it is attached beneath the female's operculum and is without a digestive tube of its own; it is solely devoted to reproduction. In all these cases the female is just as enslaved as the male: she is a slave to the species; while the male is fastened to his spouse, his spouse is also fastened, either to a living organism on which she feeds as a parasite or to a mineral substratum; she is consumed by producing eggs the minuscule male fertilizes. As life takes on more complex forms, individual autonomy develops with the loosening of the link uniting the sexes; but insects of both sexes remain tightly subordinate to the eggs. In the case of ephemerals, both spouses often die after coitus and laying; and in the case of rotifers and mosquitoes, the male, lacking a digestive apparatus, sometimes perishes after fertilization, while the female can feed herself and survive: egg formation and laying take time; the mother dies as soon as the next generation's future has been assured. The privilege of many female insects comes from the fact that fertilization is generally a rapid process while ovulation and incubation of the eggs demand a long period of time. For termites, the enormous mush-stuffed queen that lays an egg a second until she is sterile—and then is pitilessly massacred—is no less a slave than the dwarf male attached to her abdomen that fertilizes the eggs as they are expelled. In bee and ant matriarchies, males are intruders that are massacred each season: at the time of the wedding flight, all the male ants escape from the anthill and fly toward the females; if they reach and fertilize them, they die immediately, exhausted; if not, the female workers refuse them entry. They kill them in front of the entrances or let them starve to death; but the fertilized female has a sad fate: she digs herself into the earth alone and often dies from exhaustion while laying the first eggs; if she manages to reconstitute a colony, she is imprisoned for twelve years laying eggs ceaselessly; the female workers whose sexuality has been atrophied live for four years, but their whole life is devoted to raising the larvae. Likewise for the bees: the drone that catches the queen in her wedding flight crashes to the ground eviscerated; the other drones return to their colony, where they are unproductive and in the way; at the beginning of the winter, they are killed. But the sterile worker bees trade their right to life for incessant work; the queen is really the hive's slave: she lays eggs ceaselessly; and the old queen dies; some larvae are nourished so they can try to succeed her. The first one hatched kills the others in the cradle. The female giant spider carries her eggs in a bag until they reach maturity: she is bigger and stronger than the male, and she sometimes devours him after coupling; the same practices can be seen in the praying mantis, which has taken shape as the myth of devouring femininity: the egg castrates the sperm, and the praying mantis assassinates her spouse; these facts prefigure a woman's dream of castration. But in truth, the praying mantis only manifests such cruelty in captivity: free and with rich enough food around, she rarely makes a meal out of the male; if she does, it is like the solitary ant that often eats some of her own eggs in order to have the strength to lay eggs and perpetuate the species. Seeing in these facts the harbinger of the "battle of the sexes" that sets individuals as such against each other is just rambling. Neither for the ants, nor the honeybees, nor the termites, nor the spider, nor the praying mantis can one say that the female enslaves and devours the male: it is the species that devours both of them in different ways. The female lives longer and seems to have more importance; but she has no autonomy; laying, incubation, and care of the larvae make up her whole destiny; her other functions are totally or partially atrophied. By contrast, an individual existence takes shape in the male. He very often takes more initiative than the female in fertilization; it is he who seeks her out, who attacks, palpates, seizes her and imposes coitus on her; sometimes he has to fight off other males. Accordingly, the organs of locomotion, touch, and prehension are also often more developed; many female butterflies are apterous, whereas their males have wings; males have more developed colors, elytrons, feet, and claws; and sometimes this profusion can also be seen in a luxurious vanity of gorgeous colors. Aside from the fleeting coitus, the male's life is useless, gratuitous: next to the diligence of worker females, the laziness of drones is a privilege worth noting. But this privilege is outrageous; the male often pays with his life for this uselessness that contains the germ of independence. A species that enslaves the female punishes the male attempting to escape: it eliminates him brutally.

In the higher forms of life, reproduction becomes the production of differentiated organisms; it has a twofold face: maintenance of the species and creation of new individuals; this innovative aspect asserts itself as the singularity of the individual is confirmed. It is thus striking that these two moments of perpetuation and creation divide; this break, already marked at the time of the egg's fertilization, is present in the generating phenomenon as a whole. The structure of the egg itself does not order this division; the female, like the male, possesses a certain autonomy, and her link with the egg loosens; the female fish, amphibian, and bird are much more than an abdomen; the weaker the mother-to-egg link, the less labor parturition involves, and the more undifferentiated is the relation between parents and their offspring. Sometimes, the newly hatched lives are the father's responsibility; this is often the case with fish. Water is an element that can carry eggs and sperm and enables their meeting; fertilization in the aquatic milieu is almost always external; fish do not mate: at best some rub against each other for stimulation. The mother expels the ova and the father the sperm: they have identical roles. There is no more reason for the mother to recognize the eggs as her own than the father. In some species, parents abandon the eggs, which develop without help; sometimes the mother has prepared a nest for them; sometimes she watches over them after fertilization; but very often the father takes charge of them: as soon as he has fertilized them, he chases away the female, who tries to devour them; he fiercely defends them from anything that approaches; there are those that put up a kind of protective nest by emitting air bubbles covered with an isolating substance; they also often incubate the eggs in their mouths or, like the sea horse, in the folds of the stomach. Analogous phenomena can be seen in toads: they do not have real coitus; the male embraces the female and this embrace stimulates the laying: while the eggs are coming out of the cloaca, the male lets out his sperm. Very often—and in particular in the toad known as the midwife toad—the father winds the strings of eggs around his feet and carries them around to guarantee their hatching. As for birds, the egg forms rather slowly within the female; the egg is both relatively big and hard to expel; it has much closer relations with the mother than with the father that fertilized it during a quick coitus; the female is the one who usually sits on it and then looks after the young; but very frequently the father participates in the nest's construction and the protection and nutrition of the young; there are rare cases—for example the passerine—where the male sits on the eggs and then raises the young. Male and female pigeons secrete a kind of milk in their crop that they feed to the fledglings. What is noteworthy in all these cases in which fathers play a nurturing role is that spermatogenesis stops during the period they devote to their offspring; busy with maintaining life, the father has no impetus to bring forth new life-forms.

The most complex and concretely individualized life is found in mammals. The split of the two vital moments, maintaining and creating, takes place definitively in the separation of the sexes. In this branching out—and considering vertebrates only—the mother has the closest connection to her offspring, whereas the father is more uninterested; the whole organism of the female is adapted to and determined by the servitude of maternity, while the sexual initiative is the prerogative of the male. The female is the prey of the species; for one or two seasons, depending on the case, her whole life is regulated by a sexual cycle—the estrous cycle—whose length and periodicity vary from one species to another. This cycle has two phases: during the first one the ova mature (the number varies according to the species), and a nidification process occurs in the womb; in the second phase a fat necrosis is produced, ending in the elimination of the structure, that is a whitish discharge. The estrus corresponds to the period of heat; but heat in the female is rather passive; she is ready to receive the male, she waits for him; for mammals—and some birds—she might invite him; but she limits herself to calling him by noises, displays, or exhibitions; she could never impose coitus. That decision is up to him in the end. Even for insects where the female has major privileges and consents to total sacrifice for the species, it is usually the male that provokes fertilization; male fish often invite the female to spawn by their presence or by touching; for amphibians, the male acts as a stimulator. But for birds and above all mammals, the male imposes himself on her; very often she submits to him with indifference or even resists him. Whether she is provocative or consensual, it is he who *takes* her: she is *taken*. The word often has a very precise meaning: either because he has specific organs or because he is stronger, the male grabs and immobilizes her; he is the one that actively makes the coitus movements; for many insects, birds, and mammals, he penetrates her. In that regard, she is like a raped interiority. The male does not do violence to the species, because the species can only perpetuate itself by renewal; it would perish if ova and sperm did not meet; but the female whose job it is to protect the egg encloses it in herself, and her body that constitutes a shelter for the egg removes it from the male's fertilizing action; there is thus a resistance that has to be broken down, and so by penetrating the egg the male realizes himself as activity. His domination is expressed by the coital position of almost all animals; the male is *on* the female. And the organ he uses is incontestably material too, but it is seen in an animated state: it is a tool, while the female organ in this operation is merely an inert receptacle. The male deposits his sperm; the female receives it. Thus, although she plays a fundamentally active role in procreation, she endures coitus, which alienates her from herself by penetration and internal fertilization;

although she feels the sexual need as an individual need—since in heat she might seek out the male—she nevertheless experiences the sexual adventure in its immediacy as an interior story and not in relation to the world and to others. But the fundamental difference between male and female mammals is that in the same quick instant, the sperm, by which the male's life transcends into another, becomes foreign to it and is separated from its body; thus the male, at the very moment it goes beyond its individuality, encloses itself once again in it. By contrast, the ovum began to separate itself from the female when, ripe, it released itself from the follicle to fall into the oviduct; penetrated by a foreign gamete, it implants itself in the uterus: first violated, the female is then alienated; she carries the fetus in her womb for varying stages of maturation depending on the species: the guinea pig is born almost adult; the dog close to a fetal state; inhabited by another who is nourished by her substance, the female is both herself and other than herself during the whole gestation period; after delivery, she feeds the newborn with milk from her breasts. This makes it difficult to know when it can be considered autonomous: at fertilization, birth, or weaning? It is noteworthy that the more the female becomes a separate individual, the more imperiously the living continuity is affirmed beyond any separation. The fish or the bird that expels the virgin ovum or the fertilized egg is less prey to its offspring than the female mammal. The female mammal recovers her autonomy after the birth of the young: a distance is thus established between her and them; and starting from this separation, she devotes herself to them; she takes care of them, showing initiative and invention; she fights to defend them against other animals and even becomes aggressive. But she does not usually seek to affirm her individuality; she does not oppose either males or females; she does not have a fighting instinct;[5] in spite of Darwin's assertions, disparaged today, the female in general accepts the male that presents himself. It is not that she lacks individual qualities—far from it; in periods when she escapes the servitude of maternity, she can sometimes be the male's equal: the mare is as quick as the stallion, the female hound has as keen a nose as the male, female monkeys show as much intelligence as males when tested. But this individuality is not asserted: the female abdicates it for the benefit of the species that demands this abdication.

The male's destiny is very different; it has just been shown that in his very surpassing, he separates himself and is confirmed in himself. This fea-

---

5. Some chickens fight in the barnyard for a pecking order. Cows too become head of the herd if there are no males.

ture is constant from insects to higher animals. Even fish and cetaceans that live in schools, loosely gathered within the group, tear themselves away when in heat; they isolate themselves and become aggressive toward other males. While sexuality is immediate for the female, it is indirect in the male: he actively bridges the distance between desire and its satisfaction; he moves, seeks, feels the female, caresses her, immobilizes her before penetrating; the organs for the functions of relation, locomotion, and prehension are often better developed in the male. It is noteworthy that the active impulsion that produces his sperm's multiplication is accompanied by brilliant feathers, shiny scales, horns, antlers, a crest, song, exuberance; neither the "wedding attire" he puts on in heat nor the displays of seduction are now thought to have a selective finality; but they are witness to the power of life that flourishes in him with gratuitous and magnificent splendor. This vital generosity, the activity deployed in mating and in coitus itself, the dominating affirmation of his power over the female—all of this contributes to positing the individual as such at the moment he surpasses himself. Hegel is right to see the subjective element in the male while the female remains enclosed in the species. Subjectivity and separateness immediately mean conflict. Aggressiveness is one of the characteristics of the male in heat. It cannot be explained by competition, since there are about the same number of females as males; it is rather competition that is explained by this combative will. It is as if before procreating, the male, claiming as his very own the act that perpetuates the species, confirms the reality of his individuality in his fight against his fellow creatures. The species inhabits the female and absorbs much of her individual life; the male, by contrast, integrates specific living forces in his individual life. He is undoubtedly also subject to laws that surpass him; he experiences spermatogenesis and periodic heats; but these processes affect the organism as a whole much less than the estrus cycle; neither sperm production nor ovogenesis as such is tiring: the absorbing job for the female is the development of the egg into an adult animal. Coitus is a rapid operation that does not reduce the male's vitality. He manifests almost no paternal instinct. He very often abandons the female after mating. When he remains near her as head of a family group (monogamic family, harem, or herd), he plays a protective and nurturing role vis-à-vis the whole community; it is rare for him to take a direct interest in the children. In those species that are favorable to the flourishing of individual life, the male's effort at autonomy—which, in the lower animals, leads to its ruin—is crowned with success. He is usually bigger than the female, stronger, quicker, more adventurous; he leads a more independent life whose activities are more gratuitous; he is more conquering, more imperious: in animal societies, it is he who commands.

In nature nothing is ever completely clear: the two types, male and female, are not always sharply distinguished; there is often a dimorphism—the color of the coat, the placement of the mottling—that seems absolutely contingent; it does happen, though, that the two types are not distinguishable, their functions barely differentiated, as was seen with fish. However, as a whole and especially at the top of the animal scale, the two sexes represent two diverse aspects of the species' life. Their opposition is not, as has been claimed, one of passivity and activity: not only is the ovum nucleus active, but the development of the embryo is also a living process and not a mechanical one. It would be too simple to define this opposition as one of change and permanence: the sperm creates only because its vitality is maintained in the egg; the ovum can only exist by surpassing itself or else it regresses and degenerates. But it is true that in both these active operations—maintenance and creation—the synthesis of becoming is not realized in the same way. Maintaining means denying the dispersion of instants, thereby affirming continuity in the course of their outpouring; creating means exploding an irreducible and separate present within a temporal unity, and it is also true that for the female it is the continuity of life that seeks to realize itself in spite of separation, while separation into new and individualized forces is brought about by male initiative; he can affirm himself in his autonomy; he integrates the specific energy into his own life; by contrast, female individuality is fought by the interest of the species; she seems possessed by outside forces: alienated. This explains why sexual opposition increases rather than abates when the individuality of organisms asserts itself. The male finds more and more ways to use the forces of which he is master; the female feels her subjugation more and more; the conflict between her own interests and those of the generating forces that inhabit her exasperates her. Giving birth for cows and mares is far more painful and dangerous than for female mice and rabbits. Woman, the most individualized of females, is also the most fragile, the one who experiences her destiny the most dramatically and who distinguishes herself the most significantly from her male.

In the human species as in most others, almost as many individuals of both sexes are born (100 girls for 104 boys); embryonic evolution is analogous; however, the original epithelium remains neuter longer in the female fetus; as a result, it is subjected to hormonal influence over a longer period, and its development is more often inverted; most hermaphrodites are thought to be genotypically female subjects who are masculinized later: it could be said that the male organism is immediately defined as male, whereas the female embryo is reluctant to accept its femaleness; but these tentative beginnings of fetal life are not yet well enough understood for them to be assigned a meaning. Once formed, the genital apparatus is symmetrical in both sexes; the hormones of each type belong to the same chemical family, the sterols, and when all things are considered, all of them derive from cholesterol; they order the secondary differentiation of the soma. Neither their formula nor their anatomical singularities define the human female as such. Her functional evolution is what distinguishes her from the male. Man's development is comparatively simple. From birth to puberty, he grows more or less regularly; at around fifteen or sixteen years old, spermatogenesis begins and continues until old age; hormone production occurs at the same time and marks the male constitution of the soma. When that happens, the male's sex life is normally integrated into his individual existence: in terms of desire and coitus, his surpassing toward the species is an integral part of the subjective moment of his transcendence: he *is* his body. Woman's history is much more complex. At the beginning of embryonic life, the supply of ovocytes is definitively formed; the ovary contains about fifty thousand ova, and each one is enclosed in a follicle, with about four hundred reaching maturity. At the moment of birth the species has taken possession of her and seeks to affirm itself; on coming into the world, the woman goes through a kind of first puberty; ovocytes suddenly grow bigger; then the ovary reduces by about one-fifth. One could say that the child was granted a reprieve; while its organism develops, its genital system remains more or less stationary. Some follicles swell up without reaching maturity; the girl's growth is analogous to the boy's: at the same age she is often bigger and heavier than he. But at puberty the species reasserts its rights: influenced by ovarian secretions, the number of growing follicles increases, the ovary becomes congested and grows, one of the ova reaches maturity, and the menstrual cycle begins; the genital system attains its definitive size and form, the soma becomes feminized, and the endocrine balance is set up. It is worth noting that this event has all the characteristics of a crisis; the woman's body does not accept the species' installation in her without a fight; and this fight weakens and endangers her; before puberty, about the same number of girls die for every 100 boys: from fourteen to eighteen, 128 girls die for every 100 boys, and from eighteen to twenty-two 105 girls for every 100 boys. This is the period when chlorosis, tuberculosis, scoliosis, osteomyelitis, and such strike. Puberty is abnormally early for some subjects: it can occur at four or five years of age. For others, it does not begin at all: the subject is infantile, suffering from amenorrhea or dysmenorrhea. Some women manifest virile characteristics: too many secretions from the adrenal glands give them masculine characteristics. These anomalies are absolutely not a victory of the individual over the tyranny of the species: there is no way to escape that tyranny because it enslaves individual life at the same time that it nourishes it; this duality can be seen in the ovarian functions; the woman's vitality takes root in the ovary, that of the man in the testicles: in both cases the castrated individual is not only sterile: it regresses and degenerates; un-"formed" and badly formed, the whole organism is impoverished and out of balance; it can only flourish with the flourishing of the genital system; and yet many genital phenomena are not in the interest of the subject's individual life and even put it in danger. The mammary glands that develop at puberty have no role in the woman's individual economy: they can be removed at any moment in her life. The finality of many ovarian secretions is in the egg, in its maturity, in the adaptation of the uterus for its needs: for the organism as a whole, they are a factor of imbalance more than regulation; the woman is more adapted to the egg's needs than to herself. From puberty to menopause she is the principal site of a story that takes place in her and does not concern her personally. Anglo-Saxons call menstruation "the curse," and it is true that there is no individual finality in the menstrual cycle. It was thought in Aristotle's time that the blood that flowed each month, if fertilization occurred, was to constitute the flesh and blood of the child; the truth of this old theory is that women endlessly start up the labor of gestation. For other mammals, this estrous cycle plays itself out during one season; there is no bloody flow: only in higher monkeys and women does this cycle take place in pain and blood.[6] For about fourteen days one of the Graafian follicles that envelops the eggs increases in volume and ripens at the same time that the ovary secretes the hormone folliculin at the level of the follicle. Ovulation takes place on the fourteenth day: the walls of the follicle disintegrate (sometimes causing a slight hemorrhage); the egg falls into the fallopian tubes while the opening evolves into the yellow body. Then begins the second or corpus luteum phase characterized by the secretion of the hormone progesterone that acts on the uterus. The uterus changes in that the wall's capillary system swells, creases, and waffles, forming a kind of lacework; this is the construction of a cradle in the womb

---

6. The analysis of these phenomena has been advanced in the last few years by comparing the phenomena occurring in women with those in the higher monkeys, especially for the Rh factor. "It is obviously easier to experiment on the latter animals," writes Louis Gallien (*La sexualité* [*Sexual Reproduction*]).

meant to receive the fertilized egg. As these cellular transformations are irreversible, this construction is not reabsorbed in cases where there is no fertilization: in other mammals the useless debris is possibly carried off by the lymph vessels. But for woman when the endometrial lace collapses, there is an exfoliation of the lining, the capillaries open up, and a bloody mass seeps out. Then, while the corpus luteum is reconstituted, a new follicular phase begins. This complex process, whose details are still quite mysterious, sets the whole body in motion as it is accompanied by hormonal secretions that act on the thyroid and pituitary glands, the central and peripheral nervous systems, and thus on all the organs. Almost all women—more than 85 percent—show signs of distress during this period. Blood pressure rises before the beginning of the flow of blood and then falls; the pulse rate and often the temperature increase; there are frequent cases of fever; the abdomen is painful; there is often constipation and then diarrhea, an increase in the liver volume, urea retention, albumin deficiency, or micro albumin; many women have hyperemia of the pituitary gland (sore throat), and others complain of auditory and visual problems; there is a rise in perspiration secretions accompanied by a sometimes strong sui generis odor at the beginning of and often throughout the menstrual period. Basal metabolism increases. The number of red blood cells decreases; however, the blood carries substances usually kept in reserve in the tissues, in particular calcium salts; these salts act on the ovary, on the thyroid that is overactive, and on the pituitary gland that regulates the metamorphosis of the activated uterine tissue; this glandular instability weakens the nervous system: the central nervous system is affected, often causing headaches, and the peripheral nervous system overreacts: the automatic control by the central nervous system is reduced, which relaxes the reflexes and the convulsive complexes and is manifested in great mood changes: woman is more emotional, nervous, and irritable than usual and can manifest serious psychological problems. This is when she feels most acutely that her body is an alienated opaque thing; it is the prey of a stubborn and foreign life that makes and unmakes a crib in her every month; every month a child is prepared to be born and is aborted in the flow of the crimson tide; woman *is* her body as man *is* his,[7] but her body is something other than her.

---

7. "I am thus my body, at least inasmuch as I have experience, and reciprocally, my body is like a natural subject, like a tentative draft of my total being" (Merleau-Ponty, *Phenomenology of Perception*).

Woman experiences an even stronger alienation when the fertilized egg drops into the uterus and develops there; gestation is, of course, a normal phenomenon that is not harmful to the mother if normal conditions of health and nutrition prevail: certain beneficial interactions develop between her and the fetus; however, contrary to an optimistic theory that is so obviously useful socially, gestation is tiring work that offers woman no benefit as an individual but that demands serious sacrifices.[8] In the early months, it often brings with it appetite loss and vomiting that is not observed in any other domestic female and shows the body's revolt against the species taking possession of it; the body loses phosphorus, calcium, and iron, the last of these losses being very hard to overcome later; the metabolic hyperactivity excites the endocrine system; the negative nervous system is in a heightened state of excitability; the specific weight of the blood decreases, and it is anemic, like "that of people who fast, who are starving, or who have been bled many times, and convalescents."[9] All that a healthy and well-nourished woman can hope for after childbirth is to recoup her losses without too much trouble; but often serious accidents or at least dangerous disorders occur during pregnancy; and if the woman is not sturdy, if she is not careful in her personal hygiene, she will be prematurely misshapen and aged by her pregnancies: it is well-known how frequent this is in the countryside. Childbirth itself is painful; it is dangerous. This crisis shows clearly that the body does not always meet the needs of both the species and the individual; the child sometimes dies, or while coming into life, it kills the mother; or its birth can cause her a chronic illness. Breastfeeding is also an exhausting servitude; a set of factors—the main one undoubtedly being the appearance of a hormone, progesterone—brings milk secretion into the mammary glands; the arrival of the milk is painful and is often accompanied by fever, and the breast-feeder feeds the newborn to the detriment of her own strength. The conflict between the species and the individual can have dramatic consequences in childbirth, making the woman's body distressingly fragile. One often hears that women "have bellyaches"; true indeed, a hostile element is locked inside them: the species is eating away at them. Many of their illnesses are the result not of an external infection but of an internal disorder: false metritis occurs from a reaction of the uterine lining to an abnormal ovarian excitation; if the yellow

---

8. I am taking here an exclusively physiological point of view. It is evident that maternity can be very advantageous psychologically for a woman, just as it can also be a disaster.
9. Cf. H. Vignes in *Traité de physiologie normale et pathologique* (Treatise on Normal and Pathological Physiology), Volume 11, edited by Roger and Binet.

body persists instead of being reabsorbed after menstruation, it provokes salpingitis and endometritis, and so on.

Woman escapes from the grip of the species by one more difficult crisis; between forty-five and fifty, the phenomena of menopause, the opposite of those of puberty, occur. Ovarian activity decreases and even disappears: this disappearance brings about a vital impoverishment of the individual. It is thought that the catabolic glands, thyroid and pituitary, attempt to compensate for the ovaries' deficiencies; thus alongside the change-of-life depression there are phenomena of surges: hot flashes, high blood pressure, nervousness; there is sometimes an increase in the sex drive. Some women retain fat in their tissues; others acquire male traits. For many there is a new endocrine balance. So woman finds herself freed from the servitudes of the female; she is not comparable to a eunuch, because her vitality is intact; however, she is no longer prey to powers that submerge her: she is consistent with herself. It is sometimes said that older women form "a third sex"; it is true they are not males, but they are no longer female either; and often this physiological autonomy is matched by a health, balance, and vigor they did not previously have.

Overlapping women's specifically sexual differentiations are the singularities, more or less the consequences of these differentiations; these are the hormonal actions that determine her soma. On average, she is smaller than man, lighter; her skeleton is thinner; the pelvis is wider, adapted to gestation and birth; her connective tissue retains fats, and her forms are rounder than man's; the overall look: morphology, skin, hair system, and so on is clearly different in the two sexes. Woman has much less muscular force: about two-thirds that of man; she has less respiratory capacity: lungs, trachea, and larynx are smaller in woman; the difference in the larynx brings about that of the voice. Women's specific blood weight is less than men's: there is less hemoglobin retention; women are less robust, more apt to be anemic. Their pulse rate is quicker, their vascular system is less stable: they blush easily. Instability is a striking characteristic of their bodies in general; for example, man's calcium metabolism is stable; women both retain less calcium salt and eliminate it during menstruation and pregnancy; the ovaries seem to have a catabolic action concerning calcium; this instability leads to disorders in the ovaries and in the thyroid, which is more developed in a woman than in a man: and the irregularity of endocrine secretions acts on the peripheral nervous system; muscles and nerves are not perfectly controlled. More instability and less control make them more emotional, which is directly linked to vascular variations: palpitations, redness, and so on; and they are thus subject to convulsive attacks: tears, nervous laughter, and hysterics.

Many of these characteristics are due to woman's subordination to the species. This is the most striking conclusion of this study: she is the most deeply alienated of all the female mammals, and she is the one that refuses this alienation the most violently; in no other is the subordination of the organism to the reproductive function more imperious nor accepted with greater difficulty. Crises of puberty and of the menopause, monthly "curse," long and often troubled pregnancy, illnesses, and accidents are characteristic of the human female: her destiny appears even more fraught the more she rebels against it by affirming herself as an individual. The male, by comparison, is infinitely more privileged: his genital life does not thwart his personal existence; it unfolds seamlessly, without crises and generally without accident. Women live, on average, as long as men, but are often sick and indisposed.

These biological data are of extreme importance: they play an all-important role and are an essential element of woman's situation: we will be referring to them in all further accounts. Because the body is the instrument of our hold on the world, the world appears different to us depending on how it is grasped, which explains why we have studied these data so deeply; they are one of the keys that enable us to understand woman. But we refuse the idea that they form a fixed destiny for her. They do not suffice to constitute the basis for a sexual hierarchy; they do not explain why woman is the Other; they do not condemn her forever to this subjugated role.

It has often been claimed that physiology alone provides answers to these questions: Does individual success have the same chances in the two sexes? Which of the two in the species plays the greater role? But the first question does not apply to woman and other females in the same way, because animals constitute given species and it is possible to provide static descriptions of them: it is simply a question of collating observations to decide if the mare is as quick as the stallion, if male chimpanzees do as well on intelligence tests as their female counterparts; but humanity is constantly in the making. Materialist scholars have claimed to posit the problem in a purely static way; full of the theory of psychophysiological parallelism, they sought to make mathematical comparisons between male and female organisms: and they imagined that these measurements directly defined their functional abilities. I will mention one example of these senseless discussions that this method prompted. As it was supposed, in some mysterious way, that the brain secreted thinking, it seemed very important to decide if the average weight of the female brain was larger or smaller than that of the male. It was found that the former weighs, on average, 1,220 grams, and the latter 1,360, the weight of the female brain varying from 1,000 to 1,500 grams and that of the male from 1,150 to 1,700. But the absolute weight is not significant; it was thus decided that the relative weight should be taken into account. It is $1/48.4$ for the man and $1/44.2$ for the woman. She is thus supposed to be advantaged. No. This still has to be corrected: in such comparisons, the smallest organism always seems to be favored; to compare two individuals correctly while not taking into account the body, one must divide the weight of the brain by the power of 0.56 of the body weight if they belong to the same species. It is considered that men and women are of two different types, with the following results:

For man: $\quad$ W 0.56 = 498 $\qquad \dfrac{1,360}{498} = 2.73$

For woman: $\quad$ W 0.56 = 446 $\qquad \dfrac{1,220}{446} = 2.74$

Equality is the result. But what removes much of the interest of these careful debates is that no relation has been established between brain weight and the development of intelligence. Nor could one give a psychic interpretation of chemical formulas defining male and female hormones. We categorically reject the idea of a psychophysiological parallelism; the bases of this doctrine have definitively and long been weakened. I mention it because although it is philosophically and scientifically ruined, it still haunts a large number of minds: it has already been shown here that some people are carrying around antique vestiges of it. We also repudiate any frame of reference that presupposes the existence of a *natural* hierarchy of values—for example, that of an evolutionary hierarchy; it is pointless to wonder if the female body is more infantile than the male, if it is closer to or further from that of the higher primates, and so forth. All these studies that confuse a vague naturalism with an even vaguer ethic or aesthetic are pure verbiage. Only within a human perspective can the female and the male be compared in the human species. But the definition of man is that he is a being who is not given, who makes himself what he is. As Merleau-Ponty rightly said, man is not a natural species: he is a historical idea. Woman is not a fixed reality but a becoming; she has to be compared with man in her becoming; that is, her *possibilities* have to be defined: what skews the issues so much is that she is being reduced to what she was, to what she is today, while the question concerns her capacities; the fact is that her capacities manifest themselves clearly only when they have been realized: but the fact is also that when one considers a being who is transcendence and surpassing, it is never possible to close the books.

However, one might say, in the position I adopt—that of Heidegger, Sartre, and Merleau-Ponty—that if the body is not a *thing*, it is a situation: it is our grasp on the world and the outline for our projects. Woman is weaker than man; she has less muscular strength, fewer red blood cells, a lesser respiratory capacity; she runs less quickly, lifts less heavy weights—there is practically no sport in which she can compete with him; she cannot enter into a fight with the male. Added to that are the instability, lack of control, and fragility that have been discussed: these are facts. Her grasp of the world is thus more limited; she has less firmness and perseverance in projects that she is also less able to carry out. This means that her individual life is not as rich as man's.

In truth these facts cannot be denied: but they do not carry their meaning in themselves. As soon as we accept a human perspective, defining the body starting from existence, biology becomes an abstract science; when the physiological given (muscular inferiority) takes on meaning, this meaning immediately becomes dependent on a whole context; "weakness" is weakness only in light of the aims man sets for himself, the instruments at his disposal, and the laws he imposes. If he did not want to apprehend the world, the very idea of a *grasp* on things would have no meaning; when, in this apprehension, the full use of body force—above the usable minimum—is not required, the differences cancel each other out; where customs forbid violence, muscular energy cannot be the basis for domination: existential, economic, and moral reference points are necessary to define the notion of *weakness* concretely. It has been said that the human species was an antiphysis; the expression is not really exact, because man cannot possibly contradict the given; but it is in how he takes it on that he constitutes its truth; nature only has reality for him insofar as it is taken on by his action: his own nature is no exception. It is not possible to measure in the abstract the burden of the generative function for woman, just as it is not possible to measure her grasp on the world: the relation of maternity to individual life is naturally regulated in animals by the cycle of heat and seasons; it is undefined for woman; only society can decide; woman's enslavement to the species is tighter or looser depending on how many births the society demands and the hygienic conditions in which pregnancy and birth occur. So if it can be said that among the higher animals individual existence is affirmed more imperiously in the male than in the female, in humanity individual "possibilities" depend on the economic and social situation.

In any case, it is not always true that the male's individual privileges confer upon him superiority in the species; the female regains another kind of autonomy in maternity. Sometimes he imposes his domination: this is the case in the monkeys studied by Zuckerman; but often the two halves of the couple lead separate lives; the lion and the lioness share the care of the habitat equally. Here again, the case of the human species cannot be reduced to any other; men do not define themselves first as individuals; men and women have never challenged each other in individual fights; the couple is an original *Mitsein;* and it is always a fixed or transitory element of a wider collectivity; within these societies, who, the male or the female, is the more necessary for the species? In terms of gametes, in terms of the biological functions of coitus and gestation, the male principle creates to maintain and the female principle maintains to create: What becomes of this division in social life? For species attached to foreign bodies or to the substrata, for those to whom nature grants food abundantly and effortlessly, the role of the male is limited to fertilization; when it is necessary to search, chase, or fight to provide food needed for offspring, the male often helps with their maintenance; this help becomes absolutely indispensable in a species where children remain incapable of taking care of their own needs for a long period after the mother stops nursing them: the male's work then takes on an extreme importance; the lives he brought forth could not maintain themselves without him. One male is enough to fertilize many females each year: but males are necessary for the survival of children after birth, to defend them against enemies, to extract from nature everything they need. The balance of productive and reproductive forces is different depending on the different economic moments of human history, and they condition the relation of the male and the female to children and later among them. But we are going beyond the field of biology: in purely biological terms, it would not be possible to posit the primacy of one sex concerning the role it plays in perpetuating the species.

But a society is not a species: the species realizes itself as existence in a society; it transcends itself toward the world and the future; its customs cannot be deduced from biology; individuals are never left to their nature; they obey this second nature, that is, customs in which the desires and fears that express their ontological attitude are reflected. It is not as a body but as a body subjected to taboos and laws that the subject gains consciousness of and accomplishes himself. He valorizes himself in the name of certain values. And once again, physiology cannot ground values: rather, biological data take on those values the existent confers on them. If the respect or fear woman inspires prohibits man from using violence against her, the male's muscular superiority is not a source of power. If customs desire—as in some Indian tribes—that girls choose husbands, or if it is the father who decides on marriages, the male's sexual aggressiveness does not grant him any initiative, any privilege. The mother's intimate link to the child will be a source of dignity or indignity for her, depending on the very variable value given to the child; this very link, as has already been said, will be recognized or not according to social biases.

Thus we will clarify the biological data by examining them in the light of ontological economic, social, and psychological contexts. Woman's enslavement to the species and the limits of her individual abilities are facts of extreme importance; the woman's body is one of the essential elements of the situation she occupies in this world. But her body is not enough to define her; it has a lived reality only as taken on by consciousness through actions and within a society; biology alone cannot provide an answer to the question that concerns us: why is woman the *Other*? The question is how, in her, nature has been taken on in the course of history; the question is what humanity has made of the human female.

CHAPTER 2

The Psychoanalytical Point of View

The enormous advance psychoanalysis made over psychophysiology is in its consideration that no factor intervenes in psychic life without having taken on human meaning; it is not the body-object described by scientists that exists concretely but the body lived by the subject. The female is a woman, insofar as she feels herself as such. Some essential biological givens are not part of her lived situation: for example, the structure of the ovum is not reflected in it; by contrast, an organ of slight biological importance like the clitoris plays a primary role in it. Nature does not define woman: it is she who defines herself by reclaiming nature for herself in her affectivity.

An entire system has been erected based on this outlook: we do not intend here to criticize it as a whole, but only to examine its contribution to the study of woman. Discussing psychoanalysis as such is not an easy undertaking. Like all religions—Christianity or Marxism—it displays an unsettling flexibility against a background of rigid concepts. Sometimes words are taken in their narrowest meanings, the term "phallus," for example, designating very precisely the fleshy growth that is the male sex organ; at other times, infinitely broadened, they take on a symbolic value: the phallus would express all of the virile character and situation as a whole. If one criticizes the doctrine to the letter, the psychoanalyst maintains that its spirit has been misunderstood; if one approves of the spirit, he immediately wants to limit you to the letter. The doctrine is unimportant, he says: psychoanalysis is a method; but the success of the method strengthens the doctrinaire in his faith. After all, where would the true features of psychoanalysis be found if not with psychoanalysts themselves? But among them, as among Christians and Marxists, there are heretics: more than one psychoanalyst has declared that "the worst enemies of psychoanalysis are psychoanalysts themselves." Many ambiguities remain to be dissolved, in spite of an often-pedantic scholastic precision. As Sartre and Merleau-Ponty have observed, the proposition "sexuality is coextensive with existence" can be understood in two very different ways; it could mean that every avatar of the existent has a sexual signification, or that every sexual phenomenon has an existential meaning: these two affirmations can be reconciled; but often one tends to slip from one to the other. Besides, as soon as "sexual" and "genital" are distinguished, the notion of sexuality becomes blurred. "The sexual for Freud is the intrinsic aptitude to trigger the genital," says Dalbiez.* But nothing is murkier than the notion of "aptitude," or of possibility: only reality can indubitably prove possibility. Not being a philosopher, Freud refused to justify his system philosophically; his disciples maintain that he thus eludes any attacks of a metaphysical sort. There are, however, metaphysical postulates behind all of his affirmations: to use his language is to adopt a philosophy. It is this very confusion that, while making criticism awkward, demands it.

Freud was not very concerned with woman's destiny; it is clear that he modeled his description of it on that of masculine destiny, merely modifying some of the traits. Before him, the sexologist Marañón had declared: "As differentiated energy, the libido is, one might say, a force of virile significance. We can say as much for the orgasm." According to him, women who attain orgasm are "viriloid" women; sexual fulfillment is a "one-way street" and woman is only at the halfway point.[1] Freud does not go that far; he accepts that woman's sexuality is as developed as man's; but he barely studies it in itself. He writes: "The libido is constantly and regularly male in essence, whether in man or in woman." He refuses to posit the feminine libido in its originality: he will thus necessarily see it as a complex deviation from the human libido in general. And this, he thinks, develops first identically in both sexes: all children go through an oral phase that fixes them upon their mother's breast, then an anal phase, and finally the genital phase; it is then that they become differentiated. Freud brought out a fact whose importance had not previously been recognized: male eroticism is definitively centered on the penis, while the woman has two distinct erotic systems, one that is clitoral and develops in infancy and another that is vaginal and develops only after puberty; when the boy gets to the genital phase, he completes his development; he has to move from the autoerotic attitude,

---

* *La méthode psychanalytique et la doctrine freudienne* (*Psychoanalytical Method and the Doctrine of Freud*).—TRANS.

1. Curiously, this theory is found in D. H. Lawrence. In *The Plumed Serpent*, Don Cipriano sees to it that his mistress never reaches orgasm: she must vibrate along with the man, and not find individualized pleasure.

where subjective pleasure is sought, to a hetero-erotic attitude that will link pleasure to an object, usually a woman; this passage will occur at puberty through a narcissistic phase: but the penis will remain, as in infancy, the favored erotic organ. Woman, also passing through a narcissistic phase, must make man the object of her libido; but the process will be far more complex as she must pass from clitoral to vaginal pleasure. There is but one genital step for man, while there are two for woman; she runs a greater risk of not completing her sexual development, and of remaining at the infantile stage, and consequently of developing neuroses.

At the autoerotic stage, the child is already more or less strongly attached to an object: a boy is fixated on his mother and wants to identify with his father; he is afraid of this ambition and fears that his father will punish him for it by mutilating him; the castration complex emanates from the Oedipus complex; so he develops aggressive feelings toward his father, while at the same time interiorizing his father's authority: thus develops the superego that censures incestuous tendencies; these tendencies are repressed, the complex is liquidated, and the son is freed from the father, whom he in fact has installed in himself in the form of moral precepts. The more defined and strongly fought the Oedipus complex is, the stronger the superego. Freud first described the history of the girl in a completely symmetrical way; later he named the feminine form of the infant complex the Electra complex; but clearly he defined it less in itself than based on a masculine model; yet he accepts a very important difference between the two: the little girl first has a maternal fixation, while the boy is at no time sexually attracted by the father; this fixation is a carryover from the oral phase; the infant then identifies with the father; but around the age of five, she discovers the anatomical difference between the sexes, and she reacts to the absence of a penis by a castration complex: she imagines having been mutilated, and suffers from it; she must therefore renounce her virile pretensions; she identifies with her mother and tries to seduce her father. The castration complex and the Electra complex reinforce each other; the feeling of frustration for girls is all the more painful as, loving her father, the girl would like to resemble him; and inversely regret strengthens her love: through the tenderness she inspires in her father, she can compensate for her inferiority. The girl experiences feelings of rivalry and hostility toward her mother. Then her superego is constituted as well, repressing her incestuous tendencies; but her superego is more fragile: the Electra complex is less clear than the Oedipus complex, because her first fixation was maternal; and since the father was himself the object of this love that he condemned, his prohibitions had less force than in the case of the rival son. It can be seen that, as with her genital development, the little girl's overall sexual drama is more complex than her brother's: she might be tempted to react to the castration complex by rejecting her femininity, obstinately coveting a penis, and identifying with her father; this attitude will lead her to remain at the clitoral stage, to become frigid, or to turn to homosexuality.

The two essential objections to this description stem from the fact that Freud copied it from a masculine model. He assumes that a woman feels like a mutilated man; but the notion of mutilation implies comparison and valorization; many psychoanalysts accept today that girls miss having a penis without assuming they were ever stripped of one; this regret is not even generalized among all girls; and it could not arise from a simple anatomical encounter; many little girls discover the masculine constitution very late; and if they do discover it, it is only by seeing it; the boy has a living experience from his penis that allows him to take pride in it, but this pride has no immediate correlation with the humiliation of his sisters since they only know the masculine organ in its exteriority; this growth, this delicate stalk of skin, can only inspire their indifference and even disgust; the girl's envy, when it appears, is the result of a prior valorization of virility: Freud takes this for granted when instead he should account for it.[2] Besides, because there is no original description of the feminine libido, the notion of the Electra complex is very vague. Even the presence of a specifically genital Oedipus complex in boys is by no means general; but, apart from very rare exceptions, it cannot be stated that the father is a source of genital excitation for his daughter; one of the great problems of female eroticism is that clitoral pleasure is localized: it is only in puberty, in connection with vaginal eroticism, that many erogenous zones develop in the woman's body; to say that in a child of ten a father's kisses and caresses have an "intrinsic aptitude" to arouse clitoral pleasure is an assertion that in most cases makes no sense. If it is accepted that the "Electra complex" has only a very diffuse and affective nature, then the whole question of affectivity is raised, a question that Freudianism does not provide the means to define, once it is distinguished from sexuality. In any case, it is not the feminine libido that deifies the father: the mother is not deified by the desire she arouses in her son; the fact that feminine desire is focused on a sovereign being gives it a unique character; but the girl is not constitutive of her object, she submits to it. The father's sovereignty is a fact of social order: Freud fails to account for this; he himself admits that it is impossible to

---

2. This discussion will be taken up again in more detail in Volume II, Chapter 12.

know what authority decided at what moment in history that the father would prevail over the mother: according to him, this decision represents progress, but its causes are unknown. "[In this case] it cannot be the father himself, since it is only this progress that raises him to the rank of an authority," he writes in his last work.[3]

Adler departed from Freud because he understood the inadequacies of a system that bases the development of human life on sexuality alone: he means to reintegrate sexuality into the total personality; while for Freud all behavior is driven by desire, that is, by seeking pleasure, Adler sees man as aiming at certain goals; he replaces drives with motives, finality, and plans; he raises intelligence to such heights that for him sexuality often has only symbolic value. According to his theories, the human drama is divided into three steps: each individual has a will to power but along with it an inferiority complex; this conflict leads him to use countless ruses rather than confront real-life obstacles that he fears may be insurmountable; the subject establishes a distance between himself and the society he fears: thus develop neuroses that are disturbances of the social sense. As for woman, her inferiority complex manifests itself in a rejection out of shame of her femininity: it is not the absence of a penis that unleashes this complex but the total situation; the girl envies the phallus only as a symbol of the privileges granted to boys; the father's place in the family, the universal predominance of males, and upbringing all confirm her idea of masculine superiority. Later, in the course of sexual relations, even the coital posture that places the woman underneath the man is an added humiliation. She reacts by a "masculine protest"; she either tries to masculinize herself or uses her feminine wiles to go into battle against man. Through motherhood she can find in her child the equivalent of the penis. But this supposes that she must first accept herself completely as woman, and thus accept her inferiority. She is far more deeply divided against herself than is man.

It is unnecessary to underline here the theoretical differences between Adler and Freud or the possibilities of reconciliation: neither the explanation based on drive nor the one based on motive is ever sufficient: all drives posit a motive, but motive is never grasped except through drives; a synthesis of Adlerism and Freudianism thus seems possible. In fact, while bringing in notions of aim and finality, Adler retains in full the idea of psychic causality; his relation to Freud resembles somewhat the relation of energeticism to mechanism: whether it is a question of impact or force of

---

3. Cf. *Moses and Monotheism.*

attraction, the physicist always recognizes determinism. This is the postulate common to all psychoanalysts: for them, human history is explained by an interplay of determined elements. They all allot the same destiny to woman. Her drama is summed up in a conflict between her "viriloid" and her "feminine" tendencies; the former are expressed in the clitoral system, the latter in vaginal eroticism; as a very young girl, she identifies with her father; she then experiences feelings of inferiority relative to man and is faced with the alternative of either maintaining her autonomy, becoming virilized—which, with an underlying inferiority complex, provokes a tension that risks bringing on neuroses—or else finding happy self-fulfillment in amorous submission, a solution facilitated by the love she felt for her sovereign father; it is he whom she is looking for in her lover or husband, and her sexual love is mingled with her desire to be dominated. Maternity will be her reward, restoring to her a new kind of autonomy. This drama seems to be endowed with its own dynamism; it continues to work itself out through all the mishaps that distort it, and every woman passively endures it.

Psychoanalysts have no trouble finding empirical confirmations of their theories: it is known that if Ptolemy's system is subtly complicated, his version of the position of the planets could be upheld for a long time; if an inverse Oedipus complex is superimposed onto the Oedipus complex and by showing a desire in every anxiety, the very facts that contradicted Freudianism will be successfully integrated into it. For a figure to be perceived, it must stand out from its background, and how the figure is perceived brings out the ground behind it in positive delineation; thus if one is determined to describe a particular case from a Freudian perspective, one will find the Freudian schema as the background behind it; but when a doctrine demands the multiplication of secondary explanations in an indefinite and arbitrary way, when observation uncovers as many anomalies as normal cases, it is better to give up the old frameworks. Today as well, every psychoanalyst works at adapting Freudian concepts to suit himself; he attempts compromises; for example, a contemporary psychoanalyst writes: "Whenever there is a complex, there are by definition several components . . . The complex consists in grouping these disparate elements and not in representing one of them by the others."[4] But the idea of a simple grouping of elements is unacceptable: psychic life is not a mosaic; it is altogether complete in every one of its moments, and this unity must be

---

4. Baudouin, *L'âme enfantine et la psychanalyse* (The Child's Soul and Psychoanalysis).

respected. This is possible only by recovering the original intentionality of existence through the disparate facts. Without going back to this source, man appears a battlefield of drives and prohibitions equally devoid of meaning and contingent. All psychoanalysts systematically refuse the idea of choice and its corollary, the notion of value; and herein lies the intrinsic weakness of the system. Cutting out drives and prohibitions from existential choice, Freud fails to explain their origin: he takes them as givens. He tried to replace the notion of value with that of authority; but he admits in *Moses and Monotheism* that he has no way to account for this authority. Incest, for example, is forbidden because the father forbade it: But why did he forbid it? It is a mystery. The superego interiorizes orders and prohibitions emanating from an arbitrary tyranny; instinctive tendencies exist, but we do not know why; these two realities are heterogeneous because morality is posited as foreign to sexuality; human unity appears as shattered, there is no passage from the individual to the society: Freud is forced to invent strange fictions to reunite them.[5] Adler saw clearly that the castration complex could be explained only in a social context; he approached the problem of valorization, but he did not go back to the ontological source of values recognized by society, and he did not understand that values were involved in sexuality itself, which led him to misunderstand their importance.

Sexuality certainly plays a considerable role in human life: it could be said to penetrate it completely; physiology has already demonstrated how the activity of testes and ovaries is intermixed with that of the soma. The existent is a sexed body; in its relations with other existents that are also sexed bodies, sexuality is thus always involved; but as the body and sexuality are concrete expressions of existence, it is also from here that their significance can be ascertained: without this perspective, psychoanalysis takes unexplained facts for granted. For example, a young girl is said to be "ashamed" of urinating in a squatting position, with her bottom exposed; but what is shame? Likewise, before asking if the male is proud because he has a penis or if his penis is the expression of his pride, we need to know what pride is and how the subject's aspirations can be embodied in an object. Sexuality must not be taken as an irreducible given; the existent possesses a more primary "quest for being"; sexuality is only one of these aspects. Sartre demonstrates this in *Being and Nothingness;* Bachelard also says it in his works on Earth, Air, and Water: psychoanalysts believe that man's quintessential truth lies in his relation to his own body and that of

---

5. Freud, *Totem and Taboo.*

others like him within society; but man has a primordial interest in the substance of the natural world surrounding him that he attempts to discover in
work, play, and all experiences of the "dynamic imagination"; man seeks to
connect concretely with existence through the whole world, grasped in all
possible ways. Working the soil and digging a hole are activities as primal
as an embrace or coitus: it is an error to see them only as sexual symbols; a
hole, slime, a gash, hardness, and wholeness are primary realities; man's
interest in them is not dictated by libido; instead, the libido will be influenced by the way these realities were revealed to him. Man is not fascinated
by wholeness because it symbolizes feminine virginity: rather, his love for
wholeness makes virginity precious. Work, war, play, and art define ways
of being in the world that cannot be reduced to any others; they bring to
light features that impinge on those that sexuality reveals; it is both through
them and through these erotic experiences that the individual chooses himself. But only an ontological point of view can restore the unity of this
choice.

Psychoanalysts vehemently reject this notion of choice in the name of
determinism and "the collective unconscious"; this unconscious would
provide man with ready-made imagery and universal symbolism; it would
explain analogies found in dreams, lapses, delusions, allegories, and human
destinies; to speak of freedom would be to reject the possibility of explaining these disturbing concordances. But the idea of freedom is not incompatible with the existence of certain constants. If the psychoanalytical
method is often productive in spite of errors in theory, it is because there
are givens in every individual case so generalized that no one would dream
of denying them: situations and behavior patterns recur; the moment of
decision springs out of generality and repetition. "Anatomy is destiny,"
said Freud; and this phrase is echoed by Merleau-Ponty: "The body is generality." Existence is one, across and through the separation of existents,
manifesting itself in analogous organisms; so there will be constants in the
relationship between the ontological and the sexual. At any given period,
technology and the economic and social structure of a group reveal an
identical world for all its members: there will also be a constant relation of
sexuality to social forms; analogous individuals, placed in analogous conditions, will grasp analogous significations in the given; this analogy is not
the basis of a rigorous universality, but it can account for finding general
types in individual cases. A symbol does not emerge as an allegory worked
out by a mysterious unconscious: it is the apprehension of a signification
through an analogue of the signifying object; because of the identity of the
existential situation cutting across all existents and the identity of the fac-

symbolism

ticity they have to cope with, significations are revealed to many individuals in the same way; symbolism did not fall out of heaven or rise out of subterranean depths: it was elaborated like language, by the human reality that is at once *Mitsein* and separation; and this explains that singular invention also has its place: in practice the psychoanalytical method must accept this whether or not doctrine authorizes it. This approach enables us to understand, for example, the value generally given to the penis.[6] It is impossible to account for this without starting from an existential fact: the subject's tendency toward *alienation;* the anxiety of his freedom leads the subject to search for himself in things, which is a way to flee from himself; it is so fundamental a tendency that as soon as he is weaned and separated from the Whole, the infant endeavors to grasp his alienated existence in the mirror, in his parents' gaze. Primitive people alienate themselves in their mana, their totem; civilized people in their individual souls, their egos, their names, their possessions, and their work: here is the first temptation of inauthenticity. The penis is singularly adapted to play this role of "double" for the little boy: for him it is both a foreign object and himself; it is a plaything, a doll, and it is his own flesh; parents and nurses treat it like a little person. So, clearly, it becomes for the child "an alter ego usually craftier, more intelligent, and more clever than the individual";[7] because the urinary function and later the erection are midway between voluntary processes and spontaneous processes, because it is the impulsive, quasi-foreign source of subjectively experienced pleasure, the penis is posited by the subject as himself and other than himself; specific transcendence is embodied in it in a graspable way, and it is a source of pride; because the phallus is set apart, man can integrate into his personality the life that flows from it. This is why, then, the length of the penis, the force of the urine stream, the erection, and the ejaculation become for him the measure of his own worth.[8] It is thus a constant that the phallus is the fleshly incarnation of transcendence; since it is also a constant that the child feels transcended, that is, frustrated in his transcendence by his father, the Freudian idea of the castration complex will persist. Deprived of this alter ego, the little girl does not alienate herself in a graspable thing, does not reclaim herself: she

---

6. We will come back to this subject in more detail in Volume II, Chapter 1.

7. Alice Bálint, *The Psychoanalysis of the Nursery.*

8. The case of little peasant boys who entertain themselves by having excrement contests has been brought to my attention: the one producing the biggest and most solid feces enjoys a prestige that no other success, in games or even in fighting, could replace. Fecal matter here played the same role as the penis: it was a matter of alienation in both cases.

is thus led to make her entire self an object, to posit herself as the Other; the question of knowing whether or not she has compared herself with boys is secondary; what is important is that, even without her knowing it, the absence of a penis keeps her from being aware of herself as a sex; many consequences result from this. But these constants we point out nevertheless do not define a destiny: the phallus takes on such importance because it symbolizes a sovereignty that is realized in other areas. If woman succeeded in affirming herself as subject, she would invent equivalents of the phallus: the doll that embodies the promise of the child may become a more precious possession than a penis.[9] There are matrilineal societies where the women possess the masks in which the collectivity alienates itself; the penis then loses much of its glory. Only within the situation grasped in its totality does anatomical privilege found a truly human privilege. Psychoanalysis could only find its truth within a historical context.

Likewise, woman can no more be defined by the consciousness of her own femininity than by merely saying that woman is a female: she finds this consciousness within the society of which she is a member. Interiorizing the unconscious and all psychic life, the very language of psychoanalysis suggests that the drama of the individual unfolds within him: the terms "complex," "tendencies," and so forth imply this. But a life is a relation with the world; the individual defines himself by choosing himself through the world; we must turn to the world to answer the questions that preoccupy us. In particular, psychoanalysis fails to explain why woman is the *Other*. Even Freud accepts that the prestige of the penis is explained by the father's sovereignty, and he admits that he does not know the source of male supremacy.

Without wholly rejecting the contributions of psychoanalysis, some of which are productive, we will nevertheless not accept its method. First of all, we will not limit ourselves to taking sexuality as a given: that this view falls short is demonstrated by the poverty of the descriptions touching on the feminine libido; I have already said that psychoanalysts have never studied it head-on, but only based on the male libido; they seem to ignore the fundamental ambivalence of the attraction that the male exercises over the female. Freudians and Adlerians explain woman's anxiety before male genitalia as an inversion of frustrated desire. Stekel rightly saw this as an original reaction; but he accounts for it only superficially: the woman would fear defloration, penetration, pregnancy, and pain, and this fear

---

9. We will come back to these ideas in Part Two; mention is made here for the sake of methodology.

would stifle her desire; this explanation is too rational.* Instead of accepting that desire is disguised as anxiety or is overcome by fear, we should consider this sort of pressing and frightened appeal that is female desire as a basic given; it is characterized by the indissoluble synthesis of attraction and repulsion. It is noteworthy that many female animals flee from coitus at the very moment they solicit it: they are accused of coquetry or hypocrisy; but it is absurd to attempt to explain primitive behaviors by assimilating them to complex ones: they are, on the contrary, at the source of attitudes called coquetry and hypocrisy in women. The idea of a passive libido is disconcerting because the libido has been defined as a drive, as energy based on the male; but one could no more conceive a priori of a light being both yellow and blue: the intuition of green is needed. Reality would be better delineated if, instead of defining the libido in vague terms of "energy," the significance of sexuality were juxtaposed with that of other human attitudes: taking, catching, eating, doing, undergoing, and so on; for sexuality is one of the singular modes of apprehending an object; the characteristics of the erotic object as it is shown not only in the sexual act but in perception in general would also have to be studied. This examination goes beyond the psychoanalytical framework that posits eroticism as irreducible.

In addition, we will pose the problem of feminine destiny quite differently: we will situate woman in a world of values, and we will lend her behavior a dimension of freedom. We think she has to choose between the affirmation of her transcendence and her alienation as object; she is not the plaything of contradictory drives; she devises solutions that have an ethical hierarchy among them. Replacing value with authority, choice with drives, psychoanalysis proposes an ersatz morality: the idea of normality. This idea is indeed highly useful from a therapeutic point of view; but it has reached a disturbing extent in psychoanalysis in general. The descriptive schema is proposed as a law; and assuredly, a mechanistic psychology could not accept the notion of moral invention; at best it can recognize *less* but never more; at best it acknowledges failures, but never creations. If a subject does not wholly replicate a development considered normal, his development will be seen as being interrupted, and this will be interpreted as a lack and a negation and never a positive decision. That, among other things, is what renders the psychoanalysis of great men so shocking: we are told that this transference or that sublimation was not successfully carried

---

* Stekel, *Frigidity in Woman*, which was published in French translation by Gallimard in 1937.—TRANS.

out in them; it is never supposed that perhaps they could have rejected it, and perhaps for good reasons; it is never considered that their behavior might have been motivated by freely posited aims; the individual is always explained through his link to the past and not with respect to a future toward which he projects himself. Therefore, we are never given more than an inauthentic picture, and in this inauthenticity no criterion other than normality can possibly be found. The description of feminine destiny is, from this point of view, altogether striking. The way psychoanalysts understand it, "to identify" with the mother or the father is to *alienate one-self* in a model, it is to prefer a foreign image to a spontaneous movement of one's own existence, it is to play at being. We are shown woman solicited by two kinds of alienations; it is very clear that to play at being a man will be a recipe for failure; but to play at being a woman is also a trap: being a woman would mean being an object, the Other; and at the heart of its abdication, the Other remains a subject. The real problem for the woman refusing these evasions is to accomplish herself as transcendence: this means seeing which possibilities are opened to her by what are called virile and feminine attitudes; when a child follows the path indicated by one or another of his parents, it could be because he freely takes on their projects: his behavior could be the result of a choice motivated by ends. Even for Adler, the will to power is only a sort of absurd energy; he calls any project that incarnates transcendence a "masculine protest"; when a girl climbs trees, it is, according to him, to be the equal of boys: he does not imagine that she likes to climb trees; for the mother, the child is anything but a "penis substitute"; painting, writing, and engaging in politics are not only "good sublimations": they are ends desired in themselves. To deny this is to falsify all of human history. Parallels can be noted between our descriptions and those of psychoanalysts. From man's point of view—adopted by both male and female psychoanalysts—behavior of alienation is considered feminine, and behavior where the subject posits his transcendence is considered masculine. Donaldson, a historian of woman, observed that the definitions "the man is a male human being, the woman is a female human being" were asymmetrically mutilated;* psychoanalysts in particular define man as a human being and woman as a female: every time she acts like a human being, the woman is said to be imitating the male. The psychoanalyst describes the child and the young girl as required to identify with the father and the mother, torn between "viriloid" and "feminine"

---

* Sir James Donaldson, *Woman, Her Position and Influence in Ancient Greece and Rome, and Among the Early Christians.*—TRANS.

tendencies, whereas we conceive her as hesitating between the role of *object*, of *Other* that is proposed to her and her claim for freedom; thus it is possible to agree on certain points: in particular when we consider the paths of inauthentic flight offered to women. But we do not give them the same Freudian or Adlerian signification. For us woman is defined as a human being in search of values within a world of values, a world where it is indispensable to understand the economic and social structure; we will study her from an existential point of view, taking into account her total situation.

CHAPTER 3

The Point of View
of Historical Materialism

The theory of historical materialism has brought to light some very important truths. Humanity is not an animal species: it is a historical reality.
Human society is an anti-physis: it does not passively submit to the presence of nature, but rather appropriates it. This appropriation is not an interior, subjective operation: it is carried out objectively in praxis. Thus
woman cannot simply be considered a sexed organism: among biological
data, only those with concrete value in action have any importance;
woman's consciousness of herself is not defined by her sexuality alone: it
reflects a situation that depends on society's economic structure, a structure
that indicates the degree of technical evolution humanity has attained. We
have seen that two essential traits characterize woman biologically: her
grasp on the world is narrower than man's; and she is more closely subjugated to the species. But these facts have a totally different value depending
on the economic and social context. Throughout human history, grasp on
the world is not defined by the naked body: the hand, with its prehensile
thumb, moves beyond itself toward instruments that increase its power;
from prehistory's earliest documents, man is always seen as armed. In the
past, when it was a question of carrying heavy clubs and of keeping wild
beasts at bay, woman's physical weakness constituted a flagrant inferiority:
if the instrument requires slightly more strength than the woman can
muster, it is enough to make her seem radically powerless. But on the other
hand, technical developments can cancel out the muscular inequality separating man and woman: abundance only creates superiority relative to a
need; having too much is not better than having enough. Thus operating
many modern machines requires only a part of masculine resources; if the
necessary minimum is not superior to woman's capacities, she becomes
man's work equal. Today enormous deployments of energy can be commanded at the touch of a switch. The burdens that come with maternity
vary greatly depending on customs: they are overwhelming if numerous

pregnancies are imposed on the woman and if she must feed and raise her children without help; if she procreates as she wishes and if society helps her during her pregnancies and provides child care, maternal duties are lighter and can be easily compensated for in the realm of work.

Engels retraces woman's history from this point of view in *The Origin of the Family;* to him, this history depends essentially on the history of technology. In the Stone Age, when the land belonged to all members of the clan, the rudimentary nature of the primitive spade and hoe limited agricultural possibilities: feminine strength was at the level of work needed for gardening. In this primitive division of labor, the two sexes already constitute two classes in a way; there is equality between these classes; while the man hunts and fishes, the woman stays at home; but the domestic tasks include productive work: pottery making, weaving, gardening; and in this way, she has an important role in economic life. With the discovery of copper, tin, bronze, and iron, and with the advent of the plow, agriculture expands its reach: intensive labor is necessary to clear the forests and cultivate the fields. So man has recourse to the service of other men, reducing them to slavery. Private property appears: master of slaves and land, man also becomes the proprietor of the woman. This is the "great historical defeat of the female sex." It is explained by the disruption of the division of labor brought about by the invention of new tools. "The same cause that had assured woman her previous authority in the home, her restriction to housework, this same cause now assured the domination of the man; domestic work thence faded in importance next to man's productive work; the latter was everything, the former an insignificant addition." So paternal right replaces maternal right: transmission of property is from father to son and no longer from woman to her clan. This is the advent of the patriarchal family founded on private property. In such a family woman is oppressed. Man reigning sovereign permits himself, among other things, his sexual whims: he sleeps with slaves or courtesans, he is polygamous. As soon as customs make reciprocity possible, woman takes revenge through infidelity: adultery becomes a natural part of marriage. This is the only defense woman has against the domestic slavery she is bound to: her social oppression is the consequence of her economic oppression. Equality can only be reestablished when both sexes have equal legal rights; but this enfranchisement demands that the whole of the feminine sex enter public industry. "Woman cannot be emancipated unless she takes part in production on a large social scale and is only incidentally bound to domestic work. And this has become possible only within a large modern industry that not only accepts women's work on a grand scale but formally requires it."

Thus woman's fate is intimately bound to the fate of socialism as seen also in Bebel's vast work on women. "Women and the proletariat," he writes, "are both oppressed." And both must be set free by the same economic development resulting from the upheaval caused by the invention of machines. The problem of woman can be reduced to that of her capacity for work. Powerful when technology matched her possibilities, dethroned when she became incapable of benefiting from them, she finds again equality with man in the modern world. Resistance put up by the old capitalist paternalism prevents this equality from being concretely achieved: it will be achieved the day this resistance is broken down. It already has broken down in the U.S.S.R., Soviet propaganda affirms. And when socialist society is realized throughout the whole world, there will no longer be men or women, but only workers, equal among themselves.

Although the synthesis outlined by Engels marks an advance over those we have already examined, it is still disappointing: the most serious problems are dodged. The whole account pivots around the transition from a communitarian regime to one of private property: there is absolutely no indication of how it was able to occur; Engels even admits that "for now we know nothing about it";[1] not only is he unaware of its historical details, but he offers no interpretation of it. Similarly, it is unclear if private property necessarily led to the enslavement of woman. Historical materialism takes for granted facts it should explain: it posits the *interest* that attaches man to property without discussing it; but where does this interest, the source of social institutions, have its own source? This is why Engels's account remains superficial, and the truths he uncovers appear contingent. It is impossible to go deeper into them without going beyond historical materialism. It cannot provide solutions to the problems we indicated, because they concern the whole man and not this abstraction, *Homo economicus.*

It is clear, for example, that the very idea of individual possession can acquire meaning only on the basis of the original condition of the existent. For that idea to appear, it is first necessary that there be in the subject a tendency to posit himself in his radical singularity, an affirmation of his existence as autonomous and separate. Obviously this claim remained subjective, interior, and without truth as long as the individual lacked the practical means to satisfy it objectively: for lack of the right tools, at first he could not experience his power over the world, he felt lost in nature and in

---

1. Friedrich Engels, *The Origin of the Family, Private Property, and the State.*

the group, passive, threatened, the plaything of obscure forces; it was only in identifying with the whole clan that he dared to think himself: the totem, the mana, and the earth were collective realities. The discovery of bronze enabled man, tested by hard and productive work, to find himself as creator, dominating nature; no longer afraid of nature, having overcome resistance, he dares to grasp himself as autonomous activity and to accomplish himself in his singularity.[2] But this accomplishment would never have been realized if man had not originally wanted it; the lesson of labor is not inscribed in a passive subject: the subject forged and conquered himself in forging his tools and conquering the earth. On the other hand, the affirmation of the subject is not enough to explain ownership: in challenges, struggles, and individual combat, every consciousness can try to rise to sovereignty. For the challenge to have taken the form of the potlatch, that is, of economic rivalry, and from there first for the chief and then for the clan members to have laid claim to private goods, there had to be another original tendency in man: in the preceding chapter we said that the existent can only succeed in grasping himself by alienating himself; he searches for himself through the world, in the guise of a foreign figure he makes his own. The clan encounters its own alienated existence in the totem, the mana, and the territory it occupies; when the individual separates from the community, he demands a singular embodiment: the mana is individualized in the chief, then in each individual; and at the same time each one tries to appropriate a piece of land, tools, or crops. In these riches of his, man finds himself because he lost himself in them: it is understandable then that he can attribute to them an importance as basic as that of his life itself. Thus man's *interest* in his property becomes an intelligible relationship. But clearly the tool alone is not enough to explain it; the whole attitude of the tool-armed man must be grasped, an attitude that implies an ontological infrastructure.

Similarly, it is impossible to *deduce* woman's oppression from private property. Here again, the shortcomings of Engels's point of view are obvious. While he clearly understood that woman's muscular weakness was a concrete inferiority only in relation to bronze and iron tools, he failed to

2. Gaston Bachelard in *La terre et les rêveries de la volonté* (*Earth and Reveries of Will*) carries out, among others, an interesting study of the blacksmith's work. He shows how man asserts and separates himself from himself by the hammer and anvil. "The temporal existence of the blacksmith is both highly particular and larger than life. Through momentary violence, the worker, uplifted, gains mastery over time"; and further on: "Those who forge take on the challenge of the universe rising against them."

see that limits to her work capacity constituted in themselves a concrete disadvantage only from a certain perspective. Because man is transcendence and ambition, he projects new demands with each new tool: after having invented bronze instruments, he was no longer satisfied with developing gardens and wanted instead to clear and cultivate vast fields. This will did not spring from bronze itself. Woman's powerlessness brought about her ruin because man apprehended her through a project of enrichment and expansion. And this project is still not enough to explain her oppression: the division of labor by sex might have been a friendly association. If the original relation between man and his peers had been exclusively one of friendship, one could not account for any kind of enslavement: this phenomenon is a consequence of the imperialism of human consciousness, which seeks to match its sovereignty objectively. Had there not been in human consciousness both the original category of the Other and an original claim to domination over the Other, the discovery of the bronze tool could not have brought about woman's oppression. Nor does Engels account for the specific character of this oppression. He tried to reduce the opposition of the sexes to a class conflict: in fact, he did it without real conviction; this thesis is indefensible. True, the division of labor by sex and the oppression resulting from it bring to mind class division in some ways: but they should not be confused; there is no biological basis for division by class; in work the slave becomes conscious of himself against the master; the proletariat has always experienced its condition in revolt, thus returning to the essential, constituting a threat to its exploiters; and the goal of the proletariat is to cease to exist as a class. We have said in the introduction how different woman's situation is, specifically because of the community of life and interests that create her solidarity with man, and due to the complicity he encounters in her: she harbors no desire for revolution, she would not think of eliminating herself as a sex: she simply asks that certain consequences of sexual differentiation be abolished. And more serious still, woman cannot in good faith be regarded only as a worker; her reproductive function is as important as her productive capacity, both in the social economy and in her personal life; there are periods in history when it is more useful to have children than till the soil. Engels sidestepped the problem; he limits himself to declaring that the socialist community will abolish the family, quite an abstract solution; everyone knows how often and how radically the U.S.S.R. has had to change its family policy to balance out production needs of the moment with the needs of repopulation; besides, eliminating the family does not necessarily liberate woman: the example of Sparta and that of the Nazi regime prove that notwithstanding her direct attachment to the state, she might still be no less oppressed by males. A truly socialist ethic—one that seeks justice without restraining liberty, one that imposes responsibilities on individuals but without abolishing individual freedom—will find itself most uncomfortable with problems posed by woman's condition. It is impossible to simply assimilate gestation to a *job* or *service* like military service. A deeper breach is created in a woman's life by requiring her to have children than by regulating citizens' occupations: no state has ever dared institute compulsory coitus. In the sexual act and in maternity, woman engages not only time and energy but also essential values. Rationalist materialism tries in vain to ignore this powerful aspect of sexuality: sexual instinct cannot be regulated; according to Freud, it might even possess an inherent denial of its own satisfaction; what is certain is that it cannot be integrated into the social sphere, because there is in eroticism a revolt of the instant against time, of the individual against the universal: to try to channel and exploit it risks killing it, because live spontaneity cannot be disposed of like inert matter; nor can it be compelled in the way a freedom can be. There is no way to directly oblige a woman to give birth: all that can be done is to enclose her in situations where motherhood is her only option: laws or customs impose marriage on her, anticonception measures and abortion are banned, divorce is forbidden. These old patriarchal constraints are exactly the ones the U.S.S.R. has brought back to life today; it has revived paternalistic theories about marriage; and in doing so, it has asked woman to become an erotic object again: a recent speech asked Soviet women citizens to pay attention to their clothes, to use makeup, and to become flirtatious to hold on to their husbands and stimulate their desire. Examples like this prove how impossible it is to consider the woman as a solely productive force: for man she is a sexual partner, a reproducer, an erotic object, an Other through whom he seeks himself. Although totalitarian or authoritarian regimes may all try to ban psychoanalysis and declare that personal emotional conflicts have no place for citizens loyally integrated into the community, eroticism is an experience where individuality always prevails over generality. And for democratic socialism where classes would be abolished but not individuals, the question of individual destiny would still retain all its importance: sexual differentiation would retain all its importance. The sexual relation that unites woman with man is not the same as the one he maintains with her; the bond that attaches her to the child is irreducible to any other. She was not created by the bronze tool alone: the machine is not sufficient to abolish her. To demand for woman all the rights, all the possibilities of the human being in general does not mean one must be blind to her singular situation.

To know this situation, it is necessary to go beyond historical materialism, which only sees man and woman as economic entities.

So we reject Freud's sexual monism and Engels's economic monism for the same reason. A psychoanalyst will interpret all woman's social claims as a phenomenon of "masculine protest"; for the Marxist, on the other hand, her sexuality only expresses her economic situation, in a rather complex, roundabout way; but the categories clitoral and vaginal, like the categories bourgeois and proletarian, are equally inadequate to encompass a concrete woman. Underlying the personal emotional conflicts as well as the economic history of humanity there is an existential infrastructure that alone makes it possible to understand in its unity the unique form that is a life. Freudianism's value derives from the fact that the existent is a body: the way he experiences himself as a body in the presence of other bodies concretely translates his existential situation. Likewise, what is true in the Marxist thesis is that the existent's ontological claims take on a concrete form based on the material possibilities offered to him, particularly based on those that technology opens to him. But if they are not incorporated into the whole of human reality, sexuality and technology of themselves will fail to explain anything. This is why in Freud prohibitions imposed by the superego and the drives of the ego appear as contingent facts; and in Engels's account of the history of the family, the most important events seem to arise unexpectedly through the whims of mysterious chance. To discover woman, we will not reject certain contributions of biology, psychoanalysis, or historical materialism: but we will consider that the body, sexual life, and technology exist concretely for man only insofar as he grasps them from the overall perspective of his existence. The value of muscular strength, the phallus, and the tool can only be defined in a world of values: it is driven by the fundamental project of the existent transcending itself toward being.

PART TWO

HISTORY

This world has always belonged to males, and none of the reasons given for this have ever seemed sufficient. By reviewing prehistoric and ethnographic data in the light of existentialist philosophy, we can understand how the hierarchy of the sexes came to be. We have already posited that when two human categories find themselves face-to-face, each one wants to impose its sovereignty on the other; if both hold to this claim equally, a reciprocal relationship is created, either hostile or friendly, but always tense. If one of the two has an advantage over the other, that one prevails and works to maintain the relationship by oppression. It is thus understandable that man might have had the will to dominate woman: but what advantage enabled him to accomplish this will?

Ethnologists give extremely contradictory information about primitive forms of human society, even more so when they are well-informed and less systematic. It is especially difficult to formulate an idea about woman's situation in the preagricultural period. We do not even know if, in such different living conditions from today's, woman's musculature or her respiratory system was not as developed as man's. She was given hard work, and in particular it was she who carried heavy loads; yet this latter fact is ambiguous: probably if she was assigned this function, it is because within the convoy men kept their hands free to defend against possible aggressors, animals or humans; so their role was the more dangerous one and demanded more strength. But it seems that in many cases women were robust and resilient enough to participate in warrior expeditions. According to the accounts by Herodotus and the traditions of the Amazons from Dahomey as well as ancient and modern testimonies, women were known to take part in bloody wars or vendettas; they showed as much courage and cruelty as males: there are references to women who bit their teeth into their enemies' livers. In spite of this, it is likely that then as now men had the advantage of physical force; in the age of the clubs and wild animals, in the age when resistance to nature was at its greatest and tools were at their most rudimentary, this superiority must have been of extreme importance. In any case, as robust as women may have been at that time, the burdens of reproduction represented for them a severe handicap in the fight against a hostile world: Amazons were said to mutilate their breasts, which meant that at least during the period of their warrior lives they rejected maternity. As for ordinary women, pregnancy, giving birth, and menstruation diminished their work capacity and condemned them to long periods of impotence; to defend themselves against enemies or to take care of themselves and their children, they needed the protection of warriors and the catch from hunting and fishing provided by the males. As there obviously was no birth control, and as nature does not provide woman with sterile periods as it does for other female mammals, frequent pregnancies must have absorbed the greater part of their strength and their time; they were unable to provide for the lives of the children they brought into the world. This is a primary fact fraught with great consequence: the human species' beginnings were difficult; hunter, gatherer, and fishing peoples reaped meager bounty from the soil, and at great cost in effort; too many children were born for the group's resources; the woman's absurd fertility kept her from participating actively in the growth of these resources, while it was constantly creating new needs. Indispensable to the perpetuation of the species, she perpetuated it too abundantly: so it was man who controlled the balance between reproduction and production. Thus woman did not even have the privilege of maintaining life that the creator male had; she did not play the role of ovum to his spermatozoid or womb to his phallus; she played only one part in the human species' effort to persist in being, and it was thanks to man that this effort had a concrete result.

Nonetheless, as the production-reproduction balance always finds a way of stabilizing itself—even at the price of infanticide, sacrifices, or wars—men and women are equally indispensable from the point of view of group survival; it could even be supposed that at certain periods when food was plentiful, his protective and nourishing role might have subordinated the male to the wife-mother. There are female animals that derive total autonomy from motherhood; so why has woman not been able to make a pedestal for herself from it? Even in those moments when humanity most desperately needed births—since the need for manual labor prevailed over the need for raw materials to exploit—and even in those times when motherhood was the most venerated, maternity was not enough for women to conquer the highest rank.[1] The reason for this is that humanity is

---

1. Sociology no longer gives credit to Bachofen's lucubrations.

not a simple natural species: it does not seek to survive as a species; its project is not stagnation: it seeks to surpass itself.

The primitive hordes were barely interested in their posterity. Connected to no territory, owning nothing, embodied in nothing stable, they could formulate no concrete idea of permanence; they were unconcerned with survival and did not recognize themselves in their descendants; they did not fear death and did not seek heirs; children were a burden and not of great value for them; the proof is that infanticide has always been frequent in nomadic peoples; and many newborns who are not massacred die for lack of hygiene in a climate of total indifference. So the woman who gives birth does not take pride in her creation; she feels like the passive plaything of obscure forces, and painful childbirth a useless and even bothersome accident. Later, more value was attached to children. But in any case, to give birth and to breast-feed are not *activities* but natural functions; they do not involve a project, which is why the woman finds no motive there to claim a higher meaning for her existence; she passively submits to her biological destiny. Because housework alone is compatible with the duties of motherhood, she is condemned to domestic labor, which locks her into repetition and immanence; day after day it repeats itself in identical form from century to century; it produces nothing new. Man's case is radically different. He does not provide for the group in the way worker bees do, by a simple vital process, but rather by acts that transcend his animal condition. *Homo faber* has been an inventor since the beginning of time: even the stick or the club he armed himself with to knock down fruit from a tree or to slaughter animals is an instrument that expands his grasp of the world; bringing home freshly caught fish is not enough for him: he first has to conquer the seas by constructing dugout canoes; to appropriate the world's treasures, he annexes the world itself. Through such actions he tests his own power; he posits ends and projects paths to them: he realizes himself as existent. To maintain himself, he creates; he spills over the present and opens up the future. This is the reason fishing and hunting expeditions have a sacred quality. Their success is greeted by celebration and triumph; man recognizes his humanity in them. This pride is still apparent today when he builds a dam, a skyscraper, or an atomic reactor. He has not only worked to preserve the given world: he has burst its borders; he has laid the ground for a new future.

His activity has another dimension that endows him with supreme dignity: it is often dangerous. If blood were only a food, it would not be worth more than milk: but the hunter is not a butcher: he runs risks in the struggle against wild animals. The warrior risks his own life to raise the prestige of the horde—his clan. This is how he brilliantly proves that life is not the supreme value for man but that it must serve ends far greater than itself. The worst curse on woman is her exclusion from warrior expeditions; it is not in giving life but in risking his life that man raises himself above the animal; this is why throughout humanity, superiority has been granted not to the sex that gives birth but to the one that kills.

· Here we hold the key to the whole mystery. On a biological level, a species maintains itself only by re-creating itself; but this creation is nothing but a repetition of the same Life in different forms. By transcending Life through Existence, man guarantees the repetition of Life: by this surpassing, he creates values that deny any value to pure repetition. With an animal, the gratuitousness and variety of male activities are useless because no project is involved; what it does is worthless when it is not serving the species; but in serving the species, the human male shapes the face of the earth, creates new instruments, invents and forges the future. Positing himself as sovereign, he encounters the complicity of woman herself: because she herself is also an existent, because transcendence also inhabits her and her project is not repetition but surpassing herself toward another future; she finds the confirmation of masculine claims in the core of her being. She participates with men in festivals that celebrate the success and victories of males. Her misfortune is to have been biologically destined to repeat Life, while in her own eyes Life in itself does not provide her reasons for being, and these reasons are more important than life itself.

Certain passages where Hegel's dialectic describes the relationship of master to slave would apply far better to the relationship of man to woman. The Master's privilege, he states, arises from the affirmation of Spirit over Life in the fact of risking his life: but in fact the vanquished slave has experienced this same risk, whereas the woman is originally an existent who gives *Life* and does not risk *her* life; there has never been combat between the male and her; Hegel's definition applies singularly to her. "The other [consciousness] is the dependent consciousness for which essential reality is animal life, that is, life given by another entity." But this relationship differs from the relationship of oppression because woman herself aspires to and recognizes the values concretely attained by males. It is the male who opens up the future toward which she also transcends; in reality, women have never pitted female values against male ones: it is men wanting to maintain masculine prerogatives who invented this division; they wanted to create a feminine domain—a rule of life, of immanence—only to lock woman in it. But it is above and beyond all sexual specification that the existent seeks self-justification in the movement of his transcendence: the very submission of women proves this. Today what women claim is to be recognized as existents just like men, and not to subordinate existence to life or the man to his animality.

Thus an existential perspective has enabled us to understand how the biological and economic situation of primitive hordes led to male supremacy. The female, more than the male, is prey to the species; humanity has always tried to escape from its species' destiny; with the invention of the tool, maintenance of life became activity and project for man, while motherhood left woman riveted to her body like the animal. It is because humanity puts itself into question in its being—that is, values reasons for living over life—that man has set himself as master over woman; man's project is not to repeat himself in time: it is to reign over the instant and to forge the future. Male activity, creating values, has constituted existence itself as a value; it has prevailed over the indistinct forces of life; and it has subjugated Nature and Woman. We must now see how this situation has continued and evolved through the centuries. What place has humanity allotted to this part of itself that has been defined in its core as Other? What rights have been conceded to it? How have men defined it?

We have just seen that women's fate is very harsh in primitive hordes; in female animals the reproductive function is limited naturally, and when it occurs, the particular animal is more or less released from other toil; only domestic females are sometimes exploited to the point of exhaustion of their forces as reproducers and in their individual capacities by a demanding master. This was undoubtedly the case of woman at a time when the struggle against a hostile world demanded the full employment of community resources; added to the fatigues of incessant and unregulated procreation were those of hard domestic duties. Nevertheless, some historians maintain that precisely at that time, male superiority was the least marked; which means that this superiority is lived in an immediate form, not yet posited and willed; no one tries to compensate for the cruel disadvantages that handicap woman; but neither does anyone try to break her down, as will later happen in paternalistic regimes. No institution actually ratifies the inequality of the sexes; in fact, there are no institutions: no property, no inheritance, no legal system. Religion is neutral; the totems that are worshipped are asexual.

It is when nomads settled the land and became farmers that institutions and law appeared. Man no longer has to limit himself to combating hostile forces; he begins to express himself concretely through the figure he imposes on the world, thinking the world and thinking himself; at that juncture, sexual differentiation is reflected in the group structure, and it takes on a particular character: in agricultural communities, woman is often vested with extraordinary prestige. This prestige is explained essentially by the new importance that children assume in a civilization based on working the land; by settling a territory, men begin to appropriate it. Property appears in a collective form; it demands posterity from its owners; mother-hood becomes a sacred function. Many tribes live under a communal regime: this does not mean that women belong to all the men in the community; it is no longer thought today that promiscuous marriage was ever practiced; but men and women only have a religious, social, and economic existence as a group: their individuality remains a purely biological fact; marriage, whatever its form—monogamy, polygamy, polyandry—is itself nothing but a secular incident that does not create a mystical link. For the wife it is in no way a source of servitude, as she remains an integral part of her clan. The clan as a whole, gathered under the same totem, mystically shares the same mana and materially shares the common enjoyment of a territory. But in the alienation process mentioned before, the clan grasps itself in this territory in the guise of an objective and concrete figure; through the permanence of the land, the clan thus realizes itself as a unity whose identity persists throughout the passage of time. Only this existential process makes it possible to understand the identification that has survived to this day among the clan, the gens, the family, and property. In the thinking of nomadic tribes, only the moment exists; the agricultural community replaces this thinking with the concept of a life rooted in the past and incorporating the future: the totem ancestor who gives his name to the clan members is venerated; and the clan takes an abiding interest in its descendants: it will survive through the land that he bequeaths to them and that they will exploit. The community conceives of its unity and wills its existence beyond the present: it sees itself in its children, it recognizes them as its own, and it accomplishes and surpasses itself through them.

But many primitives are unaware of the father's role in the procreation of children, who are thought to be the reincarnation of ancestral larvae floating around certain trees, certain rocks, in certain sacred places, and descending into the woman's body; in some cases, they believe she must not be a virgin if this infiltration is to take place; but other peoples believe that it also takes place through the nostrils or mouth; at any rate, defloration is secondary here, and for mystical reasons the prerogative is rarely the husband's. The mother is clearly necessary for the birth of the child; she is the one who keeps and nourishes the germ within her, and so the life of the clan is propagated in the visible world through her. This is how she finds herself playing the principal role. Very often, children belong to their mother's clan, bear her name, and share her rights, particularly the use of the land belonging to the clan. So communal property is transmitted through women: through them the fields and their harvests are reserved to members of the clan, and inversely it is through their mothers that members are destined to a given piece of land. The land can thus be considered as mystically belonging to women: their hold on the soil and its fruits is both religious and legal. The tie that binds them is stronger than one of ownership; maternal right is characterized by a true assimilation of woman to the land; in each, through its avatars, the permanence of life is achieved, life that is essentially generation. For nomads, procreation seems only an accident, and the riches of the earth are still unknown; but the farmer admires the mystery of fertilization that burgeons in the furrows and in the maternal womb. He knows that he was conceived like the cattle and the harvests, and he wants his clan to conceive other humans who will perpetuate it in perpetuating the fertility of the fields; nature as a whole seems like a mother to him; the earth is woman, and the woman is inhabited by the same obscure forces as the earth.[1] This is part of the reason agricultural work is entrusted to woman: able to call up the ancestral larvae within her, she also has the power to make fruit and wheat spring from the sowed fields. In both cases it is a question of a magic conjuration, not of a creative act. At this stage, man no longer limits himself to gathering the products of the earth: but he does not yet understand his power; he hesitates between technical skill and magic; he feels passive, dependent on Nature that doles out existence and death by chance. To be sure, he recognizes more or less the function of the sexual act as well as the techniques for cultivating the soil: but children and crops still seem like supernatural gifts; and the mysterious emanations flowing from the feminine body bring forth into this world the riches latent in the mysterious sources of life. Such beliefs are still alive today among numerous Indian, Australian, and Polynesian tribes, and become all the more important as they match the practical interests of the collectivity.[2] Motherhood relegates woman to a sedentary existence; it is natural for her to stay at home while men hunt, fish, and go to war. But primitive people rarely cultivate more than a modest garden contained within their own village limits, and its cultivation is a domestic task; Stone Age instruments require little effort; economics and mystical belief agree to leave agricultural work to women. Domestic work, as it is taking

---

1. "Hail, Earth, mother of all men, may you be fertile in the arms of God and filled with fruits for the use of man," says an old Anglo-Saxon incantation.

2. For the Bhantas of India, or in Uganda, a sterile woman is considered dangerous for gardens. In Nicobar, it is believed that the harvest will be better if it is brought in by a pregnant woman. In Borneo, seeds are chosen and preserved by women. "One seems to feel in women a natural affinity with the seeds that are said by the women to be in a state of pregnancy. Sometimes women will spend the night in the rice fields during its growth period" (Hose and MacDougall). In India of yore, naked women pushed the plow through the field at night. Indians along the Orinoco left the sowing and planting to women because "women knew how to conceive seed and bear children, so the seeds and roots planted by them bore fruit far more abundantly than if they had been planted by male hands" (Frazer). Many similar examples can be found in Frazer.

shape, is also their lot: they weave rugs and blankets; they shape pottery. And they are often in charge of barter; commerce is in their hands. The life of the clan is thus maintained and extended through them; children, herds, harvests, tools, and the whole prosperity of the group of which they are the soul depend on their work and their magic virtues. Such strength inspires in men a respect mingled with fear, reflected in their worship. It is in women that the whole of foreign Nature is concentrated.

It has already been said here that man never thinks himself without thinking the Other; he grasps the world under the emblem of duality, which is not initially sexual. But being naturally different from man, who posits himself as the same, woman is consigned to the category of Other; the Other encompasses woman; at first she is not important enough to incarnate the Other alone, so a subdivision at the heart of the Other develops: in ancient cosmographies, a single element often has both male and female incarnations; thus for the Babylonians, the Ocean and the Sea were the double incarnation of cosmic chaos. When the woman's role grows, she comes to occupy nearly the whole region of the Other. Then appear the feminine divinities through whom fertility is worshipped. A discovery made in Susa shows the oldest representation of the Great Goddess, the Great Mother in a long robe and high coiffure, which other statues show crowned with towers; excavations in Crete have yielded several effigies of her. She can be steatopygous and crouched, or thin and standing, sometimes clothed, and often naked, her arms pressed beneath her swollen breasts. She is the queen of heaven, a dove is her symbol; she is also the empress of hades, she comes out slithering, symbolized by a serpent. She can be seen in mountains, woods, the sea, and springs. She creates life everywhere; if she kills, she resurrects. Fickle, lascivious, and cruel like Nature, propitious and yet dangerous, she reigns over all of Asia Minor, over Phrygia, Syria, Anatolia, and over all of western Asia. She is known as Ishtar in Babylon, Astarte to Semitic peoples, and Gaea, Rhea, or Cybele to the Greeks; she is found in Egypt in the form of Isis; male divinities are subordinated to her. Supreme idol in faraway regions of heaven and hades, woman on earth is surrounded by taboos like all sacred beings—she is herself taboo; because of the powers she holds, she is seen as a magician or a sorceress; she is included in prayers, and she can be at times a priestess like the druids among the ancient Celts; in certain cases she participates in the government of the tribe, and at times she even governs on her own. These distant ages have left us no literature. But the great patriarchal periods conserve in their mythology, monuments, and traditions the memory of times when women occupied very high positions. From a feminine point of view, the Brahman period is a regression from that of Rig-Veda, and the latter a regression from the primitive stage that preceded it. The pre-Islamic bedouin women had a much higher status than that accorded them by the Koran. The great figures of Niobe and Medea evoke an era when mothers, considering their children to be their own property, took pride in them. And in the Homeric poems, Andromache and Hecuba have an importance that classic Greece no longer granted to women hidden in the shadows of the gynaeceum.

These facts all lead to the supposition that in primitive times a veritable reign of women existed; this hypothesis, proposed by Bachofen, was adopted by Engels; the passage from matriarchy to patriarchy seems to him to be "the great historical defeat of the feminine sex." But in reality this golden age of Woman is only a myth. To say that woman was the *Other* is to say that a relationship of reciprocity between the sexes did not exist: whether Earth, Mother, or Goddess, she was never a peer for man; her power asserted itself *beyond* human rule: she was thus *outside* of this rule. Society has always been male; political power has always been in men's hands. "Political authority, or simply social authority, always belongs to men," Lévi-Strauss affirms at the end of his study of primitive societies. For men, the counterpart—or the other—who is also the same, with whom reciprocal relationships are established, is always another male individual. The duality that can be seen in one form or another at the heart of society pits one group of men against another; and women are part of the goods men possess and a means of exchange among themselves: the mistake comes from confusing two forms of mutually exclusive alterity. Insofar as woman is considered the absolute Other, that is—whatever magic powers she has—as the inessential, it is precisely impossible to regard her as another subject.[3] Women have thus never constituted a separate group that posited itself *for-itself* before a male group; they have never had a direct or autonomous relationship with men. "The relationship of reciprocity which is the basis of marriage is not established between men and women, but between men by means of women, who are merely the occasion of this relationship," said Lévi-Strauss.[4] Woman's concrete condition is not

---

3. It will be seen that this distinction has been perpetuated. Periods that regard woman as *Other* are those that refuse most harshly to integrate her into society as a human being. Today she only becomes an *other* peer by losing her mystical aura. Antifeminists have always played on this ambiguity. They readily agree to exalt the woman as Other in order to make her alterity absolute and irreducible, and to refuse her access to the human *Mitsein*.

4. Lévi-Strauss, *The Elementary Structures of Kinship*.

affected by the type of lineage that prevails in the society to which she belongs; whether the regime is patrilineal, matrilineal, bilateral, or undifferentiated (undifferentiation never being precise), she is always under men's guardianship; the only question is if, after marriage, she is still subjected to the authority of her father or her oldest brother—authority that will also extend to her children—or of her husband. In any case: "The woman is never anything more than the symbol of her lineage. Matrilineal descent is the authority of the woman's father or brother extended to the brother-in-law's village."[5] She only mediates the law; she does not possess it. In fact, it is the relationship of two masculine groups that is defined by the system of filiation, and not the relation of the two sexes. In practice, woman's concrete condition is not consistently linked to any given type of law. It may happen that in a matrilineal system she has a very high position: but—beware—the presence of a woman chief or a queen at the head of a tribe absolutely does not mean that women are sovereign: the reign of Catherine the Great changed nothing in the fate of Russian peasant women; and they lived no less frequently in a state of abjection. And cases where a woman remains in her clan and her husband makes rapid, even clandestine visits to her are very rare. She almost always goes to live under her husband's roof: this fact is proof enough of male domination. "Behind the variations in the type of descent," writes Lévi-Strauss, "the permanence of patrilocal residence attests to the basic asymmetrical relationship between the sexes which is characteristic of human society." Since she keeps her children with her, the result is that the territorial organization of the tribe does not correspond to its totemic organization: the former is contingent, the latter rigorously constructed; but in practice, the first was the more important because the place where people work and live counts more than their mystical connection. In the more widespread transitional regimes, there are two kinds of rights, one based on religion and the other on the occupation and labor on the land, and they overlap. Though only a secular institution, marriage nevertheless has great social importance, and the conjugal family, though stripped of religious signification, is very alive on a human level. Even within groups where great sexual freedom is found, it is considered conventional for a woman who brings a child into the world to be married; alone with an offspring, she cannot constitute an autonomous group; and her brother's religious protection does not suffice; a husband's presence is required. He often has many heavy responsibilities for the children; they do not belong to his clan, but it is nonetheless he who

---

5. Ibid.

- Catherine the Great

feeds and raises them; between husband and wife, and father and son, bonds of cohabitation, work, common interest, and tenderness are formed. Relations between this secular family and the totemic clan are extremely complex, as the diversity of marriage rites attests. In primitive times, a husband buys a wife from a foreign clan, or at least there is an exchange of goods from one clan to another, the first giving over one of its members and the second delivering cattle, fruits, or work in return. But as husbands take charge of wives and their children, it also happens that they receive remuneration from their brides' brothers. The balance between mystical and economic realities is an unstable one. Men often have a closer attachment to their sons than to their nephews; it is as a father that a man will choose to affirm himself when such affirmation becomes possible. And this is why every society tends toward a patriarchal form as its development leads man to gain awareness of himself and to impose his will. But it is important to emphasize that even at times when he was still confused by the mysteries of Life, Nature, and Woman, he never relinquished his power; when, terrified by the dangerous magic woman possesses, he posits her as the essential, it is he who posits her, and he who realizes himself thereby as the essential in this alienation he grants; in spite of the fecund virtues that infuse her, man remains her master, just as he is master of the fertile earth; she is destined to be subordinated, possessed, and exploited, as is also Nature, whose magic fertility she incarnates. The prestige she enjoys in the eyes of men comes from them; they kneel before the Other, they worship the Goddess Mother. But as powerful as she may appear, she is defined through notions created by the male consciousness. All of the idols invented by man, however terrifying he may have made them, are in fact dependent upon him, and this is why he is able to destroy them. In primitive societies, this dependence is not acknowledged and posited, but its existence is implicit, in itself: and it will readily become mediatory as soon as man develops a clearer consciousness of self, as soon as he dares to assert himself and stand in opposition. And in fact, even when man grasps himself as given, passive, and subject to the vagaries of rain and sun, he still realizes himself as transcendence, as project; already, spirit and will assert themselves within him against life's confusion and contingencies. The totem ancestor, of which woman assumes multiple incarnations, is more or less distinctly a male principle under its animal or tree name; woman perpetuates carnal existence, but her role is only that of nourisher, not of creator; in no domain whatsoever does she create; she maintains the life of the tribe by providing children and bread, nothing more; she lives condemned to immanence; she incarnates only the static aspect of society, closed in on itself. Meanwhile, man continues to monopolize the functions that open this society to nature and to the whole of humanity; the only efforts worthy of him are war, hunting, and fishing; he conquers foreign prey and annexes it to the tribe; war, hunting, and fishing represent an expansion of existence, his going beyond into the world; the male is still the only incarnation of transcendence. He does not yet have the practical means to totally dominate Woman-Earth, he does not yet dare stand up to her: but already he wants to tear himself away from her. I think the profound reason for the well-known custom of exogamy, so widespread in matrilineal societies, is to be found in this determination. Even though man is unaware of the role he plays in procreation, marriage has great importance for him; this is where he attains adult dignity and receives his share of a piece of the world; through his mother he is bound to the clan, his ancestors, and everything that constitutes his own subsistence; but in all of these secular functions—work or marriage—he aspires to escape this circle and assert transcendence against immanence, to open up a future different from the past where he is rooted; depending on the types of relations recognized in different societies, the banning of incest takes on different forms, but from primitive times to our days it has remained the same: man wishes to possess that which he *is* not; he unites himself to what appears to him to be Other than himself. The wife must not be part of the husband's mana, she must be foreign to him: thus foreign to his clan. Primitive marriage is sometimes founded on abduction, real or symbolic: because violence done to another is the clearest affirmation of another's alterity. Taking his wife by force, the warrior proves he is able to annex the riches of others and burst through the bounds of the destiny assigned to him at birth; purchasing her under various forms—paying tribute, rendering services—has, less dramatically, the same signification.[6]

6. In Lévi-Strauss's thesis already cited, there is, in a slightly different form, a confirmation of this idea. What comes out of this study is that the prohibition of incest is in no way the primal factor underlying exogamy; but it reflects the positive desire for exogamy in a negative form. There is no intrinsic reason that it be improper for a woman to have intercourse with men in her clan; but it is socially useful that she be part of the goods by which each clan, instead of closing in on itself, establishes a reciprocal relationship with another clan: "Exogamy has a value less negative than positive . . . it prohibits endogamous marriage . . . certainly not because a biological danger is attached to consanguineous marriage, but because exogamous marriage results in a social benefit." The group should not for its own private purposes consume women who constitute one of its possessions, but should use them as an instrument of communication; if marriage with a woman of the same clan is forbidden, "the sole reason is that she is *same* whereas she must (and therefore can) become *other* . . . the same women that were originally offered can be exchanged in return. All that is necessary on either side is the *sign of otherness*, which is the outcome of a certain position in a structure and not of any innate characteristic."

man wishes to possess that which he is not

Little by little, man mediated his experience, and in his representations, as in his practical existence, the male principle triumphed. Spirit prevailed over Life, transcendence over immanence, technology over magic, and reason over superstition. The devaluation of woman represents a necessary stage in the history of humanity: for she derived her prestige not from her positive value but from man's weakness; she incarnated disturbing natural mysteries: man escapes her grasp when he frees himself from nature. In passing from stone to bronze, he is able to conquer the land through his work and conquer himself as well. The farmer is subjected to the vagaries of the soil, of germination, and of seasons; he is passive, he beseeches, and he waits: this explains why totem spirits peopled the human world; the peasant endured the whims of these forces that took possession of him. On the contrary, the worker fashions a tool according to his own design; he imposes on it the form that fits his project; facing an inert nature that defies him but that he overcomes, he asserts himself as sovereign will; if he quickens his strokes on the anvil, he quickens the completion of the tool, whereas nothing can hasten the ripening of grain; his responsibility develops with what he makes: his movement, adroit or maladroit, makes it or breaks it; careful, skillful, he brings it to a point of perfection he can be proud of: his success depends not on the favor of the gods but on himself; he challenges his fellow workers, he takes pride in his success; and while he still leaves some place for rituals, applied techniques seem far more important to him; mystical values become secondary, and practical interests take precedence; he is not entirely liberated from the gods, but he distances himself by distancing them from himself; he relegates them to their Olympian heaven and keeps the terrestrial domain for himself; the great Pan begins to fade at the first sound of his hammer, and man's reign begins. He discovers his power. He finds cause and effect in the relationship between his creating arm and the object of his creation: the seed planted germinates or not, while metal always reacts in the same way to fire, to tempering, and to mechanical treatment; this world of tools can be framed in clear concepts: rational thinking, logic, and mathematics are thus able to emerge. The whole representation of the universe is overturned. Woman's religion is bound to the reign of agriculture, a reign of irreducible duration, contingencies, chance, anticipation, and mystery; the reign of *Homo faber* is the reign of time that can be conquered like space, the reign of necessity, project, action, and reason. Even when he contends with the earth, he will henceforth contend with it as a worker; he discovers that the soil can be fertilized, that it is good to let it lie fallow, that certain seeds should be treated certain ways: it is he who makes the crops grow; he digs canals, he irrigates or drains the land, he lays out roads, he builds temples: he creates the world anew. The peoples who remained under the heel of the Mother Goddess where matrilineal filiation was perpetuated were also those arrested in a primitive state of civilization. Woman was venerated only inasmuch as man was a slave to his own fears, a party to his own impotence: it was out of fear and not love that he worshipped her. Before he could accomplish himself, he had to begin by dethroning her.[7] It is the male principle of creative force, light, intelligence, and order that he will henceforth recognize as a sovereign. Standing beside the Mother Goddess emerges a god, a son, or a lover who is still inferior to her, but who looks exactly like her, and who is associated with her. He also incarnates the fertility principle: he is a bull, the Minotaur, or the Nile fertilizing the plains of Egypt. He dies in autumn and is reborn in spring after the spouse-mother, invulnerable yet tearful, has devoted her forces to searching for his body and bringing him back to life. Appearing in Crete, this couple can also be found all along the banks of the Mediterranean: Isis and Horus in Egypt, Astarte and Adonis in Phoenicia, Cybele and Attis in Asia Minor, and Rhea and Zeus in Hellenic Greece. And then the Great Mother was dethroned. In Egypt, where woman's condition is exceptionally favorable, the goddess Nout, incarnating the sky, and Isis, the fertile land, wife of the Nile, Osiris, continue to be extremely important; but it is nonetheless Ra, the sun god, virile light and energy, who is the supreme king. In Babylon, Ishtar is only the wife of Bel-Marduk; and it is he who created things and guaranteed harmony. The god of the Semites is male. When Zeus reigns in heaven, Gaea, Rhea, and Cybele have to abdicate: all that is left to Demeter is a still imposing but secondary divinity. The Vedic gods have wives, but these are not worshipped as they are. The Roman Jupiter has no equal.[8]

Thus, the triumph of patriarchy was neither an accident nor the result of a violent revolution. From the origins of humanity, their biological

---

7. Of course, this condition is necessary but not sufficient: there are patrilineal civilizations immobilized in a primitive stage; others, like the Mayas, regressed. There is no absolute hierarchy between societies of maternal right and those of paternal right: but only the latter have evolved technically and ideologically.

8. It is interesting to note (according to H. Bégouën, *Journal of Psychology*, 1934) that in the Aurignacian period there were numerous statuettes representing women with overly emphasized sexual attributes: they are noteworthy for their plumpness and the size accorded to their vulvas. Moreover, grossly sketched vulvas on their own were also found in caves. In the Solutrean and Magdalenian epochs, these effigies disappear. In the Aurignacian, masculine statuettes are very rare, and there are never any representations of the male organ. In the Magdalenian epoch, some representations of vulvas are still found, though in small quantities, but a great quantity of phalluses was discovered.

Dethorning the Great Mother

privilege enabled men to affirm themselves alone as sovereign subjects; they never abdicated this privilege; they alienated part of their existence in Nature and in Woman; but they won it back afterward; condemned to play the role of the Other, woman was thus condemned to possess no more than precarious power: slave or idol, she was never the one who chose her lot. "Men make gods and women worship them," said Frazer; it is men who decide if their supreme divinities will be females or males; the place of woman in society is always the one they assign her; at no time has she imposed her own law.

Perhaps, however, if productive work had remained at the level of her strength, woman would have achieved the conquest of nature *with* man; the human species affirmed itself against the gods through male and female individuals; but she could not obtain the benefits of tools for herself. Engels only incompletely explained her decline: it is insufficient to say that the invention of bronze and iron profoundly modified the balance of productive forces and brought about women's inferiority; this inferiority is not in itself sufficient to account for the oppression she has suffered. What was harmful for her was that, not becoming a labor partner for the worker, she was excluded from the human *Mitsein:* that woman is weak and has a lower productive capacity does not explain this exclusion; rather, it is because she did not participate in his way of working and thinking and because she remained enslaved to the mysteries of life that the male did not recognize in her an equal; by not accepting her, once she kept in his eyes the dimension of *other,* man could only become her oppressor. The male will for expansion and domination transformed feminine incapacity into a curse. Man wanted to exhaust the new possibilities opened up by new technology: he called upon a servile workforce, and he reduced his fellow man to slavery. Slave labor being far more efficient than work that woman could supply, she lost the economic role she played within the tribe. And in his relationship with the slave, the master found a far more radical confirmation of his sovereignty than the tempered authority he exercised on woman. Venerated and revered for her fertility, being *other* than man, and sharing the disquieting character of the *other,* woman, in a certain way, kept man dependent on her even while she was dependent on him; the reciprocity of the master-slave relationship existed *in the present* for her, and it was how she escaped slavery. As for the slave, he had no taboo to protect him, being nothing but a servile man, not just different, but inferior: the dialectic of the slave-master relationship will take centuries to be actualized; within the organized patriarchal society, the slave is only a beast of burden with a human face: the master exercises tyrannical authority over him; this exalts his pride: and he turns it against the woman. Everythin[

against her; the more powerful he becomes, the more s[

ticular, when he acquires ownership of land,[9] he als[

property. Formerly he was possessed by *the* mana, by *[

a soul, *property;* freed from *Woman,* he now lays clai[

posterity of his own. He wants the family labor he [

his fields to be totally *his,* and for this to happen, the workers mus[

to him: he subjugates his wife and his children. He must have heirs who will extend his life on earth because he bequeaths them his possessions, and who will give him in turn, beyond the tomb, the necessary honors for the repose of his soul. The cult of the domestic gods is superimposed on the constitution of private property, and the function of heirs is both economic and mystical. Thus, the day agriculture ceases to be an essentially magic operation and becomes creative labor, man finds himself to be a generative force; he lays claim to his children and his crops at the same time.[10]

There is no ideological revolution more important in the primitive period than the one replacing matrilineal descent with agnation; from that time on, the mother is lowered to the rank of wet nurse or servant, and the father's sovereignty is exalted; he is the one who holds rights and transmits them. Apollo, in Aeschylus's *Eumenides,* proclaims these new truths: "The mother is no parent of that which is called her child, but only nurse of the new-planted seed that grows. The parent is he who mounts. A stranger she preserves a stranger's seed, if no god interfere." It is clear that these affirmations are not the results of scientific discoveries; they are acts of faith. Undoubtedly, the experience of technical cause and effect from which man draws the assurance of his creative powers makes him recognize he is as necessary to procreation as the mother. Idea guided observation; but the latter is restricted to granting the father a role equal to that of the mother: it led to the supposition that, as for nature, the condition for conception was the encounter of sperm and menses; Aristotle's idea that woman is merely matter, and "the principle of movement which is male in all living beings is better and more divine," is an idea that expresses a will to power that goes beyond all of what is known. In attributing his posterity exclu-

---

9. See Part One, Chapter 3, in this volume.

10. In the same way that woman was identified with furrows, the phallus was identified with the plow, and vice versa. In a drawing representing a plow from the Kassite period, there are traces of the symbols of the generative act; afterward, the phallus-plow identity was frequently reproduced in art forms. The word *lak* in some Austro-Asian languages designates both phallus and plow. An Assyrian prayer addresses a god whose "plow fertilized the earth."

to himself, man frees himself definitively from subjugation by men, and he triumphs over woman in the domination of the world. Doomed to procreation and secondary tasks, stripped of her practical importance and her mystical prestige, woman becomes no more than a servant.

Men represented this triumph as the outcome of a violent struggle. One of the most ancient cosmologies, belonging to the Assyro-Babylonians, tells of their victory in a text that dates from the seventh century but that recounts an even older legend. The Sun and the Sea, Aton and Tiamat, gave birth to the celestial world, the terrestrial world, and the great gods; but finding them too turbulent, they decided to destroy them; and Tiamat, the woman-mother, led the struggle against the strongest and most fine-looking of her descendants, Bel-Marduk; he, having challenged her in combat, killed her and slashed her body in two after a frightful battle; with one half he made the vault of heaven, and with the other the foundation for the terrestrial world; then he gave order to the universe and created humanity. In the *Eumenides* drama, which illustrated the triumph of patriarchy over maternal right, Orestes also assassinates Clytemnestra. Through these bloody victories, the virile force and the solar forces of order and light win over feminine chaos. By absolving Orestes, the tribunal of the gods proclaims he is the son of Agamemnon before being the son of Clytemnestra. The old maternal right is dead: the audacious male revolt killed it. But we have seen that in reality, the passage to paternal rights took place through gradual transitions. Masculine conquest was a reconquest: man only took possession of that which he already possessed; he put law into harmony with reality. There was neither struggle, nor victory, nor defeat. Nevertheless, these legends have profound meaning. At the moment when man asserts himself as subject and freedom, the idea of the Other becomes mediatory. From this day on, the relationship with the Other is a drama; the existence of the Other is a threat and a danger. The ancient Greek philosophy, which Plato, on this point, does not deny, showed that alterity is the same as negation, thus Evil. To posit the Other is to define Manichaeism. This is why religions and their codes treat woman with such hostility. By the time humankind reaches the stage of writing its mythology and laws, patriarchy is definitively established: it is males who write the codes. It is natural for them to give woman a subordinate situation; one might imagine, however, that they would consider her with the same benevolence as children and animals. But no. Afraid of woman, legislators organize her oppression. Only the harmful aspects of the ambivalent virtues attributed to her are retained: from sacred she becomes unclean.

Eve, given to Adam to be his companion, lost humankind; to punish men, the pagan gods invent women, and Pandora, the firstborn of these female creatures, is the one who unleashes all the evil that humanity endures. The Other is passivity confronting activity, diversity breaking down unity, matter opposing form, disorder resisting order. Woman is thus doomed to Evil. "There is a good principle that created order, light, and man and a bad principle that created chaos, darkness, and woman," says Pythagoras. The Laws of Manu define her as a vile being to be held in slavery. Leviticus assimilates her to beasts of burden, owned by the patriarch. The laws of Solon confer no rights on her. The Roman code puts her in guardianship and proclaims her "imbecility." Canon law considers her "the devil's gateway." The Koran treats her with the most absolute contempt.

And yet Evil needs Good, matter needs the idea, and night needs light. Man knows that to satisfy his desires, to perpetuate his existence, woman is indispensable to him; he has to integrate her in society: as long as she submits to the order established by males, she is cleansed of her original stain. This idea is forcefully expressed in the Laws of Manu: "Whatever be the qualities of the man with whom a woman is united according to the law, such qualities even she assumes, like a river united with the ocean, and she is admitted after death to the same celestial paradise." The Bible too praises the "virtuous woman." Christianity, in spite of its loathing of the flesh, respects the devoted virgin and the chaste and docile wife. Within a religious group, woman can even hold an important religious position: Brahmani in India and Flaminica in Rome are as holy as their husbands; in a couple, the man is dominant, but both male and female principles remain essential to the childbearing function, to life, and to the social order.

This very ambivalence of the Other, of the Female, will be reflected in the rest of her history; until our times she will be subordinated to men's will. But this will is ambiguous: by total annexation, woman will be lowered to the rank of a thing; of course, man attempts to cover with his own dignity what he conquers and possesses; in his eyes the Other retains some of her primitive magic; one of the problems he will seek to solve is how to make his wife both a servant and a companion; his attitude will evolve throughout the centuries, and this will also entail an evolution in woman's destiny.[11]

---

11. We will examine this evolution in the Western world. The history of the woman in the East, in India, and in China was one of long and immutable slavery. From the Middle Ages to today, we will center this study on France, where the situation is typical.

Once woman is dethroned by the advent of private property, her fate is linked to it for centuries: in large part, her history is intertwined with the history of inheritance. The fundamental importance of this institution becomes clear if we keep in mind that the owner alienated his existence in property; it was more important to him than life itself; it goes beyond the strict limits of a mortal lifetime, it lives on after the body is gone, an earthly and tangible incarnation of the immortal soul; but this continued survival can occur only if property remains in the owner's hands: it can remain his after death only if it belongs to individuals who are extensions of himself and recognized, who are *his own*. Cultivating paternal lands and worshipping the father's spirit are one and the same obligation for the heir: to ensure the survival of ancestors on earth and in the underworld. Man will not, therefore, agree to share his property or his children with woman. He will never really be able to go that far, but at a time when patriarchy is powerful, he strips woman of all her rights to hold and transmit property. It seems logical, in fact, to deny her these rights. If it is accepted that a woman's children do not belong to her, they inevitably have no link with the group the woman comes from. Woman is no longer passed from one clan to another through marriage: she is radically abducted from the group she is born into and annexed to her husband's; he buys her like a head of cattle or a slave, he imposes his domestic divinities on her: and the children she conceives belong to her spouse's family. If she could inherit, she would thus wrongly transmit her paternal family's riches to that of her husband: she is carefully excluded from the succession. But inversely, because she owns nothing, woman is not raised to the dignity of a person; she herself is part of man's patrimony, first her father's and then her husband's. Under a strictly patriarchal regime, a father can condemn to death his male and female children at birth; but in the case of a male child, society most often put limits on this power: a normally constituted newborn male is allowed to live, whereas the custom of exposure is very widespread for girls; there was massive infanticide among Arabs: as soon as they were born, girls were thrown into ditches. Accepting a female child is an act of generosity on the father's part; the woman enters such societies only through a kind of grace bestowed on her, and not legitimately like males. In any case, the stain of birth is far more serious for the mother when a girl is born: among Hebrews, Leviticus demands twice as much cleansing as for a newborn boy. In societies where "blood money" exists, only a small sum is required when the victim is of the feminine sex: her value compared with a male's is like a slave's with a free man's. When she is a young girl, the father has total power over her; on her marriage he transmits it entirely to her spouse. Since she is his property like the slave, the beast of burden, or the thing, it is natural for a man to have as many wives as he wishes; only economic reasons put limits on polygamy; the husband can disown his wives at whim, and society barely accords them any guarantees. In return, woman is subjected to rigorous chastity. In spite of the taboos, matriarchal societies allow great freedom of behavior; prenuptial chastity is rarely demanded; and adultery not judged severely. On the contrary, when woman becomes man's property, he wants a virgin, and he demands total fidelity at the risk of severe penalty; it would be the worst of crimes to risk giving heritage rights to a foreign offspring: this is why the paterfamilias has the right to put a guilty wife to death. As long as private property lasts, conjugal infidelity on the part of a woman is considered a crime of high treason. All codes up to our time have perpetuated inequality in issues concerning adultery, arguing the seriousness of the fault committed by the woman who might bring an illegitimate child into the family. And though the right to take the law into one's own hands has been abolished since Augustus, the Napoleonic Code still holds out the promise of the jury's leniency for a husband who avenges himself. When woman belonged to both a patrilineal clan and a conjugal family, she was able to preserve a good amount of freedom, as the two series of bonds overlapped and even conflicted with each other and as each system served to support her against the other: for example, she could often choose the husband of her fancy, since marriage was only a secular event and had no effect on society's deep structure. But under the patriarchal regime, she was the property of a father who married her off as he saw fit; then attached to her husband's household, she was no more than his thing and the thing of the family (*genos*) in which she was placed.

When family and private patrimony incontestably remain the bases of society, woman also remains totally alienated. This is what has happened in the Muslim world. The structure is feudal in that there has never been a state strong enough to unify and dominate the numerous tribes: no power holds in check that of the patriarch chief. The religion that was created when the Arab people were warriors and conquerors professed the utmost disdain toward women. "Men are superior to women on account of the qualities with which God has gifted the one above the other, and on account of the outlay they make from their substance for them," says the Koran; the woman has never held real power or mystic prestige. The bedouin woman works hard, she plows and carries burdens: this is how she sets up a reciprocal bond with her husband; she moves around freely, her face uncovered. The Muslim woman, veiled and shut in, is still today a kind of slave in most levels of society. I recall an underground cave in a troglodyte village in Tunisia where four women were squatting: the old, one-eyed, and toothless wife, her face ravaged, was cooking dough on a small brazier surrounded by acrid smoke; two slightly younger but equally disfigured wives were rocking children in their arms; one was breast-feeding; seated before a weaver's loom was a young idol, magnificently dressed in silk, gold, and silver, knotting strands of wool. Leaving this gloomy den—realm of immanence, womb, and tomb—in the corridor leading up toward the light, I met the male, dressed in white, sparklingly clean, smiling, sunny. He was returning from the market, where he had bantered about world affairs with other men; he would spend a few hours in this retreat of his own, in the heart of this vast universe to which he belonged and from which he was not separated. For the old withered crea-tures, for the young bride doomed to the same degeneration, there was no other universe but the murky cave from which they would emerge only at night, silent and veiled.

The Jews of biblical times have more or less the same customs as the Arabs. The patriarchs are polygamous and can renounce their wives almost at whim; at the risk of harsh punishment, the young bride has to be deliv-ered to her spouse as a virgin; in cases of adultery, she is stoned; she is con-fined to domestic labor, as the image of virtuous women demonstrates: "She seeketh wool and flax . . . she riseth also while it is yet night . . . her candle goeth not off at night . . . she eateth not the bread of idleness." Even chaste and industrious, she is impure and burdened with taboos; she cannot testify in court. Ecclesiastes treats her with the deepest disgust: "And I find more bitter than death the woman, whose heart is snares and nets, and her hands as bands . . . one man among a thousand have I found; but a woman among all those have I not found." When her husband dies, custom and even law require her to marry a brother of the deceased.

This custom called levirate is found among many Oriental peoples. In all regimes where woman is under guardianship, one of the problems is what to do with widows. The most radical solution is to sacrifice them on their husbands' tombs. But it is not true that even in India the law imposes such holocausts; the Laws of Manu permit a wife to survive a husband; spectacular suicides have never been more than an aristocratic fashion. It is far more frequent for the widow to be handed over to her husband's heirs. The levirate sometimes takes the form of polyandry; to avoid the ambiguities of widowhood, all the brothers in the family become the husbands of the woman, a custom that serves to preserve the clan against the possible infertility of the husband. According to a text of Caesar's, in Brittany all the men of one family had a certain number of women in common.

This form of radical patriarchy was not established everywhere. In Babylon, Hammurabi's Code recognized certain rights of woman: she receives a share of the paternal inheritance, and when she marries, her father provides her with a dowry. In Persia, polygamy is customary; woman is bound to absolute obedience to the husband her father chooses for her as soon as she is nubile; but she is more respected than among most Oriental peoples; incest is not forbidden, and marriage takes place frequently among sisters and brothers; she is in charge of educating the children up to the age of seven for boys and until marriage for girls. Woman can share in her husband's estate if the son proves himself unworthy; if she is a "privileged wife," she is entrusted with the guardianship of minor children in the case of her husband's death and with the business management in the absence of an adult son. The rules of marriage clearly point out the importance posterity has for the head of a family. It is likely that there were five forms of marriage:[1] (1) The woman married with the consent of her parents; she was then called the "privileged wife"; her children belonged to her husband. (2) When the woman was an only child, her firstborn would be given up to her parents to replace their daughter; then she would become a "privileged wife." (3) If a man died unmarried, his family would take a woman from outside, give her a dowry, and marry her: she was called an "adopted wife"; half of her children belonged to the deceased and the other half to the living husband. (4) A widow without children who remarried was called a servant wife: she owed half of the children of her second marriage to her deceased husband. (5) The woman who married without the consent of her parents could not inherit from them until the

---

1. This account is taken from Clement Huart, *La Perse antique et la civilisation iranienne* (*Ancient Persia and Iranian Civilization*).

oldest son, coming of age, would give her to his father as a "privileged wife"; if her husband died before, she was considered a minor and put under guardianship. The status of the adopted wife and the servant wife establishes the right of every man to be survived by descendants who are not necessarily connected by a blood relationship. This confirms what was said above; this relationship was in a way invented by man when he sought to annex for himself—beyond his finite life—immortality in this world and in the underworld.

In Egypt, woman's condition was the most favorable. When Goddess Mothers married, they maintained their standing; social and religious unity resides in the couple; woman is an ally, a complement to man. Her magic is so unthreatening that even the fear of incest is overcome, and no differentiation is made between a sister and a spouse.[2] She has the same rights as men, the same legal power; she inherits, and she owns property. This uniquely fortunate situation is in no way haphazard: it stems from the fact that in ancient Egypt the land belonged to the king and the higher castes of priests and warriors; for private individuals, landed property was only usufructuary; the land was inalienable, property transmitted by inheritance had little value, and there was no problem about sharing it. Because of this absence of personal patrimony, woman maintained the dignity of a person. She married whom she wanted, and as a widow she could remarry as she wished. The male practiced polygamy, but although all of his children were legitimate, he had only one real wife, the only one associated with religion and linked to him legally: the others were mere slaves, deprived of all rights. The chief wife did not change status by marrying: she remained mistress of her possessions and was free to engage in contracts. When the pharaoh Bocchoris established private property, woman's position was too strong to be dislodged; Bocchoris opened the era of contracts, and marriage itself became contractual. There were three types of contracts: one dealt with servile marriage; woman became man's thing, but she could specify that he would not have a concubine other than her; nonetheless, the legal spouse was considered equal to man, and all their property was held in common; the husband would often agree to pay her a sum of money in the case of divorce. Later, this custom led to a type of contract remarkably favorable to women; the husband agreed to absolve her of her debt. There were serious punishments for adultery, but divorce was fairly open for the two spouses. The presence of contracts soundly restrained polygamy;

---

2. In some cases the brother *had to* marry his sister.

women got possession of the wealth and transmitted it to their children, which brought about the creation of a plutocratic class. Ptolemy Philopator decreed that women could no longer alienate their property without marital authorization, which kept them as eternal minors. But even in times when they had a privileged status, unique in the ancient world, they were not socially equal to men; taking part in religion and government, they could have the role of regent, but the pharaoh was male; priests and warriors were males; woman's role in public life was a secondary one; and in private life, fidelity was required of her without reciprocity.

The customs of the Greeks are very similar to Oriental ones; yet they do not practice polygamy. No one knows exactly why. Maintaining a harem always entails heavy costs: only the ostentatious Solomon, the sultans from *The Thousand and One Nights,* kings, chiefs, or rich property owners could afford the luxury of a vast seraglio; an ordinary man had to be satisfied with three or four women; a peasant rarely possessed more than two. Besides—except in Egypt, where there was no specific landed property— the concern for preserving the patrimony intact led to granting the oldest son special rights on paternal inheritance; from this stemmed a hierarchy among women, the mother of the principal heir invested with dignity far superior to that of his other wives. If the wife herself has property of her own or if she is dowered, she is considered a person by her husband: he is joined to her by both a religious and an exclusive bond. From there on, the custom that only recognizes one wife was undoubtedly established: but the reality was that the Greek citizen continued to be comfortably "polygamous" since he could find the satisfaction of his desires from street prostitutes or gynaeceum servants. "We have hetarias for spiritual pleasures," says Demosthenes, "concubines (*pallakes*) for sensual pleasure, and wives to give us sons." The *pallakis* replaced the wife in the master's bed if she was ill, indisposed, pregnant, or recovering from childbirth; so there was no great difference between a gynaeceum and a harem. In Athens, the wife is shut up in her quarters, held by law under severe constraint, and watched over by special magistrates. She spends her whole life as a minor; she is under the control of her guardian: either her father, or her husband, or her husband's heir or, by default, the state, represented by public officials; here are her masters, and they use her like merchandise, the guardian's control extending over both her person and her property; the guardian can transmit her rights as he wishes: the father gives his daughter up for adoption or in marriage; the husband can repudiate his wife and hand her over to another husband. But Greek law assures woman of a dowry used to support her and that must be restored in full to her if the marriage is dissolved;

the law also authorizes the woman to file for divorce in certain rare cases; but these are the only guarantees that society grants. Of course, all inheritance is bequeathed to the male children, and the dowry is considered not acquired property but a kind of duty imposed on the guardian. However, thanks to this dowry custom, the widow no longer passes for a hereditary possession in the hands of her husband's heirs: she returns to her family's guardianship.

One of the problems arising from societies based on agnation is the fate of inheritance in the absence of any male descendants. The Greeks had instituted the custom of *epiklerate:* the female heir had to marry her oldest relative in the paternal family (*genos*); thus the property her father bequeathed to her would be transmitted to children belonging to the same group, and the estate remained the property of the paternal *genos;* the *epikleros* was not a female heir but only a machine to procreate a male heir; this custom placed her entirely at man's mercy as she was automatically handed over to the firstborn of her family's men, who most often turned out to be an old man.

Since the cause of women's oppression is found in the resolve to perpetuate the family and keep the patrimony intact, if she escapes the family, she escapes this total dependence as well; if society rejects the family by denying private property, woman's condition improves considerably. Sparta, where community property prevailed, was the only city-state where the woman was treated almost as the equal of man. Girls were brought up like boys; the wife was not confined to her husband's household; he was only allowed furtive nocturnal visits; and his wife belonged to him so loosely that another man could claim a union with her in the name of eugenics: the very notion of adultery disappears when inheritance disappears; as all the children belonged to the city as a whole, women were not jealously enslaved to a master: or it can be explained inversely, that possessing neither personal wealth nor individual ancestry, the citizen does not possess a woman either. Women underwent the burdens of maternity as men did war: but except for this civic duty, no restraints were put on their freedom.

Along with the free women just discussed and slaves living within the *genos*—unconditionally owned by the family head—are the prostitutes found in Greece. Primitive people were familiar with hospitality prostitution, turning over a woman to a guest passing through, which undoubtedly had mystical explanations; and with sacred prostitution, intended for the common good by releasing the mysterious forces of fertility. These customs existed in classical antiquity. Herodotus reports that in the fifth century B.C., every woman in Babylon had to give herself once in her life to a stranger in the temple of Mylitta for a coin she contributed to the temple's coffers; she then returned home to live in chastity. Religious prostitution has continued to our day among Egyptian almahs and Indian *bayadères*, who make up respectable castes of musicians and dancers. But most often, in Egypt, India, and western Asia, sacred prostitution slipped into legal prostitution, the priestly class finding this trade profitable. There were venal prostitutes even among the Hebrews. In Greece, especially along the coast or on the islands where many foreigners stopped off, temples of "young girls hospitable to strangers," as Pindar called them, could be found: the money they earned was intended for religious establishments, that is, for priests and indirectly for their maintenance. In reality, in a hypocritical way, sailors' and travelers' sexual needs—in Corinth and other places—were exploited; and this was already venal prostitution. Solon was the one who turned this into an institution. He bought Asian slaves and shut them up in *dicterions* located in Athens near the temple of Venus, not far from the port, under the management of *pornotropos* in charge of the financial administration of the establishment; each girl received wages, and the net profit went to the state. After that, *kapaileia*, private establishments, were opened: a red Priapus served as their display sign. Soon, in addition to slaves, poor Greek women were taken in as residents. The *dicterions* were considered so necessary that they were recognized as inviolable places of asylum. Nonetheless, courtesans were marked with infamy, they had no social rights, and their children were exempted from providing for them; they had to wear specific outfits made of multicolored cloth decorated with flower bouquets, and their hair was dyed with saffron. Besides the women shut up in *dicterions*, there were free courtesans, who could be placed in three categories: *dicteriads*, much like today's registered prostitutes; *auletrids*, who were dancers and flute players; and hetaeras, demimondaines who often came from Corinth having had official liaisons with high-ranking Greek men and who played the social role of modern-day "worldly women." The first ones were found among freed women or lower-class Greek girls; exploited by procurers, they led a pitiful life. The second type succeeded in getting rich thanks to their musical talent: the most famous of all was Lamia, mistress of Ptolemy of Egypt, then of his vanquisher, the king of Macedonia, Demetrius Poliorcetes. As for the last category, many were well-known for sharing in the glory of their lovers. Disposing of themselves and their fortunes freely, intelligent, cultivated, and artistic, they were treated like persons by the men who were captivated by their charms. And because they escaped from their families, because they lived on the margins of society, they also escaped men: they could seem to be their counterparts, almost their equals. In Aspasia, in Phryne, and in Lais, the superiority of the free woman asserted itself over the virtuous mother of a family.

These brilliant exceptions aside, the Greek woman is reduced to semi-slavery; she does not even have the freedom to complain: Aspasia and the more passionate Sappho are barely able to make a few grievances heard. In Homer, there are remnants of the heroic period when women had some power: still, the warriors roundly send them off to their chambers. The same scorn is found in Hesiod: "He who confides in a woman confides in a thief." In the great classical period, woman is resolutely confined to the gynaeceum. "The best woman is she of whom men speak the least," said Pericles. Plato, who proposed admitting a council of matrons to the Republic's administration and giving girls a liberal education, is an exception; he provoked Aristophanes' raillery; to a woman who questions him about public affairs, a husband responds, in *Lysistrata:* "This is none of your business. Shut up, or you'll be beaten . . . go back to your weaving." Aristotle expresses the common point of view in declaring that woman is woman because of a deficiency, that she must live closed up at home and obey man. "The slave is entirely deprived of the freedom to deliberate; woman does have it, but she is weak and powerless," he states. According to Xenophon, a woman and her spouse are complete strangers to each other: "Are there people you communicate with less than your wife?—There are not many"; all that is required of a woman in *Oeconomicus* is to be an attentive, prudent, economical housewife, busy as a bee, a model of organization. The modest status to which women are reduced does not keep the Greeks from being deeply misogynist. In the seventh century B.C., Archilochus writes biting epigrams against women; Simonides of Amorgos says, "Women are the greatest evil God ever created: if they sometimes seem useful, they soon change into trouble for their masters." For Hipponax: "There are but two days in life when your wife brings you joy: her wedding day and her funeral." But it is the Ionians who, in Miletus's stories, are the most spiteful: for example, the tale of the matron of Ephesus. Mostly women are attacked for being lazy, shrewish, or spendthrift, in fact precisely the absence of the qualities demanded of them. "There are many monsters on the earth and in the sea, but the greatest is still woman," wrote Menander. "Woman is a pain that never goes away." When the institution of the dowry brought a certain importance to women, it was her arrogance that was deplored; this is one of Aristophanes'—and notably Menander's—familiar themes. "I married a witch with a dowry. I took her for her fields and her house, and that, O

Apollo, is the worst of evils!" "Damn him who invented marriage and then the second, the third, the fourth, and the rest who followed them." "If you are poor and you marry a rich woman, you will be reduced to being both a slave and poor." The Greek woman was too closely controlled to be attacked for her conduct; and it was not the flesh in her that was vilified. It was more the responsibilities and duties of marriage that weighed on men; this leads to the supposition that in spite of her rigorous conditions, and although she had almost no recognized rights, she must have held an important place in the household and enjoyed some authority; doomed to obedience, she could disobey; she could bombard her husband with tantrums, tears, nagging, and insults; marriage, meant to enslave woman, was a ball and chain for the husband as well. In the character of Xanthippe is embodied all the grievances of the Greek citizen against the shrewish wife and the adversities of conjugal life.

The conflict between family and state defines the history of the Roman woman. The Etruscans constituted a matrilineal filiation society, and it is probable that at the time of the monarchy Rome still practiced exogamy linked to a matriarchal regime: the Latin kings did not transmit power through heredity. What is certain is that after Tarquinius's death, patriarchy asserts itself: agricultural property and the private estate—thus the family—become society's nucleus. Woman will be strictly subservient to the patrimony and thus to the family group: laws deprive her of even those guarantees accorded to Greek women; she lives her life in powerlessness and servitude. She is, of course, excluded from public affairs and prohibited from any "masculine office"; she is a perpetual minor in civil life. She is not directly deprived of her paternal inheritance but, through circuitous means, is kept from using it: she is put under the authority of a guardian. "Guardianship was established in the interest of the guardians themselves," said Gaius, "so that woman—of whom they are the presumptive heirs—could not rob them of their inheritance with a will, nor diminish the inheritance by alienations or debts." Woman's first guardian is her father; in his absence, paternal male relatives fulfill that function. When the woman marries, she passes "into the hands" of her husband; there are three types of marriage: the *confarreatio,* where the spouses offer a spelt cake to the Capitoline Jupiter in the presence of the *flamen dialis;* the *coemptio,* a fictitious sale in which the plebeian father "mancipated" his daughter to her husband; and the *usus,* the result of a cohabitation of one year; all three were with *manu,* meaning that the male spouse replaces the father or his male relatives; his wife is considered one of his daughters, and he thenceforth has complete power over her person and her property. But from the time of the Law of the Twelve Tables, because the Roman woman belonged to both paternal and conjugal clans, conflicts arose, giving rise to her legal emancipation. As a result, the *manu* marriage dispossesses her male agnates. To defend the paternal relatives' interests, *sine manu* marriage comes into being; in this case, the woman's property remains under the guardians' control, and the husband's rights are only over her person; and even this power is shared with the paterfamilias, who keeps his daughter under his absolute authority. The family court is in charge of settling disputes arising between father and husband: such an institution gives the woman recourse from her father to her husband or from her husband to her father; she is not one individual's thing. Moreover, although a gens is very powerful—as the existence of this court proves—independent of public courts, the father, as head of the family, is above all a citizen: his authority is unlimited, he rules absolutely over wife and children; but they are not his property; rather, he administers their existence for the public good; the woman, who brings his children into the world and whose domestic duties often extend to agricultural tasks, is very useful to the country and deeply respected. Here is an important fact that recurs throughout history: abstract rights cannot sufficiently define the concrete situation of woman; this situation depends in great part on the economic role she plays; and very often, abstract freedom and concrete powers vary inversely. Legally more enslaved than the Greek woman, the Roman is more deeply integrated in society; at home she sits in the atrium, which is the center of the domicile, rather than being relegated to the gynaeceum; it is she who presides over the slaves' work; she oversees the children's education, and her influence on them often extends to an advanced age; she shares her husband's work and his concerns, she is considered a co-owner of his property; the marriage formula "*Ubi tu Gaius, ego Gaia*" is not an empty formula;* the matron is called *domina;* she is mistress of the home, associate in religion, not a slave but man's companion; the tie that unites her to him is so sacred that in five centuries not one divorce is recorded. She is not confined to her quarters: she is present at meals and celebrations, she goes to the theater; men give her right-of-way on the street, consuls and lictors stand aside for her. Legend accords her an eminent role in history: those of the Sabine women, Lucretia, and Virginia are well-known; Coriolanus yields to the supplications of his mother's and his wife's pleas; the law of

---

* "Where you are Gaius, I am Gaia."—TRANS.

Licinius consecrating the triumph of Roman democracy is said to have been inspired by his wife; Cornelia forges the soul of the Gracchi. "Everywhere men govern women," said Cato, "and we who govern all men are governed by our women."

Little by little the legal situation of Roman women adapts to their practical situation. During the patrician oligarchy, each paterfamilias is an independent ruler within the Republic; but when state power becomes established, it opposes the concentration of wealth and the arrogance of powerful families. Family courts bow to public justice. And woman acquires ever greater rights. Four powers originally limited her freedom: the father and the husband controlled her person, her guardian and *manus* her property. The state takes authority over the opposition of father and husband to restrict their rights: the state court will now rule over adultery cases, divorce, and so on. In the same way, guardians and *manus* destroy each other. In the interest of the guardian, the *manus* had already been separated from marriage; later, the *manus* becomes an expedient that women use to escape their guardians, either by contracting fictitious marriages or by securing obliging guardians from their father or from the state. Under imperial legislation, guardianship will be entirely abolished. Woman simultaneously gains a positive guarantee of her independence: her father is obliged to provide her with a dowry; and it will not go back to the agnates after the marriage's dissolution, nor does it ever belong to her husband; a woman can at any moment demand restitution by a sudden divorce, which puts man at her mercy. "In accepting the dowry, he sold his power," said Plautus. From the end of the Republic on, the mother's right to her children's respect was recognized as equal to the father's; she is granted custody of her children in case of guardianship or of the husband's bad conduct. When she had three children and the deceased had no heirs, a Senate decree, under Hadrian, entitled her to an *ab intestat* succession right for each of them. And under Marcus Aurelius the Roman family's evolution was completed: from 178 on, the mother's children become her heirs, over her male relatives; from then on, the family is based on *coniunctio sanguinis*, and the mother is equal to the father; the daughter inherits like her brothers.

Nevertheless, the history of Roman law shows a tendency that contradicts the one just described: rendering the woman independent of the family, the central power takes her back under its guardianship and subjects her to various legal restraints.

In fact, she would assume an unsettling importance if she could be both rich and independent; so what is conceded with one hand is taken away from her with the other. The Oppian Law that banned luxury was voted when Hannibal threatened Rome; when the danger passed, women demanded its abrogation; in a famous speech, Cato asked that it be upheld: but a demonstration by matrons assembled in the public square carried the repeal against him. More severe laws were proposed as mores loosened, but without great success: they did little more than give rise to fraud. Only the Velleian Senate decree triumphed, forbidding woman to "intercede" for others,[3] depriving her of nearly every legal capacity. It is when woman is probably the most emancipated that the inferiority of her sex is proclaimed, a remarkable example of the male justification process already discussed: when her rights as girl, wife, or sister are no longer limited, she is refused equality with men because of her sex; the pretext for persecuting her becomes "imbecility and fragility of the sex."

The fact is that matrons did not put their newfound freedom to the best use; but it is also true that they were forbidden to take the best advantage of it. These two contradictory strains—an individualistic strain that tears woman from the family and a state-controlled strain that abuses her as an individual—result in an unbalanced situation for her. She can inherit, she has equal rights with the father concerning the children, she can will her property thanks to the institution of the dowry, she escapes conjugal restraints, she can divorce and remarry as she wishes: but she is emancipated only in a negative way because she is offered no employment for her vital forces. Economic independence remains abstract since it yields no political capacity; therefore, lacking the power to *act*, Roman women *demonstrate:* they cause a ruckus in towns, they besiege the courts, they brew, they foment plots, they lay down prescriptions, they inflame civil wars, they march along the Tiber carrying the statue of the Mother of the Gods, thus introducing Oriental divinities to Rome; in the year 114 the scandal of the vestal virgins breaks out, and their college is then disbanded. As public life and virtue are out of reach, and when the dissolution of the family renders the former private virtues useless and outdated, there is no longer any moral code for women. They have two choices: either to respect the same values as their grandmothers or to no longer recognize any. The end of the first century and beginning of the second see numerous women living as companions and partners of their spouses, as in the time of the Republic: Plotina shares the glory and responsibilities of Trajan; Sabina becomes so famous for her good deeds that statues deify her while she is

---

3. That is, to enter into contracts with another.

still alive; under Tiberius, Sextia refuses to live on after Aemilius Scaurus, and Pascea to live on after Pomponius Labeus; Paulina opens her veins at the same time as Seneca; Pliny the Younger makes Arria's "Paete, non dolet" famous; Martial admires the irreproachable wives and devoted mothers Claudia Rufina, Virginia, and Sulpicia. But numerous women refuse motherhood, and many women divorce; laws continue to ban adultery: some matrons even go so far as to register as prostitutes to avoid being constrained in their debaucheries.[4] Until then, Latin literature had always respected women: then satirists went wild against them. They attacked, in fact, not women in general but mainly contemporary women. Juvenal reproaches their hedonism and gluttony; he accuses them of aspiring to men's professions: they take an interest in politics, immerse themselves in court cases, debate with grammarians and rhetoricians, develop passions for hunting, chariot racing, fencing, and wrestling. But in fact they rival men mainly because of their own taste for amusement and vice; they lack sufficient education for higher aims; and besides, no objective is even proposed to them; action remains forbidden to them. The Roman woman of the ancient Republic has a place on earth, but she is still chained to it by lack of abstract rights and economic independence; the Roman woman of the decline is typical of false emancipation, possessing, in a world where men are still the only masters, nothing but empty freedom: she is free "for nothing."

---

4. Rome, like Greece, officially tolerated prostitution. There were two categories of courtesans: those living closed up in brothels, and others, *bonae meretrices,* freely exercising their profession. They did not have the right to wear the clothing of matrons; they had a certain influence on fashion, customs, and art, but they never held a position as lofty as the hetaeras of Athens.

CHAPTER 4

The evolution of the feminine condition was not a continuous process. With the great invasions, all of civilization is put into question. Roman law itself is under the influence of a new ideology, Christianity; and in the centuries that follow, barbarians impose their laws. The economic, social, and political situation is overturned: and women's situation suffers the consequences.

Christian ideology played no little role in women's oppression. Without a doubt, there is a breath of charity in the Gospels that spread to women as well as to lepers; poor people, slaves, and women are the ones who adhere most passionately to the new law. In the very early days of Christianity, women who submitted to the yoke of the Church were relatively respected; they testified along with men as martyrs; but they could nonetheless worship only in secondary roles; deaconesses were authorized only to do lay work: caring for the sick or helping the poor. And although marriage is considered an institution demanding mutual fidelity, it seems clear that the wife must be totally subordinate to the husband: through Saint Paul the fiercely antifeminist Jewish tradition is affirmed. Saint Paul commands self-effacement and reserve from women; he bases the principle of subordination of women to man on the Old and New Testaments. "The man is not of the woman; but the woman of the man"; and "Neither was man created for the woman; but the woman for the man." And elsewhere: "For the husband is the head of the wife, even as Christ is the head of the church." In a religion where the flesh is cursed, the woman becomes the devil's most fearsome temptation. Tertullian writes: "Woman! You are the devil's gateway. You have convinced the one the devil did not dare to confront directly. It is your fault that God's Son had to die. You should always dress in mourning and rags." Saint Ambrose: "Adam was led to sin by Eve and not Eve by Adam. It is right and just that he whom she led into sin, she shall receive as master." And Saint John Chrysostom: "Of all the wild animals, none can be found as harmful as woman." When canon law is written in the fourth century, marriage is treated as a concession to human failings, incompatible with Christian perfection. "Take up the hatchet and cut the roots of the sterile tree of marriage," writes Saint Jerome. In the time of Gregory VI, when celibacy was imposed on priests, woman's dangerous character was more harshly asserted: all the Fathers of the Church proclaim her wretchedness. Saint Thomas will remain true to this tradition, declaring that woman is only an "occasional" and incomplete being, a sort of failed man. "Man is the head of woman just as Christ is the head of man," he writes. "It is a constant that woman is destined to live under the authority of man and has no authority of her own." Thus, the only marriage regime canon law recognizes is by dowry, rendering woman helpless and powerless. Not only is she prohibited from male functions, but she is also barred from making court depositions, and her testimony holds no weight. The emperors are more or less under the influence of the Church Fathers; Justinian's legislation honors woman as spouse and mother but subjugates her to those functions; her helplessness is due not to her sex but to her situation within the family. Divorce is prohibited, and marriage has to be a public event; the mother has the same authority over her children as the father, and she has equal rights to their inheritance; if her husband dies, she becomes their legal tutor. The Velleian Senate decree is modified: from that time on she can intercede for the benefit of a third party; but she cannot contract for her husband; her dowry becomes inalienable; it is her children's patrimony, and she is forbidden to dispose of it.

In barbarian-occupied territories, these laws are juxtaposed with Germanic traditions. The German customs were unique. They had chiefs only in wartime; in peacetime the family was an autonomous society; it seemed to be midway between matrilineal filiation clans and patriarchal gens; the mother's brother had the same power as the father and the same authority over their niece and daughter as her husband. In a society where all capacity was rooted in brute force, woman was entirely powerless; but the rights that were guaranteed to her by the twofold domestic powers on which she depended were recognized; subjugated, she was nonetheless respected; her husband purchased her, but the price of this purchase constituted a dowry that belonged to her; and besides, her father dowered her; she received her portion of the paternal inheritance and, in the case of parents being murdered, a portion of the fine paid by the murderer. The family was monogamous, adultery being severely punished and marriage respected. The woman still lived under wardship, but she was a close partner of her husband. "In peace and in war, she shares his lot; she lives with him, she dies

with him," says Tacitus. She went to war with him, brought food to the soldiers, and encouraged them by her presence. As a widow, part of her
deceased husband's power was transmitted to her. Since her incapacity was
rooted in her physical frailty, it was not considered an expression of moral
inferiority. Some women were priestesses and prophets, so it could be
assumed that their education was superior to men's. Among the objects
that legally reverted to women in questions of inheritance were, later, jewelry and books.

This is the tradition that continues into the Middle Ages. The woman is
absolutely dependent on her father and husband: during Clovis's time, the
mundium weighs on her throughout her life;* but the Franks rejected Germanic chastity: under the Merovingians and Carolingians polygamy
reigns; the woman is married without her consent and can be repudiated by
her husband, who holds the right of life or death over her according to his
whim. She is treated like a servant. Laws protect her but only inasmuch as
she is the man's property and the mother of his children. Calling her a
prostitute without having proof is considered an insult liable to a fine fifteen times more than any insult to a man; kidnapping a married woman is
equivalent to a free man's murder; taking a married woman's hand or arm
is liable to a fine of fifteen to thirty-five sous; abortion is forbidden under
threat of a hundred-sou fine; murder of a pregnant woman costs four times
that of a free man; a woman who has proved herself fertile is worth three
times a free man; but she loses all worth when she can no longer be a
mother; if she marries a slave, she becomes an outlaw, and her parents have
the right to kill her. She has no rights as an individual. But while the state is
becoming powerful, the shift that had occurred in Rome occurs here as
well: the wardship of the disabled, children, and women no longer belongs
to family law but becomes a public office; starting from Charlemagne, the
mundium that weighs down the woman belongs to the king; he only intervenes at first in cases in which the woman is deprived of her natural
guardians; then, little by little, he confiscates the family powers; but this
change does not bring about the Frank woman's emancipation. The
mundium becomes the guardian's responsibility; his duty is to protect his
ward: this protection brings about the same slavery for woman as in the
past.

When feudalism emerges out of the convulsions of the early Middle
Ages, woman's condition looks very uncertain. What characterizes feudal

---

* *Mundium:* almost total legal guardianship over women by father and husband.—TRANS.

law is the confusion between sovereign and property law, between public and private rights. This explains why woman is both put down and raised up by this system. She first finds herself denied all private rights because she lacks political capacity. Until the eleventh century, order is based on force alone and property on armed power. A fief, legal experts say, is "property held against military service"; woman cannot hold feudal property, because she is incapable of defending it. Her situation changes when fiefs become hereditary and patrimonial; in Germanic law some aspects of maternal law survived, as has already been shown: if there were no male heirs, the daughter could inherit. This leads, around the eleventh century, to the feudal system's acceptance of female succession. However, military service is still required of the vassals; and woman's lot does not improve with her ability to inherit; she still needs a male guardian; the husband plays that role: he is invested with the title, holds the fief, and has the usufruct of the goods. Like the Greek *epikleros,* woman is the instrument and not the bearer through which the domain is transmitted; that does not emancipate her; in a way she is absorbed by the fief, she is part of the real property. The domain is no longer the family's thing as it was for Roman gens: it is the lord's property, and the woman also belongs to the lord. He is the one who chooses a spouse for her; when she has children, she gives them to him rather than to her husband: they will be vassals who will defend his property. She is therefore a slave of the domain and of its master through the "protection" of a husband who was imposed on her: few periods of history seem harsher for woman's lot. An heiress means land and a château: suitors fight over this prey, and the girl is sometimes not even twelve years old when her father or his lord gives her to some baron as a gift. The more marriages, the more domains for a man; and thus the more repudiations; the Church hypocritically authorizes them; as marriage was forbidden between relatives up to the seventh degree, and as kinship was defined by spiritual relations such as godmother and godfather as well as by blood relations, some pretext or other can always be found for an annulment; many women in the eleventh century were repudiated four or five times. Once widowed, the woman immediately has to accept a new master. In the chansons de geste Charlemagne has, all at once, the widows of his barons who had died in Spain remarry; in *Girard de Vienne,* the Burgundy duchess goes herself to the king to demand a new spouse. "My husband has just died, but what good is mourning? Find me a powerful husband because I need to defend my land"; many epics show the king or lord dealing tyrannically with girls and widows. One also sees the husband treating the woman given to him as a gift without any respect; he abuses and slaps her, drags her by her hair, and beats her; all that Beaumanoir in *Coutumes de Beauvaisis* (Customs of Beauvaisis) asks is that the husband "punish his wife reasonably." This warlike civilization has only scorn for women. The knight is not interested in women: his horse is a treasure of much higher value to him; in the epics, girls are always the ones to make the first step toward young men; once married, they alone are expected to be faithful; the man dissociates them from his life. "Cursed be the knight who takes counsel from a lady on when to joust." And in Renaud de Montauban, there is this diatribe: "Go back into your painted and golden quarters, sit ye down in the shade, drink, eat, embroider, dye silk, but do not busy yourself with our affairs. Our business is to fight with the sword and steel. Silence!" The woman sometimes shares the males' harsh life. As a girl, she excels in all physical exercises, she rides, hunts, hawks; she barely receives any education and is raised with no regard for modesty: she welcomes the château's guests, takes care of their meals and baths, and she "pleasures" them to sleep; as a woman, she sometimes has to hunt wild animals, undertake long and difficult pilgrimages; when her husband is far away, it is she who defends the seigneury. These ladies of the manor, called viragoes, are admired because they behave exactly like men: they are greedy, treacherous, and cruel, and they tyrannize their vassals. History and legend have bequeathed the memory of several of them: the chatelaine Aubie, after having a tower built higher than any donjon, then had the architect's head cut off so her secret would be kept; she chased her husband from his domain: he stole back and killed her. Mabel, Roger de Montgomerie's wife, delighted in reducing her seigneury's nobles to begging: their revenge was to decapitate her. Juliane, bastard daughter of Henry I of England, defended the château of Breteuil against him, luring him into an ambush for which he punished her severely. Such acts remain exceptional, however. Ordinarily, the lady spent her time spinning, praying for the dead, waiting for her spouse, and being bored.

It has often been claimed that courtly love, born in the twelfth century in the Mediterranean south of France, brought about an improvement in woman's lot. There are several opposing hypotheses as to its origins: according to some people, "courtliness" comes from the lord's relations with his young vassals; others link it to Cathar heresies and the cult of the Virgin; still others say that profane love derives from the love of God in general. It is not so sure that courts of love ever existed. What is sure is that faced with Eve the sinner, the Church comes to glorify the Mother of the Redeemer: she has such a large following that in the thirteenth century it can be said that God was made woman; a mysticism of woman thus develops in religion. Moreover, leisure in château life enables the noble ladies to promote and nurture the luxury of conversation, politeness, and poetry; women of letters such as Béatrice de Valentinois, Eleanor of Aquitaine and her daughter Marie of France, Blanche of Navarre, and many others attract and patronize poets; first in the Midi and then in the North culture thrives, giving women new prestige. Courtly love was often described as platonic; Chrétien de Troyes, probably to please his protector, banishes adultery from his novels: the only guilty love he depicts is that of Lancelot and Guinevere; but in fact, as the feudal husband was both a guardian and a tyrant, the wife sought a lover outside of marriage; courtly love was a compensation for the barbarity of official customs. "Love in the modern sense does not exist in antiquity except outside of official society," notes Engels: at the very point where antiquity broke off its penchant for sexual love, the Middle Ages took it up again with adultery. And this is the form that love will take as long as the institution of marriage lasts.

While courtly love might ease woman's lot, it does not modify it substantially. Ideologies like religion and poetry do not lead to female liberation; woman gains a little ground at the end of the feudal age for other reasons entirely. When the supremacy of royal power is imposed on feudatories, the lord loses a large part of his rights: his right, in particular, to decide on his vassals' marriages is progressively suppressed; at the same time, the feudal lord loses the use of his ward's property; the benefits attached to wardship fall into disuse; and when the service of the fief is converted to a monetary fee, wardship itself disappears; woman was unable to perform military service, but she was as capable as a man of paying the financial obligations; the fief is then little more than a simple patrimony, and there is no longer any reason for the two sexes not to be placed on an equal footing. In fact, women in Germany, Switzerland, and Italy remain subjected to a perpetual wardship; but France accepts, in Beaumanoir's words, that "a girl is worth a man." Germanic tradition gave women a defender as a guardian; when she no longer needs a defender, she goes without a guardian; as a sex, she is no longer taxed with incapacity. Unmarried or widowed, she has all the rights of man; property grants her sovereignty: she governs the fief that she owns, meaning she dispenses justice, signs treaties, and decrees laws. She is even seen playing a military role, commanding troops, taking part in fighting; before Joan of Arc there were women soldiers, and however surprising La Pucelle is, she is not shocking.

Nonetheless, so many factors converge to thwart woman's independence that they are never all abolished simultaneously; physical weakness is no longer an issue; but feminine subordination remains useful to society in cases where the woman is married. Thus marital power outlives the feudal regime. The paradox still being perpetuated today is established: the woman most fully integrated into society is the one with the fewest privileges in the society. In civil feudality, marriage has the same features as in military feudality: the husband remains the wife's guardian. When the bourgeoisie is formed, it observes the same laws. In common law as in feudal law, the only emancipation is outside marriage; the daughter and the widow have the same capacities as the man; but by marrying, the woman falls under the husband's guardianship and administration; he can beat her; he watches over her behavior, relations, and correspondence and disposes of her fortune, not through a contract, but by the very fact of marriage. "As soon as the marriage is consummated," Beaumanoir says, "the possessions of each party are held in common by virtue of the marriage and the man is the guardian of them." It is in the interest of property that the nobility and the bourgeoisie demand one master to administer it. The wife is not subordinated to the husband because she is judged basically incapable: when nothing else prevents it, woman's full capacities are recognized. From feudality to today, the married woman is deliberately sacrificed to private property. It is important to see that the greater the property owned by the husband, the greater this servitude: the propertied classes are those in which woman's dependence has always been the most concrete; even today, the patriarchal family survives among rich landowners; the more socially and economically powerful man feels, the more he plays the paterfamilias with authority. On the contrary, shared destitution makes the conjugal link reciprocal. Neither feudality nor the Church enfranchised woman. Rather, it was from a position of servitude that the patriarchal family moved to an authentically conjugal one. The serf and his wife owned nothing; they simply had the common use of their house, furniture, and utensils: man had no reason to want to become master of woman who owned nothing; but the bonds of work and interest that joined them raised the spouse to the rank of companion. When serfdom is abolished, poverty remains; in small rural communities and among artisans, spouses live on an equal footing; woman is neither a thing nor a servant: those are the luxuries of a rich man; the poor man experiences the reciprocity of the bond that attaches him to his other half; in freely contracted work, woman wins concrete autonomy because she has an economic and social role. The farces and fabliaux of the Middle Ages reflect a society of artisans, small merchants, and peasants in which the husband's only privilege over his wife is to be able to beat her: but she pits craftiness against force to reestablish equality. However, the rich woman pays for her idleness with submission.

In the Middle Ages, the woman still retained some privileges: she took part in local meetings in the villages, she participated in the primary meetings for the deputies' election to the Estates-General; her husband could exercise his own authority only over movables: his wife's consent was necessary to alienate real estate. The sixteenth century sees the codification of the laws perpetuated throughout the ancien régime; by that time feudal habits and customs had totally disappeared, and nothing protects women from men's claims that they should be chained to the household. The influence of Roman law, so condescending for women, can be perceived here; as in Roman times, the violent diatribes against the stupidity and fragility of the sex were not at the root of the code but are used as justifications; it is after the fact that men find reasons to act as it suits them. "Among all the bad characteristics that women possess," one reads in the *Songe du verger*,*

> I find that there are nine principal ones: To begin with, a woman
> hurts herself as a result of her own nature; second, women are by
> nature extremely stingy; third, they are driven by sudden whims;
> fourth, they are bad by their own volition; fifth, they are impostors.
> Women are known to be false, and according to civil law a woman
> may not be accepted as a witness to a will. A woman always does
> the opposite of what she is commanded to do . . . Women accuse
> themselves willingly and announce their own vituperation and
> shame. They are crafty and malicious. Saint Augustine said that "A
> woman is a beast who is neither firm nor stable"; she is hateful, to the
> confusion of her husband; she nourishes wrongdoing and stands at
> the beginning of all the pleas and tensions; and is the path and road
> of all iniquity.

Similar texts abound around this time. The interest of this one is that each accusation is meant to justify one of the provisions of the code against women and the inferior situation in which they are kept. Naturally, any "male office" is forbidden to them; the Velleian decree of the Senate is reinstated, depriving them of all civil capacity; birthright and masculine privilege place them second in line for the paternal inheritance. Unmarried, the daughter remains under the father's guardianship; if he does not marry her off, he generally sends her to a convent. An unwed mother has the right

---

* The *Songe du verger* is a treatise of political doctrine, written first in Latin (1370) and then in French (1378). Title usually kept in French.—TRANS.

to seek out the father, but such a right merely provides for the costs of lying-in and the infant's food; a married woman becomes subject to the husband's authority: he determines the place of residence, directs the household, repudiates the adulteress wife, shuts her up in a monastery, or later obtains a lettre de cachet to send her to the Bastille;* no deed is valid without his authorization; everything the wife brings to the marriage becomes part of the dowry in the Roman meaning of the word; but as marriage is indissoluble, the husband has to die before the wife can recover her property, giving rise to the adage "*Uxor non est proprie socia sed speratur fore.*"† As she does not manage her capital, although she has rights to it, she does not have the responsibility for it; it does not provide any substance to her action: she has no concrete grasp on the world. Even her children belong to the father rather than to her, as in the time of the *Eumenides:* she "gives" them to her spouse, whose authority is far greater than hers and who is the real master of her posterity; even Napoleon will use this argument, declaring that just as a pear tree is the property of the owner of the pears, the wife is the property of the man to whom she provides children. The status of the French wife remains as such throughout the ancien régime; little by little jurisprudence will abolish the Velleian decree, but not until the Napoleonic Code does it disappear definitively. The husband is responsible for the wife's debts as well as her behavior, and she is accountable to him alone; she has almost no direct relations with public authorities or autonomous relations with anyone outside her family. She looks more like a servant in work and motherhood than an associate: objects, values, and human beings that she creates are not her own property but her family's, that is, man's, as he is the head. Her situation is far from being more liberal in other countries—it is, on the contrary, less liberal; some maintained guardianship; and in all of them, the married woman's capacities are nonexistent and moral standards strict. All the European codes were drafted on the basis of canon, Roman, and Germanic law, all were unfavorable to the woman, and all the countries recognized private property and the family, deferring to the demands of these institutions.

In all these countries, one of the consequences of the "honest wife's" servitude to the family is prostitution. Hypocritically kept on society's fringes, prostitutes fill a highly important role. Christianity pours scorn on them but accepts them as a necessary evil. "Getting rid of the prostitutes," said Saint Augustine, "will trouble society by dissoluteness." Later, Saint

---

* Lettre de cachet: letter with a seal. It carries an official seal, usually signed by the king of France, authorizing the imprisonment without trial of a named person.—TRANS.
†"The wife is not exactly a partner, but it is hoped she will become one."—TRANS.

Thomas—or at least the theologian that signed his name to Book IV of *De regimine principium*—asserted: "Remove public women from society and debauchery will disrupt it by disorder of all kinds. Prostitutes are to a city what a cesspool is to a palace: get rid of the cesspool and the palace will become an unsavory and loathsome place." In the early Middle Ages, moral license was such that women of pleasure were hardly necessary; but when the bourgeois family became institutionalized and monogamy rigorous, man obviously had to go outside the home for his pleasure.

In vain did one of Charlemagne's capitularies vigorously forbid it, in vain did Saint Louis order prostitutes to be chased out of the city in 1254 and brothels to be destroyed in 1269: in the town of Damietta, Joinville tells us, prostitutes' tents were adjacent to the king's. Later, attempts by Charles IX of France and Marie-Thérèse of Austria in the eighteenth century also failed. The organization of society made prostitution necessary. "Prostitutes," Schopenhauer would pompously say later, "are human sacrifices on the altar of monogamy." And Lecky, a historian of European morality, expressed the same idea: "Supreme type of vice, prostitutes are the most active guardians of virtue." Their situation and the Jews' were often rightly compared:[1] usury and money lending were forbidden by the Church exactly as extra-conjugal sex was; but society can no more do without financial speculators than free love, so these functions fell to the damned castes: they were relegated to ghettos or reserved neighborhoods. In Paris, loose women worked in pens where they arrived in the morning and left after the curfew had tolled; they lived on special streets and did not have the right to stray, and in most other cities brothels were outside town walls. Like Jews, they had to wear distinctive signs on their clothes. In France the most common one was a specific-colored aglet hung on the shoulder; silk, fur, and honest women's apparel were often prohibited. They were *by law* taxed with infamy, had no recourse whatsoever to the police and the courts, and could be thrown out of their lodgings on a neighbor's simple claim. For most of them, life was difficult and wretched. Some were closed up in public houses. Antoine de Lalaing, a French traveler, left a description of a Spanish establishment in Valencia in the late fifteenth century. "The place," he said, was

about the size of a small city, surrounded by walls with only one door. And in front of it there were gallows for criminals that might be inside; at the door, a man appointed to this task takes the canes of

1. "Those coming to Sisteron by the Peipin passage, like the Jews, owed a toll of five sols to the ladies of Sainte-Claire" (Bahutaud).

those wishing to enter and tells them that if they want to hand over their money, and if they have the money, he will give it to the porter. If it is stolen overnight, the porter will not answer for it. In this place there are three or four streets full of small houses, in each of which are prettily and cleanly dressed girls in velvet and satin. There are almost three hundred of them; their houses are well kept and decorated with good linens. The decreed price is four pennies of their money, which is the equivalent of our gros . . . There are taverns and cabarets. It is not easy to recognize these houses by daylight, while at night or in the evening the girls are seated at their doorways, with pretty lamps hanging near them in order to make it easier to see them at leisure. There are two doctors appointed and paid by the town to visit the girls every week in order to discover if they have any disease or intimate illness. If the town is stricken with any sickness, the lords of the place are required to maintain the girls at their expense and the foreigners are sent away to any place they wish to go.[2]

The author even marvels at such effective policing. Many prostitutes lived freely; some of them earned their living well. As in the period of the courtesans, high gallantry provided more possibilities for feminine individualism than the life of an "honest woman."

A condition unique to France is that of the unmarried woman; legal independence is in stark and shocking contrast to the wife's servitude; she is an oddity and so customs hasten to withdraw everything law grants her; she has total civil capacity: but those laws are abstract and empty; she has no economic autonomy, no social dignity, and generally the spinster remains hidden in the shadow of the paternal family or finds others like her behind convent walls: there she knows no other form of freedom but disobedience and sin—just as decadent Roman women were emancipated only by vice. Negativity continues to be women's lot as long as their emancipation remains negative.

In such conditions it is clear how rare it was for a wife to act or merely to make her presence felt: among the working classes, economic oppression cancels out sexual inequality; but it deprives the individual of opportunities; among the nobility and bourgeoisie, the wife is abused because of her sex; she has a parasitic existence; she is poorly educated; she needs excep-

---

2. De Reiffenberg, *Dictionnaire de la conversation*, "Femmes et filles de folles vie" (*Dictionary of Conversation*, "Women and Girls of the Low Life"). [Translation of Old French by Gabrielle Spiegel.—TRANS.]

tional circumstances if she is to envisage and carry out any concrete project. Queens and regents have that rare good fortune: their sovereignty exalts them above their sex; French Salic law denies women the right of access to the throne; but they sometimes play a great role beside their husbands or after their deaths: for example, Saint Clotilda, Saint Radegunda, and Blanche of Castile. Convent life makes woman independent of man: some abbesses wield great power; Héloïse gained fame as an abbess as much as a lover. In the mystical, thus autonomous, relation that binds them to God, feminine souls draw their inspiration and force from a virile soul; and the respect society grants them enables them to undertake difficult projects. Joan of Arc's adventure is something of a miracle: and it is, moreover, a very brief adventure. But Saint Catherine of Siena's story is meaningful; she creates a great reputation in Sienna for charitable activity and for the visions that testify to her intense inner life within a very normal existence; she thus acquires the necessary authority for success generally lacking in women; her influence is invoked to hearten those condemned to death, to bring back to the fold those who are lost, to appease quarrels between families and towns. She is supported by the community that recognizes itself in her, which is how she is able to fulfill her pacifying mission, preaching submission to the pope from city to city, carrying on a vast correspondence with bishops and sovereigns, and finally chosen by Florence as ambassador to go and find the pope in Avignon. Queens, by divine right, and saints, by their shining virtues, are assured of support in the society that allows them to be men's equal. Of others, a silent modesty is required. The success of a Christine de Pizan is due to exceptional luck: even so, she had to be widowed and burdened with children for her to decide to earn her living by her pen.

Altogether, men's opinion in the Middle Ages is not favorable to women. Courtly poets did exalt love; many codes of courtly love appear, such as André le Chapelain's poem and the famous *Roman de la Rose*, in which Guillaume de Lorris encourages young men to devote themselves to the service of ladies. But against this troubadour-inspired literature are pitted bourgeois-inspired writings that cruelly attack women: fabliaux, farces, and plays criticize women for their laziness, coquetry, and lust. Their worst enemies are the clergy. They incriminate marriage. The Church made it a sacrament and yet prohibited it for the Christian elite: this is the source of the contradiction of the *querelle des femmes*.* It is denounced with singular

---

* *Querelle des femmes:* a literary quarrel traced to Christine de Pizan's objection to the portrayal of women in the *Roman de la Rose*, voiced in her *Epître au dieu d'amours* (1399; *Epistle to the God of Love*), a debate that helped nurture literary production throughout the early modern period.—TRANS.

vigor in *The Lamentations of Matheolus*, famous in its time, published fifteen years after the first part of the *Roman de la Rose*, and translated into French one hundred years later. Matthew lost his "clergy" by taking a wife; he cursed his marriage, cursed women and marriage in general. Why did God create woman if there is this incompatibility between marriage and clergy? Peace cannot exist in marriage: it had to be the devil's work; or else God did not know what he was doing. Matthew hopes that woman will not rise on Judgment Day. But God responds to him that marriage is a purgatory thanks to which heaven is reached; and carried to the heavens in a dream, Matthew sees a legion of husbands welcoming him to the shouts of "Here, here the true martyr!" Jean de Meung, another cleric, is similarly inspired; he enjoins young men to get out from under the yoke of women; first he attacks love:

> *Love is hateful country*
> *Love is amorous hate.*

He attacks marriage that reduces man to slavery, that dooms him to be cuckolded; and he directs a violent diatribe against woman. In return, woman's champions strive to demonstrate her superiority. Here are some of the arguments apologists for the weaker sex drew on until the seventeenth century:

> Mulier perfetur viro scilicet. *Materia:* quia Adam factus esst de limo terrae, Eva de costa Adae. *Loco:* quia Adam factus est extra paradisum, Eva in paradiso. *In conceptione:* quia mulier concepit Deum, quid homo non potuit. *Apparicione:* quia Christus apparuit mulieri post mortem resurrectionem, scilicet Magdalene. *Exaltatione:* quia mulier exaltata est super chorus angelorum, scilicet beata Maria.[3]

To which their opponents replied that if Christ first appeared to women, it is because he knew they were talkative, and he was in a hurry to make his resurrection known.

---

3. "Woman is superior to man, namely: *Materially:* because Adam was made of clay, Eve from one of Adam's ribs. *In terms of place:* because Adam was created outside of paradise, Eve in paradise. *In terms of conception:* because woman conceived God, something man couldn't do. *In terms of appearance:* because Christ after his death appeared to a woman, namely Magdalene. *In terms of glorification:* because a woman was glorified above the choir of angels, namely blessed Mary."

The quarrel continues throughout the fifteenth century. The author of *The Fifteen Joys of Marriage* indulgently describes the misfortunes of poor husbands. Eustache Deschamps writes an interminable poem on the same theme. It is here that the "quarrel of the *Roman de la Rose*" begins. This is the first time a woman takes up her pen to defend her sex: Christine de Pizan attacks the clerics energetically in *The Epistle to the God of Love*. The clerics rise up immediately to defend Jean de Meung; but Gerson, chancellor of the University of Paris, takes Christine's side; he writes his treatise in French to reach a wide public. Martin Le Franc throws the indigestible *Ladies' Chaperon*—still being read two hundred years later—onto the battlefield.* And Christine intervenes once again. Her main demand is for women's right to education: "If the custom were to put little girls in school and they were normally taught sciences like the boys, they would learn as perfectly and would understand the subtleties of all the arts and sciences as they do."

In truth this dispute concerns women only indirectly. No one dreams of demanding a social role for them other than what they are assigned. It is more a question of comparing the life of the cleric to the state of marriage; it is a masculine problem brought up by the Church's ambiguous attitude to marriage. Luther settles this conflict by rejecting the celibacy of priests. Woman's condition is not influenced by this literary war. While railing against society as it is, the satire of farces and fabliaux does not claim to change it: it mocks women but does not plot against them. Courtly poetry glorifies femininity: but such a cult does not in any way imply the assimilation of the sexes. The *querelle* is a secondary phenomenon in which society's attitude is reflected but which does not modify it.

It has already been said that the wife's legal status remained practically unchanged from the early fifteenth century to the nineteenth century; but in the privileged classes her concrete condition does change. The Italian Renaissance is a period of individualism propitious to the burgeoning of strong personalities, regardless of sex. There were some women at that time who were powerful sovereigns, like Jean of Aragon, Joan of Naples, and Isabella d'Este; others were adventurer condottieri who took up arms like men: thus Girolamo Riario's wife fought for Forli's freedom; Hippolyta Fioramenti commanded the Duke of Milan's troops and during the siege of Pavia led a company of noblewomen to the ramparts. To defend their city

---

* The correct title is *Le champion des dames* (c. 1441; The Ladies' Champion).—TRANS.

against Montluc, Sienese women marshaled three thousand female troops commanded by women. Other Italian women became famous thanks to their culture or talents: for example, Isotta Nogarola, Veronica Gambara, Gaspara Stampa, Vittoria Colonna, who was Michelangelo's friend, and especially Lucrezia Tornabuoni, mother of Lorenzo and Giuliano de' Medici, who wrote, among other things, hymns and a life of Saint John the Baptist and the Virgin. A majority of these distinguished women were courtesans; joining free moral behavior with freethinking, ensuring their economic autonomy through their profession, many were treated by men with deferential admiration; they protected the arts and were interested in literature and philosophy, and they themselves often wrote or painted: Isabella da Luna, Caterina di San Celso, and Imperia, who was a poet and musician, took up the tradition of Aspasia and Phryne. For many of them, though, freedom still takes the form of license: the orgies and crimes of these great Italian ladies and courtesans remain legendary.

This license is also the main freedom found in the following centuries for women whose rank or fortune liberates them from common morality; in general, it remains as strict as in the Middle Ages. As for positive accomplishments, they are possible only for a very few. Queens are always privileged: Catherine de Medici, Elizabeth of England, and Isabella the Catholic are great sovereigns. A few great saintly figures are also worshipped. The astonishing destiny of Saint Teresa of Avila is explained approximately in the same way as Saint Catherine's: her self-confidence is inspired by her confidence in God; by carrying the virtues connected with her status to the highest, she garners the support of her confessors and the Christian world: she is able to emerge beyond a nun's ordinary condition; she founds and runs monasteries, she travels, takes initiatives, and perseveres with a man's adventurous courage; society does not thwart her; even writing is not effrontery: her confessors order her to do it. She brilliantly shows that a woman can raise herself as high as a man when, by an astonishing chance, a man's possibilities are granted to her.

But in reality such possibilities are very unequal; in the sixteenth century, women are still poorly educated. Anne of Brittany summons many women to the court, where previously only men had been seen; she strives to form a retinue of girls of honor: but she is more interested in their upbringing than in their culture. Among women who a little later distinguish themselves by their minds, intellectual influence, and writings, most are noblewomen: the duchess of Retz, Mme de Lignerolles, the Duchess of Rohan and her daughter Anne; the most famous were princesses: Queen Margot and Margaret of Navarre. Pernette Du Guillet seems to have been a bourgeois; but Louise Labé is undoubtedly a courtesan: in any case, she felt free to behave unconventionally.

Women in the seventeenth century will continue to distinguish themselves essentially in intellectual spheres; social life and culture are spreading; women play a considerable role in salons; by the very fact they are not involved in the construction of the world, they have the leisure to indulge in conversation, the arts, and literature; they are not formally educated, but through discussions, readings, and instruction by private preceptors or public lectures they succeed in acquiring greater knowledge than their husbands: Mlle de Gournay, Mme de Rambouillet, Mlle de Scudéry, Mme de La Fayette, and Mme de Sévigné enjoy great reputations in France; and outside France similar renown is associated with the names of Princess Elisabeth, Queen Christine, and Mlle de Schurman, who corresponded with the whole scholarly world. Thanks to this culture and the ensuing prestige, women manage to encroach on the masculine universe; from literature and amorous casuistry many ambitious women slide toward political intrigue. In 1623 the papal nuncio wrote: "In France all the major events, all the important plots, most often depend on women." The princesse de Condé foments the "women's conspiracy"; Anne of Austria readily takes the advice of the women surrounding her; Richelieu lends an indulgent ear to the duchesse d'Aiguillon; the roles played by Mme de Montbazon, the duchesse de Chevreuse, Mlle de Montpensier, the duchess de Longueville, Anne de Gonzague, and many others in the Fronde are well-known. Lastly, Mme de Maintenon is a brilliant example of the influence a skillful woman adviser could wield on state affairs. Organizers, advisers, and schemers, women assure themselves of a highly effective role by oblique means: the princesse des Ursins in Spain governs with more authority but her career is brief. Alongside these great noblewomen, a few personalities assert themselves in a world that escapes bourgeois constraints; a hitherto unknown species appears: the actress. The presence of a woman onstage is noted for the first time in 1545; in 1592 there is still only one; at the beginning of the seventeenth century most of them are actors' wives; they then become more and more independent both onstage and in their private lives. As far as the courtesan is concerned, after being Phryne or Imperia, she finds her highest incarnation in Ninon de Lenclos: from capitalizing on her femininity, she surpasses it; from living among men, she takes on virile qualities; her independent moral behavior disposes her to independent thinking: Ninon de Lenclos brought freedom to the highest point a woman could at that time.

In the eighteenth century, woman's freedom and independence continue to grow. Customs remained strict in principle: girls receive no more than a cursory education; they are married off or sent to a convent without being consulted. The bourgeoisie, the rising class that is being consolidated, imposes a strict morality on the wife. But on the other hand, with the nobility breaking up, the greatest freedom of behavior is possible for women of the world, and even the *haute bourgeoisie* is contaminated by these examples; neither convent nor conjugal home can contain the woman. Once again, for the majority of women, this freedom remains negative and abstract: they limit themselves to the pursuit of pleasure. But those who are intelligent and ambitious create avenues for action for themselves. Salon life once again blossoms: The roles played by Mme Geoffrin, Mme du Deffand, Mlle de Lespinasse, Mme d'Epinay, and Mme de Tencin are well-known; protectors and inspiration, women make up the writer's favorite audience; they are personally interested in literature, philosophy, and sciences: like Mme Du Châtelet, for example, they have their own physics workshops or chemistry laboratory; they experiment; they dissect; they intervene more actively than ever before in political life: one after the other, Mme de Prie, Mme de Mailly, Mme de Châteauneuf, Mme de Pompadour, and Mme du Barry govern Louis XV; there is barely a minister without his Egeria, to such a point that Montesquieu thinks that in France everything is done by women; they constitute, he says, "a new state within the state"; and Collé writes on the eve of 1789: "They have so taken over Frenchmen, they have subjugated them so greatly that they think about and feel only for themselves." Alongside society women there are also actresses and prostitutes who enjoy great fame: Sophie Arnould, Julie Talma, and Adrienne Lecouvreur.

Throughout the ancien régime the cultural domain is the most accessible to women who try to assert themselves. Yet none reached the summits of a Dante or a Shakespeare; this can be explained by the general mediocrity of their condition. Culture has never been the privilege of any but the feminine elite, never of the masses; and masculine geniuses often come from the masses; even privileged women encountered obstacles that barred their access to the heights. Nothing stopped the ascent of a Saint Teresa, a Catherine of Russia, but a thousand circumstances conspired against the woman writer. In her small book *A Room of One's Own*, Virginia Woolf enjoyed inventing the destiny of Shakespeare's supposed sister; while he learned a little Latin, grammar, and logic in school, she was closed up at home in total ignorance; while he poached, ran around in the countryside, and slept with local women, she was mending kitchen towels under her parents' watchful eyes; if, like him, she bravely left to seek her fortune in

London, she could not become an actress earning her living freely: either she would be brought back to her family and married off by force; or seduced, abandoned, and dishonored, she would commit suicide out of despair. She could also be imagined as a happy prostitute, a Moll Flanders, as Daniel Defoe portrayed her: but she would never have run a theater and written plays. In England, Virginia Woolf notes, women writers always engender hostility. Dr. Johnson compared them to "a dog's walking on his hinder legs. It is not done well; but you are surprised to find it done at all." Artists care about what people think more than anyone else; women narrowly depend on it: it is easy to imagine how much strength it takes for a woman artist simply to dare to carry on regardless; she often succumbs in the fight. At the end of the seventeenth century, Lady Winchilsea, a childless noblewoman, attempts the feat of writing; some passages of her work show she had a sensitive and poetic nature; but she was consumed by hatred, anger, and fear:

> *Alas! a woman that attempts the pen,*
> *Such an intruder on the rights of men,*
> *Such a presumptuous creature is esteemed,*
> *The fault by no virtue can be redeemed.* *

Almost all her work is filled with indignation about woman's condition. The Duchess of Newcastle's case is similar; also a noblewoman, she creates a scandal by writing. "Women live like cockroaches or owls, they die like worms," she furiously writes. Insulted and ridiculed, she had to shut herself up in her domain; and in spite of a generous temperament and going half-mad, she produced nothing more than wild imaginings. It is not until the eighteenth century that a bourgeois widow, Mrs. Aphra Behn,† lived by her pen like a man; others followed her example, but even in the nineteenth century they were often obliged to hide; they did not even have a "room of their own"; that is, they did not enjoy material independence, one of the essential conditions for inner freedom.

As has already been seen, because of the development of social life and its close link to intellectual life, French women's situation is a little more favorable. Nevertheless, people are largely hostile to the bluestockings. During the Renaissance, noblewomen and intellectuals inspire a movement

---

* Beauvoir shortened and paraphrased this quatrain in the French text.—Trans.
† Discrepancy: In fact, Mrs. Aphra Behn, dramatist and novelist, lived from 1640 to 1689. —Trans.

in favor of their sex; Platonic doctrines imported from Italy spiritualize love and woman. Many well-read men strive to defend her. *La nef des dames vertueuses* (The Ship of Virtuous Ladies), *Le chevalier des dames* (The Ladies' Chevalier), and so on were published. Erasmus in *Le petit sénat* (The Little Senate) gives the floor to Cornelia, who unabashedly details the grievances of her sex. "Men are tyrants . . . They treat us like toys . . . they make us their launderers and cooks." Erasmus demands that women be allowed to have an education. Cornelius Agrippa, in a very famous work, *Déclamation de la noblesse et de l'excellence du sexe féminin* (*Declamation on the Nobility and Preeminence of the Female Sex*), devotes himself to showing feminine superiority. He takes up the old cabbalistic arguments: Eve means Life and Adam Earth. Created after man, woman is more finished then he. She is born in paradise, he outside. When she falls into the water, she floats; man sinks. She is made from Adam's rib and not from earth. Her monthly cycles cure all illnesses. Eve merely wandered in her ignorance, whereas Adam sinned, which is why God made himself a man; moreover, after his resurrection he appeared to women. Then Agrippa declares that women are more virtuous than men. He lists "virtuous women" that the sex can take pride in, which is also a commonplace of these praises. Lastly, he mounts an indictment of male tyranny: "Acting against divine right and violating natural law with impunity, the tyranny of men has deprived women of the freedom they receive at birth." Yet she engenders children; she is as intelligent and even subtler than man; it is scandalous that her activities are limited, "undoubtedly done not by God's order, nor by necessity or reason, but by the force of usage, by education, work and principally by violence and oppression." He does not, of course, demand sexual equality, but wants woman to be treated with respect. The work was immensely successful; there is also *Le fort inexpugnable* (*The Impregnable Fort*), another praise of woman; and *La parfaite amye* (*The Perfect Friend*) by Héroët, imbued with Platonic mysticism. In a curious book introducing Saint-Simonian doctrine, Postel announces the coming of a new Eve, the regenerating mother of humankind: he thinks he has even met her; she is dead, and she is perhaps reincarnated in him. With more moderation, Marguerite de Valois, in her *Docte et subtil discours* (*Learned and Subtle Discourse*) proclaims that there is something divine in woman. But the writer who best served the cause of her sex was Margaret of Navarre, who proposed an ideal of sentimental mysticism and chastity without prudery to counter licentiousness, attempting to reconcile marriage and love for women's honor with happiness. Women's opponents do not, of course, give up. Among others, *Les controverses des sexes masculine* *et féminin* (Controversies over the Masculine and Feminine Sexes), in response to Agrippa, puts forward the old medieval arguments. Rabelais has a good time in *The Third Book* satirizing marriage in the tradition of Matthew and Deschamps: however, it is women who lay down the law in the privileged abbey of Thélème. Antifeminism becomes virulent once again in 1617, with the *Alphabet de l'imperfection et malice des femmes* (*A Discourse of Women, Shewing Their Imperfections Alphabetically*), by Jacques Olivier; the cover pictures an engraving of a woman with a harpy's hands, covered with the feathers of lust and perched on her feet, because, like a hen, she is a bad housewife: under every letter of the alphabet is one of her defects. Once more it was a man of the Church who rekindled the old quarrel; Mlle de Gournay answered back with *Egalité des hommes et des femmes* (*Equality of Men and Women*). This is followed by a quantity of libertine literature, including *Parnasse et cabinets satyriques* (Parnassus and Satyrical Cabinets),* that attacks women's moral behavior, while the holier-than-thous quoting Paul, the Church Fathers, and Ecclesiastes drag them down. Woman provided an inexhaustible theme for the satires of Mathurin Régnier and his friends. In the other camp, the apologists outdo themselves in taking up and commenting on Agrippa's arguments. Father du Boscq in *L'honneste femme* (*The Compleat Woman*) calls for women to be allowed to be educated. The *Astrée* and a great quantity of courtly literature praise their merits in rondeaux, sonnets, elegies, and such.

Even the successes women achieved were cause for new attacks; *Les précieuses ridicules* (*The Pretentious Young Ladies*) set public opinion against them; and a bit later *Les femmes savants* (*The Learned Ladies*) are applauded. Molière is not, however, woman's enemy: he vigorously attacks arranged marriages, he demands freedom for young girls in their love lives and respect and independence for the wife. On the other hand, Bossuet does not spare them in his sermons. The first woman, he preaches, is "only a part of Adam and a kind of diminutive. Her mind is about the same size." Boileau's satire against women is not much more than an exercise in rhetoric, but it raises an outcry: Pradon, Regnard, and Perrault counterattack violently. La Bruyère and Saint-Evremond take the part of women. The period's most determined feminist is Poulain de la Barre who in 1673 publishes a Cartesian-inspired work, *De l'égalité des deux sexes* (*The Equality of the Two Sexes*). He thinks that since men are stronger, they favor their sex and women accept this dependence out of custom. They never had their

---

* This title might be a confusion and combination of *Le cabinet satyrique* (1618) and *Le parnasse des poètes satyriques* (1622).—TRANS.

chances: in either freedom or education. Thus they cannot be judged by what they did in the past. Nothing indicates their inferiority to men. Anatomy reveals differences, but none of them constitutes a privilege for the male. And Poulain de la Barre concludes with a demand for a solid education for women. Fontenelle writes *Entretiens sur la pluralité des mondes* (*Conversations on the Plurality of Worlds*) for women. And while Fénelon, following Mme de Maintenon and Abbot Fleury, puts forward a very limited educational program, the Jansenist academic Rollin wants women to undertake serious studies.

The eighteenth century is also divided. In 1744, the author of the *Controverse sur l'âme de la femme* (*Controversy over Woman's Soul*) declares that "woman created uniquely for man will cease to be at the end of the world because she will cease to be useful for the object for which she had been created, from which follows necessarily that her soul is not immortal." In a slightly less radical way, Rousseau is the spokesman of the bourgeoisie and dooms woman to her husband and motherhood. "All the education of women should be relative to men . . . Woman is made to yield to man and to bear his injustices," he asserts. However, the democratic and individualist ideal of the eighteenth century is favorable to women; for most philosophers they are human beings equal to those of the strong sex. Voltaire denounces the injustice of their lot. Diderot considers their inferiority largely *made* by society. "Women, I pity thee!" he writes. He thinks that "in all customs the cruelty of civil laws makes common cause with the cruelty of nature against women. They have been treated as idiot beings." Montesquieu, paradoxically, believes that women should be subordinate to man in the home but that everything predisposes them to political action. "It is against reason and against nature for women to be mistresses in the house . . . but not for them to govern an empire." Helvétius shows that woman's inferiority is created by the absurdity of her education; d'Alembert is of the same opinion. Economic feminism timidly makes its appearance through a woman, Mme de Ciray.* But it is Mercier almost alone in his *Tableau de Paris* who rises up against the destitution of women workers and tackles the fundamental question of women's work. Condorcet wants women to enter political life. He considers them man's equals and defends them against classic attacks: "Women are said . . . not to have their own

---

* The name Ciray is untraceable. Emilie Du Châtelet and Voltaire lived and worked in the Château de Cirey from 1734 to 1749, giving rise to some speculation about the possibility of a misspelling or an erroneous transcription from the original manuscript of the name Ciray. But there is no conclusive evidence of this.—TRANS.

feeling of justice, that they listen to their feelings more than to their conscience . . . [But] it is not nature, it is education, it is the social existence that causes this difference." And elsewhere: "The more women have been enslaved by laws, the more dangerous their empire has been . . . It would lessen if women had less interest in keeping it, if it ceased being for them the sole means of defending themselves and escaping oppression."

CHAPTER 5

The Revolution might have been expected to change the fate of woman. It did nothing of the kind. This bourgeois revolution respected bourgeois institutions and values; and it was waged almost exclusively by men. It must be pointed out that during the entire ancien régime working-class women as a sex enjoyed the most independence. A woman had the right to run a business, and she possessed all the necessary capacities to exercise her trade autonomously. She shared in production as linen maid, laundress, burnisher, shopgirl, and so on; she worked either at home or in small businesses; her material independence allowed her great freedom of behavior: a woman of modest means could go out, go to taverns, and control her own body almost like a man; she is her husband's partner and his equal. She is oppressed on an economic and not on a sexual level. In the countryside, the peasant woman plays a considerable role in rural labor; she is treated like a servant; often she does not eat at the same table as her husband and sons; she toils harder and the burdens of maternity add to her fatigue. But as in old farming societies, since she is necessary to man, he respects her for it; their goods, interests, and concerns are shared; she enjoys great authority in the home. From within their difficult lives, these women could have asserted themselves as individuals and demanded their rights; but a tradition of timidity and submission weighed on them: the Estates-General cahiers record an insignificant number of feminine claims, limited to "Men should not engage in trades that are the prerogative of women." And it is true that women are found alongside their men in demonstrations and riots: they are the ones who go to Versailles to find "the baker, the baker's wife, and the baker's little boy."* But it is not the people who led the Revolution and

---

* The "baker, the baker's wife, and the baker's little boy" refer to King Louis XVI, the queen, and the dauphin, forced by the starving people to leave Versailles for Paris in October 1789. —TRANS.

reaped its fruits. As for bourgeois women, a few rallied ardently to the cause of freedom: Mme Roland, Lucile Desmoulins, and Théroigne de Méricourt; one of them, Charlotte Corday, significantly influenced the outcome when she assassinated Marat. There were a few feminist movements. In 1791, Olympe de Gouges proposed a "Declaration of the Rights of Woman and the Female Citizen" equivalent to the "Declaration of the Rights of Man," demanding that all masculine privileges be abolished. In 1790 the same ideas are found in *Motion de la pauvre Javotte* (Poor Javotte's Motion) and in other similar lampoons; but in spite of Condorcet's support, these efforts are abortive, and Olympe perishes on the scaffold. In addition to *L'Impatient,* the newspaper she founded, a few other short-lived papers appear. Women's clubs merge for the most part with men's and are taken over by them. On Brumaire 28, 1793, when the actress Rose Lacombe, president of the Society of Republican and Revolutionary Women, along with a delegation of women, forces the doors of the Conseil Général, the prosecutor Chaumette pronounces words in the assembly that could be inspired by Saint Paul and Saint Thomas: "Since when are women allowed to renounce their sex and become men? . . . [Nature] has told woman: Be a woman. Child care, household tasks, sundry motherhood cares, those are your tasks." Women are banned from entering the Conseil and soon even from the clubs where they had learned their politics. In 1790, the right of the firstborn and masculine privilege were eliminated; girls and boys became equals regarding succession; in 1792 divorce law was established, relaxing strict marital ties; but these were feeble conquests. Bourgeois women were too integrated into the family to find concrete grounds for solidarity with each other; they did not constitute a separate caste capable of forcing their demands: on an economic level, they existed as parasites. Thus, while women could have participated in events in spite of their sex, they were prevented by their class, and those from the agitating class were condemned to stand aside because they were women. When economic power falls into the hands of the workers, it will then be possible for the working woman to gain the capacities that the parasitic woman, noble or bourgeois, never obtained.

During the liquidation of the Revolution woman enjoys an anarchic freedom. But when society is reorganized, she is rigidly enslaved again. From the feminist point of view, France was ahead of other countries; but for the unfortunate modern French woman, her status was determined during a military dictatorship; the Napoleonic Code, which sealed her fate for a century, greatly held back her emancipation. Like all military leaders, Napoleon wants to see woman solely as a mother; but, heir to a bourgeois revolution, he does not intend to demolish the social structure by giving the mother priority over the wife: he prohibits the querying of paternity; he sets down harsh conditions for the unwed mother and the illegitimate child. Yet the married woman herself does not find recourse in her dignity as mother; the feudal paradox is perpetuated. Girls and wives are deprived of citizens' rights, prohibiting them from functions such as the practice of law or wardship. But the unmarried woman enjoys her civil role fully while marriage preserves the *mundium*. Woman owes *obedience* to her husband; he can have her confined in cases of adultery and obtain a divorce from her; if he kills the guilty wife when caught in the act, he is excusable in the eyes of the law; the husband, on the other hand, receives an infraction only if he brings a concubine into the home, and this is the only ground that would allow his wife to divorce him. Man decides where they will live, and he has many more rights over the children than the mother; and—except in cases where the woman manages a business—his authorization is necessary for her contracts. Marital power is rigorously exercised, both over the wife herself as a person and over her possessions.

Throughout the nineteenth century, the legal system continues to reinforce the code's severity, depriving, among other things, the woman of all rights of alienation. In 1826 the Restoration abolishes divorce,* and the 1848 Constitutional Assembly refuses to reestablish it; it does not reappear until 1884, and then it is still difficult to obtain. The bourgeoisie was never more powerful, yet they recognize the dangers implicit in the Industrial Revolution; they assert themselves with nervous authority. The freedom of ideas inherited from the eighteenth century never makes inroads into family moral principles; these remain as they are defined by the early-nineteenth-century reactionary thinkers Joseph de Maistre and Bonald. They base the value of order on divine will and demand a strictly hierarchical society; the family, the indissoluble social cell, will be the microcosm of society. "Man is to woman what woman is to the child"; or "power is to the minister what the minister is to the people," says Bonald. Thus the husband governs, the wife administers, and the children obey. Divorce is, of course, forbidden; and woman is confined to the home. "Women belong to the family and not to politics, and nature made them for housework and not for public service," adds Bonald. These hierarchies were respected in the family as described by Le Play in the middle of the century.

In a slightly different way, Auguste Comte also demands a hierarchy of the sexes; between men and women there are "radical differences, both physical and moral, profoundly separating one from the other, in every

---

* The correct date is 1816.—TRANS.

species of animal and *especially in the human race.*" Femininity is a kind of "prolonged childhood" that sets women apart from the "ideal type of the race." This biological infantilism expresses an intellectual weakness; the role of this purely affective being is that of spouse and housewife, no match for man: "Neither instruction nor education is suitable for her." As with Bonald, woman is confined to the family, and within this micro society the father governs because woman is "inept in all government even domestic"; she only administers and advises. Her instruction has to be limited. "Women and the proletariat cannot and must not become originators, nor do they wish to." And Comte foresees society's evolution as totally eliminating woman's work outside the family. In the second part of his work, Comte, swayed by his love for Clotilde de Vaux, exalts woman to the point of almost making her a divinity, the emanation of the Great Being; in the temple of Humanity, positivist religion will propose her for the adoration of the people, but only for her morality; man acts, while she loves: she is more deeply altruistic than he. But according to the positivist system, she is still no less confined to the family; divorce is still forbidden for her, and it would even be preferable for her widowhood to last forever; she has no economic or political rights; she is only a wife and an educator.

Balzac expresses the same ideal in more cynical ways: woman's destiny, and her only glory, is to make the hearts of men beat, he writes in *La physiologie du mariage* (*The Physiology of Marriage*). "Woman is a possession acquired by contract; she is personal property, and the possession of her is as good as a security—indeed, properly speaking, woman is only man's annexe." Here he is speaking for the bourgeoisie, which intensified its antifeminism in reaction to eighteenth-century license and threatening progressive ideas. Having brilliantly presented the idea at the beginning of *The Physiology of Marriage* that this loveless institution forcibly leads the wife to adultery, Balzac exhorts husbands to rein in wives to total subjugation if they want to avoid the ridicule of dishonor. They must be denied training and culture, forbidden to develop their individuality, forced to wear uncomfortable clothing, and encouraged to follow a debilitating dietary regime. The bourgeoisie follows this program exactly, confining women to the kitchen and to housework, jealously watching their behavior; they are enclosed in daily life rituals that hindered all attempts at independence. In return, they are honored and endowed with the most exquisite respect. "The married woman is a slave who must be seated on a throne," says Balzac; of course men must give in to women in all irrelevant circumstances, yielding them first place; women must not carry heavy burdens as in primitive societies; they are readily spared all painful tasks and worries: at the same time this relieves them of all responsibility. It is hoped that, thus duped, seduced by the ease of their condition, they will accept the role of mother and housewife to which they are being confined. And in fact, most bourgeois women capitulate. As their education and their parasitic situation make them dependent on men, they never dare to voice their claims: those who do are hardly heard. It is easier to put people in chains than to remove them if the chains bring prestige, said George Bernard Shaw. The bourgeois woman clings to the chains because she clings to her class privileges. It is drilled into her and she believes that women's liberation would weaken bourgeois society; liberated from the male, she would be condemned to work; while she might regret having her rights to private property subordinated to her husband's, she would deplore even more having this property abolished; she feels no solidarity with working-class women: she feels closer to her husband than to a woman textile worker. She makes his interests her own.

Yet these obstinate examples of resistance cannot stop the march of history; the advent of the machine ruins landed property and brings about working-class emancipation and concomitantly that of woman. All forms of socialism, wresting woman from the family, favor her liberation: Plato, aspiring to a communal regime, promised women a similar autonomy to that enjoyed in Sparta. With the utopian socialism of Saint-Simon, Fourier, and Cabet is born the utopia of the "free woman." The Saint-Simonian idea of universal association demands the abolition of all slavery: that of the worker and that of the woman; and it is because women like men are human beings that Saint-Simon, and Leroux, Pecqueur, and Carnot after him, demand their freedom. Unfortunately, this reasonable theory has no credibility in the Saint-Simonian school. Instead, woman is exalted in the name of femininity, the surest way to disserve her. Under the pretext of considering the couple as the basis of social unity, Père Enfantin tries to introduce a woman into each "director-couple" called the priest-couple; he awaits a better world from a woman messiah, and the Compagnons de la Femme embark for the East in search of this female savior. He is influenced by Fourier, who confuses the liberation of woman with the restoration of the flesh; Fourier demands the right of all individuals to follow their passionate attractions; he wants to replace marriage with love; he considers the woman not as a person but only in her amorous functions. And Cabet promises that Icarian communism will bring about complete equality of the sexes, though he accords women a limited participation in politics. In fact, women hold second place in the Saint-Simonian movement: only Claire Bazard, founder and main support for a brief period of the magazine *La Femme Nouvelle* (The New Woman), plays a relatively important role. Many other minor publications appear later, but their claims are timid; they demand education rather than emancipation for women; Carnot, and later Legouvé, is committed to raising the level of education for women. The idea of the woman partner or the woman as a regenerating force persists throughout the nineteenth century in Victor Hugo. But woman's cause is discredited by these doctrines that, instead of assimilating her, oppose her to man, emphasizing intuition and emotion instead of reason. The cause is also discredited by some of its partisans' mistakes. In 1848 women founded clubs and journals; Eugénie Niboyet published *La Voix des Femmes* (Women's Voice), a magazine that Cabet worked on. A female delegation went to the city hall to demand "women's rights" but obtained nothing. In 1849, Jeanne Deroin ran for deputy, and her campaign foundered in ridicule. Ridicule also killed the "Vesuvians" movement and the Bloomerists, who paraded in extravagant costumes. The most intelligent women of the period took no part in these movements: Mme de Staël fought for her own cause rather than her sisters'; George Sand demanded the right for free love but refused to collaborate on *La Voix des Femmes;* her claims are primarily sentimental. Flora Tristan believed in the people's redemption through woman; but she is more interested in the emancipation of the working class than that of her own sex. Daniel Stern and Mme de Girardin, however, joined the feminist movement.

On the whole, the reform movement that develops in the nineteenth century seeks justice in equality, and is thus generally favorable to feminism. There is one notable exception: Proudhon. Undoubtedly because of his peasant roots, he reacts violently against Saint-Simonian mysticism; he supports small property owners and at the same time believes in confining woman to the home. "Housewife or courtesan" is the dilemma he locks her in. Until then, attacks against women had been led by conservatives, bitterly combating socialism as well: *Le Charivari* was one of the inexhaustible sources of jokes; it is Proudhon who breaks the alliance between feminism and socialism; he protests against the socialist women's banquet presided over by Leroux, and he fulminates against Jeanne Deroin. In his work *Justice,* he posits that woman should be dependent on man; man alone counts as a social individual; a couple is not a partnership, which would suppose equality, but a union; woman is inferior to man first because her physical force is only two-thirds that of the male, then because she is intellectually and morally inferior to the same degree: she is worth $2 \times 2 \times 2$ against $3 \times 3 \times 3$ or $8/27$ of the stronger sex. When two women, Mme Adam and Mme d'Héricourt, respond to him—one quite firmly, the other less effusively—Proudhon retorts with *La pornocratie, ou Les femmes dans les temps modernes* (Pornocracy, or Women in Modern Times). But, like all antifeminists, he addresses ardent litanies to the "real woman," slave and mirror to the male;

in spite of this devotion, he has to recognize himself that the life he gave his own wife never made her happy: Mme Proudhon's letters are one long lament.

But it is not these theoretical debates that influenced the course of events; they only timidly reflected them. Woman regains the economic importance lost since prehistoric times because she escapes the home and plays a new role in industrial production. The machine makes this upheaval possible because the difference in physical force between male and female workers is canceled out in a great number of cases. As this abrupt industrial expansion demands a bigger labor market than male workers can provide, women's collaboration is necessary. This is the great nineteenth-century revolution that transforms the lot of woman and opens a new era to her. Marx and Engels understand the full impact this will have on women, promising them a liberation brought about by that of the proletariat. In fact, "women and workers both have oppression in common," says Bebel. And both will escape oppression thanks to the importance their productive work will take on through technological development. Engels shows that woman's lot is closely linked to the history of private property; a catastrophe substituted patriarchy for matriarchy and enslaved woman to the patrimony; but the Industrial Revolution is the counterpart of that loss and will lead to feminine emancipation. He writes: "Woman cannot be emancipated unless she takes part in production on a large social scale and is only incidentally bound to domestic work. And this has become possible only within a large modern industry that not only accepts women's work on a grand scale but formally requires it."

At the beginning of the nineteenth century, woman was more shamefully exploited than workers of the opposite sex. Domestic labor constituted what the English termed the "sweating system"; in spite of constant work, the worker did not earn enough to make ends meet. Jules Simon, in *L'ouvrière* (The Woman Worker), and even the conservative Leroy-Beaulieu, in *Le travail des femmes au XIXe siècle* (Women's Work in the Nineteenth Century), published in 1873, denounce loathsome abuses; the latter declares that more than 200,000 French workers earn less than fifty centimes a day. It is clear why they hasten to migrate to the factories; in fact, it is not long before nothing is left outside workshops except needlework, laundering, and housework, all slave labor paying famine wages; even lace making, millinery, and such are taken over by the factories; in return, job offers are massive in the cotton, wool, and silk industries; women are mainly used in spinning and weaving mills. Employers often prefer them to men. "They do better work for less pay." This cynical formula clearly shows the drama of feminine labor. It is through labor that woman won her dignity as a human being; but it was a singularly difficult and slow conquest. Spinning and weaving are done under lamentable hygienic conditions. "In Lyon," writes Blanqui, "in the trimmings workshops, some women are obliged to work almost hanging in a kind of harness in order to use both their feet and hands." In 1831, silk workers work in the summer from as early as three o'clock in the morning to eleven at night, or seventeen hours a day,* "in often unhealthy workshops where sunlight never enters," says Norbert Truquin. "Half of the young girls develop consumption before the end of their apprenticeship. When they complain they are accused of dissimulating."[1] In addition, the male assistants take advantage of the young women workers. "To get what they wanted they used the most revolting means, hunger and want," says the anonymous author of *La verité sur les événements de Lyon* (The Truth About the Events of Lyon). Some of the women work on farms as well as in factories. They are cynically exploited. Marx relates in a footnote of *Das Kapital:* "Mr. E., manufacturer, let me know that he employed only women on his mechanical weaving looms, and that he gave preference to married women, and among them, women who had a family to care for at home, because they were far more docile and attentive than unmarried women, and had to work until ready to drop from exhaustion to provide indispensable means of subsistence to support their families. This is how," adds Marx, "the qualities proper to woman are misrepresented to her disadvantage, and all the delicate and moral elements of her nature become means to enslave her and make her suffer." Summarizing *Das Kapital* and commenting on Bebel, G. Deville writes: "Beast of luxury or beast of burden, such is woman almost exclusively today. Kept by man when she does not work, she is still kept by him when she works herself to death." The situation of the woman worker was so lamentable that Sismondi and Blanqui called for women to be denied access to workshops. The reason is in part that women did not at first know how to defend themselves and organize unions. Feminine "associations" date from 1848 and are originally production associations. The movement progressed extremely slowly, as the following figures show:

in 1905, out of 781,392 union members, 69,405 are women;
in 1908, out of 957,120 union members, 88,906 are women;
in 1912, out of 1,1064,413 union members, 92,336 are women.

---

* Beauvoir's calculation.—TRANS.
1. Truquin, *Mémoires et aventures d'un prolétaire* (Memoirs and Adventures of a Proletarian in Times of Revolution). Cited from E. Dolléans, *Histoire du mouvement ouvrier* (History of the Working-Class Movement), Volume I.

In 1920, out of 1,580,967 workers, 239,016 are women and unionized female employees, and among 1,083,957 farmworkers, only 36,193 women are unionized; in all, 292,000 women are unionized out of a total of 3,076,585 union workers. A tradition of resignation and submission as well as a lack of solidarity and collective consciousness leaves them disarmed in front of the new possibilities available to them.

The result of this attitude is that women's work was regulated slowly and late. Legislation does not intervene until 1874, and in spite of the campaigns waged under the empire, only two provisions affect women: one banning minors from night work, requiring a day off on Sundays and holidays, and limiting the workday to twelve hours; as for women over twenty-one, all that is done is to prohibit underground mine and quarry work. The first feminine work charter, dated November 2, 1892, bans night work and limits the workday in factories; it leaves the door open for all kinds of fraud. In 1900 the workday is limited to ten hours; in 1905 a weekly day of rest becomes obligatory; in 1907 the woman worker is granted free disposal of her income; in 1909 maternity leave is granted; in 1911 the 1892 provisions are reinforced; in 1913 laws are passed for rest periods before and after childbirth, and dangerous and excessive work is prohibited. Little by little, social legislation takes shape, and health guarantees are set up for women's work; seats are required for salesgirls, long shifts at outdoor display counters are prohibited, and so on. The International Labor Office succeeded in getting international agreements on sanitary conditions for women's work, maternity leave, and such.

A second consequence of the resigned inertia of women workers was the salaries they were forced to accept. Various explanations with multiple factors have been given for the phenomenon of low female salaries. It is insufficient to say that women have fewer needs than men: that is only a subsequent justification. Rather, women, as we have seen, did not know how to defend themselves against exploitation; they had to compete with prisons that dumped products without labor costs on the market; they competed with each other. Besides, in a society based on the marital community, woman seeks emancipation through work: bound to her father's or husband's household, she is most often satisfied just to bring home some extra money; she works outside the family, but for it; and since the working woman does not have to support herself completely, she ends up accepting remuneration far inferior to that of which a man demands. With a significant number of women accepting bargain wages, the whole female salary scale is, of course, set up to the advantage of the employer.

In France, according to an 1889–93 survey, for a day of work equal to

a man's, a woman worker received only half the male's wages. A 1908 survey showed that the highest hourly rates for women working from home
never rose above twenty centimes an hour and dropped as low as five centimes: it was impossible for a woman so exploited to live without charity or
a protector. In America in 1918, women earned half men's salary. Around
this period, for the same amount of coal mined in Germany, a woman
earned approximately 25 percent less than a man. Between 1911 and 1943
women's salaries in France rose a bit more rapidly than men's, but they
nonetheless remained clearly inferior.

While employers warmly welcomed women because of the low wages
they accepted, this provoked resistance on the part of male workers.
Between the cause of the proletariat and that of women there was no such
direct solidarity as Bebel and Engels claimed. The problem was similar to
that of the black labor force in the United States. The most oppressed
minorities in a society are readily used by the oppressors as a weapon
against the class they belong to; thus they at first become enemies, and a
deeper consciousness of the situation is necessary so that blacks and whites,
women and male workers, form coalitions rather than opposition. It is
understandable that male workers at first viewed this cheap competition as
an alarming threat and became hostile. It is only when women were integrated into unions that they could defend their own interests and cease
endangering those of the working class as a whole.

In spite of all these difficulties, progress in women's work continued.
In 1900, in France, 900,000 women worked from home making clothes,
leather goods, funeral wreaths, purses, beadwork, and Paris souvenirs, but
this number diminished considerably. In 1906, 42 percent of working-age
women (between eighteen and sixty) worked in farming, industry, business, banks, insurance, offices, and liberal professions. This movement
spread to the whole world because of the 1914–18 labor crisis and the world
war. The lower middle class and the middle class were determined to follow this movement, and women also invaded the liberal professions.
According to one of the last prewar censuses, in France 42 percent of all
women between eighteen and sixty worked; in Finland, 37 percent; in Germany, 34.2 percent; in India, 27.7 percent; in England, 26.9 percent; in the
Netherlands, 19.2 percent; and in the United States, 17.7 percent. But in
France and in India, the high figures reflect the extent of rural labor.
Excluding the peasantry, France had in 1940 approximately 500,000 heads
of establishments, 1 million female employees, 2 million women workers,
and 1.5 million women working alone or unemployed. Among women
workers, 650,000 were domestic workers; 1.2 million worked in light indus-

try, including 440,000 in textiles, 315,000 in clothing, and 380,000 at home in dressmaking. For commerce, liberal professions, and public service, France, England, and the United States ranked about the same.

One of the basic problems for women, as has been seen, is reconciling the reproductive role and productive work. The fundamental reason that woman, since the beginning of history, has been consigned to domestic labor and prohibited from taking part in shaping the world is her enslavement to the generative function. In female animals there is a rhythm of heat and seasons that ensures the economy of their energies; nature, on the contrary, between puberty and menopause, places no limits on women's gestation. Some civilizations prohibit early marriage; Indian tribes are cited where women are guaranteed a two-year rest period between births; but in general over the centuries, women's fertility has not been regulated. Contraceptives have existed since antiquity, generally for women's use—potions, suppositories, or vaginal tampons—but they remained the secrets of prostitutes and doctors; maybe the secret was available to women of the Roman decadence whose sterility satirists reproached.[2] But the Middle Ages knew nothing of them; no trace is found until the eighteenth century. For many women in these times, life was an uninterrupted series of pregnancies; even women of easy virtue paid for their licentious love lives with frequent births. At certain periods, humanity felt the need to reduce the size of the population; but at the same time, nations worried about becoming weak; in periods of crisis and great poverty, postponing marriage lowered the birthrates. The general rule was to marry young and have as many children as the woman could carry, infant mortality alone reducing the number of living children. Already in the seventeenth century, the abbé de Pure protests against the "amorous dropsy" to which women are condemned; and Mme de Sévigné urges her daughter to avoid frequent pregnancies.[3] But it is in the eighteenth century that the Malthusian movement develops in France. First the well-to-do class and then the population in general deem it reasonable to limit the number of children according to parents'

---

2. "The earliest known reference to birth-control methods appears to be an Egyptian papyrus from the second millennium B.C., recommending the vaginal application of a bizarre mixture composed of crocodile excrement, honey, natron, and a rubbery substance" (P. Ariès, *Histoire des populations françaises* [History of French Populations]). Medieval Persian physicians knew of thirty-one recipes, of which only nine were intended for men. Soranus, in the Hadrian era, explains that at the moment of ejaculation, if the woman does not want a child, she should "hold her breath, pull back her body a little so that the sperm cannot penetrate the *os uteri*, get up immediately, squat down, and make herself sneeze."

3. In *La précieuse* (1656) (The Precious Woman).

resources, and anticonception procedures begin to enter into social practices. In 1778, Moreau, the demographer, writes, "Rich women are not the only ones who considered the propagation of the species the greatest old-fashioned dupe; these dark secrets, unknown to all animals except man, have already made their way into the countryside; nature is confounded even in the villages." The practice of coitus interruptus spreads first among the bourgeoisie, then among rural populations and workers; the prophylactic, which already existed as an antivenereal device, becomes a contraceptive device, widespread after the discovery of vulcanization, toward 1840.[4] In Anglo-Saxon countries, birth control is official, and numerous methods have been discovered to dissociate these two formerly inseparable functions: the sexual and the reproductive. Viennese medical research, precisely establishing the mechanism of conception and the conditions favorable to it, has also suggested methods for avoiding it. In France contraception propaganda and the sale of pessaries, vaginal tampons, and such are prohibited; but birth control is no less widespread.

As for abortion, it is nowhere officially authorized by law. Roman law granted no special protection to embryonic life; the *nasciturus* was not considered a human being, but part of the woman's body. *"Partus antequam edatur mulieris portio est vel viscerum."*[5] In the era of decadence, abortion seems to have been a normal practice, and even a legislator who wanted to encourage birthrates would never dare to prohibit it. If the woman refused a child against her husband's will, he could have her punished; but her crime was her disobedience. Generally, in Oriental and Greco-Roman civilization, abortion was allowed by law.

It was Christianity that overturned moral ideas on this point by endowing the embryo with a soul; so abortion became a crime against the fetus itself. "Any woman who does what she can so as not to give birth to as many children as she is capable of is guilty of that many homicides, just as is a woman who tries to injure herself after conception," says Saint Augustine. In Byzantium, abortion led only to a temporary relegation; for the barbarians who practiced infanticide, it was punishable only if it was carried out by violence, against the mother's will: it was redeemed by paying blood money. But the first councils issued edicts for the severest penalties against this "homicide," whatever the presumed age of the fetus. Nonetheless, one question arises that has been the object of infinite discussion: At

---

4. "Around 1930 an American firm sold twenty million prophylactics in one year. Fifteen American factories produced a million and a half of them per day" (P. Ariès, *Histoire*).

5. "The infant, before being born, is a part of the woman, a kind of organ."

what moment does the soul enter the body? Saint Thomas and most other writers settled on life beginning toward the fortieth day for males and the eightieth for females; thus was established a distinction between the animated and the non-animated fetus. A Middle Ages penitential book declares: "If a pregnant woman destroys her fruit before forty-five days, she is subject to a penitence of one year. For sixty days, three years. And finally, if the infant is already animated, she should be tried for homicide." The book, however, adds: "There is a great difference between a poor woman who destroys her infant for the pain she has to feed it and the one who has no other reason but to hide a crime of fornication." In 1556, Henry II published a well-known edict on concealing pregnancy; since the death penalty was applied for simple concealment, it followed that the penalty should also apply to abortion maneuvers; in fact, the edict was aimed at infanticide, but it was used to authorize the death penalty for practitioners and accomplices of abortion. The distinction between the quickened and the non-quickened fetus disappeared around the eighteenth century. At the end of the century, Beccaria, a man of considerable influence in France, pleaded in favor of the woman who refuses to have a child. The 1791 code excuses the woman but punishes her accomplices with "twenty years of irons." The idea that abortion is homicide disappeared in the nineteenth century: it is considered rather to be a crime against the state. The law of 1810 prohibits it absolutely under pain of imprisonment and forced labor for the woman who aborts and her accomplices; but doctors practice abortion whenever it is a question of saving the mother's life. Because the law is so strict, juries at the end of the century stopped applying it, and few arrests were made, with four-fifths of the accused acquitted. In 1923 a new law is passed, again with forced labor for the accomplices and the practitioner of the operation, but punishing the woman having the abortion with only prison or a fine; in 1939 a new decree specifically targets the technicians: no reprieve would be granted. In 1941 abortion was decreed a crime against state security. In other countries, it is a misdemeanor punishable by a short prison sentence; in England, it is a crime—a felony—punishable by prison or forced labor. Overall, codes and courts are more lenient with the woman having the abortion than with her accomplices. The Church, however, has never relaxed its severity. The March 27, 1917, code of canon law declares: "Those who procure abortions, the mother not excepted, incur excommunication *latae sententiae*, once the result has been obtained, reserved to the Ordinary." No reason can be invoked, even the danger of the mother's death. The pope again declared recently that between the mother's life and the child's the former must be sacrificed: the fact is, the mother, being baptized, can enter heaven—curiously, hell never enters into these calculations—while the fetus is condemned to perpetual limbo.[6]

Abortion was officially recognized, but only for a short time, in Germany before Nazism and in the Soviet Union before 1936. But in spite of religion and laws, it has been practiced in all countries to a large extent. In France, every year 800,000 to 1 million abortions are performed—as many as births—and two-thirds of the women are married, many already having one or two children. In spite of the prejudices, resistance, and an outdated morality, unregulated fertility has given way to fertility controlled by the state or individuals. Progress in obstetrics has considerably decreased the dangers of childbirth; childbirth pain is disappearing; at this time—March 1949—legislation has been passed in England requiring the use of certain anesthetic methods; they are already generally applied in the United States and are beginning to spread in France. With artificial insemination, the evolution that will permit humanity to master the reproductive function comes to completion. These changes have tremendous importance for woman in particular; she can reduce the number of pregnancies and rationally integrate them into her life, instead of being their slave. During the nineteenth century, woman in her turn is freed from nature; she wins control of her body. Relieved of a great number of reproductive servitudes, she can take on the economic roles open to her, roles that would ensure her control over her own person.

The convergence of these two factors—participation in production and freedom from reproductive slavery—explains the evolution of woman's condition. As Engels predicted, her social and political status necessarily had to change. The feminist movement begun in France by Condorcet and in England by Mary Wollstonecraft in *A Vindication of the Rights of Woman*, and followed up at the beginning of the century by the Saint-Simonians, never succeeded for lack of a concrete base. But now women's claims would have ample weight. They would be heard even

---

6. In Volume II, we will return to the discussion of this view. Let it just be said here that Catholics are far from keeping to the letter of Saint Augustine's doctrine. The confessor whispers to the young fiancée, on the eve of her wedding, that she can do anything with her husband, as long as "proper" coitus is achieved; positive birth-control practices—including coitus interruptus—are forbidden; but the calendar established by Viennese sexologists can be used, where the act whose only recognized aim is reproduction is carried out on the days conception is impossible for the woman. There are spiritual advisers who even indicate this calendar to their flocks. In fact, there are ample "Christian mothers" who only have two or three children and have nonetheless not interrupted their conjugal relations after the last delivery.

within the heart of the bourgeoisie. With the rapid development of industrial civilization, landed property is falling behind in relation to personal property: the principle of family group unity is losing force. The mobility of capital allows its holder to own and dispose of his wealth without reciprocity instead of being held by it. Through patrimony, woman was substantially attached to her husband: with patrimony abolished, they are only juxtaposed, and even children do not constitute as strong a bond as interest. Thus, the individual will assert himself against the group; this evolution is particularly striking in America, where modern capitalism has triumphed: divorce is going to flourish, and husbands and wives are no more than provisional associates. In France, where the rural population is large and where the Napoleonic Code placed the married woman under guardianship, evolution will be slow. In 1884, divorce was restored, and a wife could obtain it if the husband committed adultery; nonetheless, in the penal area, sexual difference was maintained: adultery was an offense only when perpetrated by the wife. The right of guardianship, granted with restrictions in 1907, was fully granted only in 1917. In 1912, the right to determine natural paternity was authorized. It was not until 1938 and 1942 that the married woman's status was modified: the duty of obedience was then abrogated, although the father remains the family head; he determines the place of residence, but the wife can oppose his choice if she advances valid arguments; her powers are increasing; but the formula is still confused: "The married woman has full legal powers. These powers are only limited by the marriage contract and law"; the last part of the article contradicts the first. The equality of spouses has not yet been achieved.

As for political rights, they have not easily been won in France, England, or the United States. In 1867, John Stuart Mill pleaded the first case ever officially pronounced before Parliament in favor of the vote for women. In his writings he imperiously demanded equality of men and women in the family and society: "The principle which regulates the existing social relations between the two sexes—the legal subordination of one sex to the other—is wrong in itself, and now one of the chief hindrances to human improvement; and . . . it ought to be replaced by a principle of perfect equality."* After that, English women organized politically under Mrs. Fawcett's leadership; French women rallied behind Maria Deraismes, who between 1868 and 1871 dealt with women's issues in a series of public lectures; she joined in the lively controversy against Alexandre Dumas fils,

---

* From John Stuart Mill, "The Subjection of Women," as reprinted in *Philosophy of Woman*, edited by Mary Briody Mahowald.

who advised the husband of an unfaithful wife, "Kill her." Léon Richer was the true founder of feminism; in 1869 he launched *Le Droit des Femmes* (*The Rights of Women*) and organized the International Congress of Women's Rights, held in 1878. The question of the right to vote was not yet dealt with; women limited themselves to claiming civil rights; for thirty years the movement remained timid in France and in England. Nonetheless, a woman, Hubertine Auclert, started a suffragette campaign; she created a group called Women's Suffrage and a newspaper, *La Citoyenne*. Many groups were organized under her influence, but they accomplished little. This weakness of feminism stemmed from its internal division; as already pointed out, women as a sex lack solidarity: they are linked to their classes first; bourgeois and proletarian interests do not intersect. Revolutionary feminism adhered to the Saint-Simonian and Marxist tradition; it is noteworthy, moreover, that a certain Louise Michel spoke against feminism because it diverted the energy that should be used entirely for class struggle; with the abolition of capital the lot of woman will be resolved.

The Socialist Congress of 1879 proclaimed the equality of the sexes, and as of that time the feminist-socialist alliance would no longer be denounced, but since women hope for their liberty through the emancipation of workers in general, their attachment to their own cause is secondary. The bourgeoisie, on the contrary, claim new rights within existing society, and they refuse to be revolutionary; they want to introduce virtuous reforms into rules of behavior: elimination of alcohol, pornographic literature, and prostitution. In 1892, the Feminist Congress convenes and gives its name to the movement, but nothing comes of it. However, in 1897 a law is passed permitting women to testify in court, but the request of a woman doctor of law to become a member of the bar is denied. In 1898, women are allowed to vote for the Commercial Court, to vote and be eligible for the National Council on Labor and Employment, to be admitted to the National Council for Public Health Services, and the Ecole des Beaux-Arts. In 1900, feminists hold a new congress, again without significant results. But in 1901, for the first time, Viviani presents the question of the woman's vote to the French parliament; he proposes limiting suffrage to unmarried and divorced women. The feminist movement gains importance at this time. In 1909 the French Union for Women's Suffrage is formed, headed by Mme Brunschvicg; she organizes lectures, meetings, congresses, and demonstrations. In 1909, Buisson presents a report on Dussaussoy's bill allowing women to vote in local assemblies. In 1910, Thomas presents a bill in favor of women's suffrage; presented again in 1918, it passes the Chamber in 1919; but it fails to pass the Senate in 1922. The situation is quite complex. Christian feminism joins forces with revolutionary feminism and Mme Brunschvicg's so-called independent feminism: in 1919, Benedict XV declares himself in favor of the women's vote, and Monsignor Baudrillart and Père Sertillanges follow his lead with ardent propaganda; Catholics believe in fact that women in France constitute a conservative and religious element; this is just what the radicals fear: the real reason for their opposition is their fear of the swing votes that women represented. In the Senate, numerous Catholics, the Union Republican group, and extreme left parties are for the women's vote: but the majority of the assembly is against it. Until 1932 delaying procedures are used by the majority, which refuses to discuss bills concerning women's suffrage; nevertheless, in 1932, the Chamber having voted the women's voting and eligibility amendment, 319 votes to 1, the Senate opens a debate extending over several sessions: the amendment is voted down. The record in *L'officiel* is of great importance; all the antifeminist arguments developed over half a century are found in the report, which fastidiously lists all the works in which they are mentioned. First of all come these types of gallantry arguments: we love women too much to let them vote; the "real woman" who accepts the "housewife or courtesan" dilemma is exalted in true Proudhon fashion; woman would lose her charm by voting; she is on a pedestal and should not step down from it; she has everything to lose and nothing to gain in becoming a voter; she governs men without needing a ballot; and so on. More serious objections concern the family's interest: woman's place is in the home; political discussions would bring about disagreement between spouses. Some admit to moderate antifeminism. Women are different from men. They do not serve in the military. Will prostitutes vote? And others arrogantly affirm male superiority: voting is a duty and not a right; women are not worthy of it. They are less intelligent and educated than men. If women voted, men would become effeminate. Women lacked political education. They would vote according to their husbands' wishes. If they want to be free, they should first free themselves from their dressmakers. Also proposed is that superbly naive argument: there are more women in France than men. In spite of the flimsiness of all these objections, French women would have to wait until 1945 to acquire political power.

New Zealand gave woman full rights in 1893. Australia followed in 1908. But in England and America victory was difficult. Victorian England imperiously isolated woman in her home; Jane Austen wrote in secret; it took great courage or an exceptional destiny to become George Eliot or Emily Brontë; in 1888 an English scholar wrote: "Women are not only not part of the race, they are not even half of the race but a sub-species des-

tined uniquely for reproduction." Mrs. Fawcett founded a suffragist movement toward the end of the century, but as in France the movement was
hesitant. Around 1903, feminist claims took a singular turn. In London, the
Pankhurst family created the Women's Social and Political Union, which
joined with the Labour Party and embarked on resolutely militant activities. It was the first time in history that women took on a cause as women:
this is what gave particular interest to the suffragettes in England and
America. For fifteen years, they carried out a policy recalling in some
respects a Gandhi-like attitude: refusing violence, they invented more or
less ingenious symbolic actions. They marched on the Albert Hall during
Liberal Party meetings, carrying banners with the words "Vote for
Women"; they forced their way into Lord Asquith's office, held meetings in
Hyde Park or Trafalgar Square, marched in the streets carrying signs, and
held lectures; during demonstrations they insulted the police or threw
stones at them, provoking their arrest; in prison they adopted the hunger
strike tactic; they raised money and rallied millions of women and men;
they influenced opinion so well that in 1907 two hundred members of Parliament made up a committee for women's suffrage; every year from then
on some of them would propose a law in favor of women's suffrage, a law
that would be rejected every year with the same arguments. In 1907 the
WSPU organized the first march on Parliament with workers covered in
shawls, and a few aristocratic women; the police pushed them back; but the
following year, as married women were threatened with a ban on work in
certain mines, the Lancashire women workers were called by the WSPU to
hold a grand meeting. There were new arrests, and the imprisoned suffragettes responded with a long hunger strike. Released, they organized
new parades: one of the women rode a horse painted with the head of
Queen Elizabeth. On July 18, 1910, the day the women's suffrage law went
to the Chamber, a nine-kilometer-long column paraded through London;
the law rejected, there were more meetings and new arrests. In 1912, they
adopted a more violent tactic: they burned empty houses, slashed pictures,
trampled flower beds, threw stones at the police; at the same time, they sent
delegation upon delegation to Lloyd George and Sir Edward Grey; they
hid in the Albert Hall and noisily disrupted Lloyd George's speeches. The
war interrupted their activities. It is difficult to know how much these
actions hastened events. The vote was granted to English women first in
1918 in a restricted form, and then in 1928 without restriction: their success
was in large part due to the services they had rendered during the war.

The American woman found herself at first more emancipated than
the European. Early in the nineteenth century, pioneer women had to share

the hard work done by men, and they fought by their sides; they were far fewer than men, and thus a high value was placed on them. But little by little, their condition came to resemble that of women in the Old World; gallantry toward them was maintained; they kept their cultural privileges and a dominant position within the family; laws granted them a religious and moral role; but the command of society resided in the males' hands. Some women began to claim their political rights around 1830. They undertook a campaign in favor of blacks. As the antislavery congress held in 1840 in London was closed to them, the Quaker Lucretia Mott founded a feminist association. On July 18, 1840,* at the Seneca Falls Convention, they drafted a Quaker-inspired declaration, which set the tone for all of American feminism: "that all men and women are created equal; that they are endowed by their Creator with certain inalienable rights . . . that to secure these rights governments are instituted . . . He [Man] has made her, if married, in the eye of the law, civilly dead . . . He has usurped the prerogative of Jehovah himself, claiming it as his right to assign for her a sphere of action, when that belongs to her conscience and her God." Three years later, Harriet Beecher Stowe wrote *Uncle Tom's Cabin*, arousing the public in favor of blacks. Emerson and Lincoln supported the feminist movement. When the Civil War broke out, women ardently participated; but in vain they demanded that the amendment giving blacks the right to vote be drafted as follows: "The right . . . to vote shall not be denied or abridged . . . on account of race, color, *sex*." Seizing on the ambiguity of one of the articles to the amendment, the great feminist leader Susan B. Anthony voted in Rochester with fourteen comrades; she was fined a hundred dollars. In 1869, she founded what later came to be called the National American Woman Suffrage Association, and that same year the state of Wyoming gave women the right to vote. But it was only in 1893 that Colorado, then in 1896 Idaho and Utah, followed this example. Progress was slow afterward. But women succeeded better economically than in Europe. In 1900, 5 million women worked, 1.3 million in industry, 500,000 in business; a large number worked in business, industry, and liberal professions. There were lawyers, doctors, and 3,373 women pastors. The famous Mary Baker Eddy founded the Christian Science Church. Women formed clubs; in 1900, they totaled about 2 million members.

Nonetheless, only nine states had given women the vote. In 1913, the

---

* The convention actually took place July 19–20, 1848.—TRANS.

suffrage movement was organized on the militant English model. Two women led it: Doris Stevens and a young Quaker, Alice Paul. From Wilson they obtained the right to march with banners and signs;* they then organized a campaign of lectures, meetings, marches, and manifestations of all sorts. From the nine states where women voted, women voters went with great pomp and circumstance to the Capitol, demanding the feminine vote for the whole nation. In Chicago, the first group of women assembled in a party to liberate their sex; this assembly became the Women's Party. In 1917, suffragettes invented a new tactic: they stationed themselves at the doors of the White House, banners in hand, and often chained to the gates so they could not be driven away. After six months, they were stopped and sent to the Occoquan penitentiary; they went on a hunger strike and were finally released. New demonstrations led to the beginning of riots. The government finally consented to naming a House Committee on Woman Suffrage. The executive committee of the Women's Party held a conference in Washington, and an amendment favoring the woman's vote went to the House and was voted on January 10, 1918. The vote still had to go to the Senate. Wilson would not promise to exert enough pressure, so the suffragettes began to demonstrate again. They held a rally at the White House doors. The president decided to address an appeal to the Senate, but the amendment was rejected by two votes. A Republican Congress voted for the amendment in June 1919. The battle for complete equality of the sexes went on for the next ten years. At the sixth International Conference of American States held in Havana in 1928, women obtained the creation of the Inter-American Commission of Women. In 1933, the Montevideo treaties elevated women's status by international convention. Nineteen American republics signed the convention giving women equality in all rights.

Sweden also had a very sizable feminist movement. Invoking old traditions, Swedish women demanded the right "to education, work, and liberty." It was largely women writers who led the fight, and it was the moral aspect of the problem that interested them at first; then, grouped in powerful associations, they won over the liberals but ran up against the hostility of the conservatives. Norwegian women in 1907 and Finnish women in 1906 obtained the suffrage that Swedish women would have to wait years to attain.

In Latin and Eastern countries woman was oppressed by customs more

---

* That is, President Woodrow Wilson.—TRANS.

than by laws. In Italy, fascism systematically hindered feminism's progress. Seeking the alliance of the Church, which continued to uphold family tradition and a tradition of feminine slavery, Fascist Italy held woman in double bondage: to public authority and to her husband. The situation was very different in Germany. In 1790, Hippel, a student, launched the first German feminist manifesto. Sentimental feminism analogous to that of George Sand flourished at the beginning of the nineteenth century. In 1848, the first German woman feminist, Louise Otto, demanded the right for women to assist in the transformation of their country: her feminism was largely nationalistic. She founded the General German Women's Association in 1865. German socialists, along with Bebel, advocated the abolition of the inequality of the sexes. In 1892, Clara Zetkin joined the party's council. Women workers and women socialists grouped together in a federation. German women failed in 1914 to establish a women's national army, but they took an active part in the war. After the German defeat, they obtained the right to vote and participated in political life: Rosa Luxemburg fought next to Liebknecht in the Spartacus group and was assassinated in 1919. The majority of German women chose the party of order; several took seats in the Reichstag. It was thus upon emancipated women that Hitler imposed the new Napoleonic ideal: "*Kinder, Küche, Kirche.*" "Woman's presence dishonors the Reichstag," he declared. As Nazism was anti-Catholic and antibourgeois, he gave the mother a privileged place; protection granted to unmarried mothers and illegitimate children greatly freed woman from marriage; as in Sparta, she was more dependent on the state than on any individual, giving her both more and less autonomy than a bourgeois woman living under a capitalist regime.

In Soviet Russia the feminist movement made the greatest advances. It began at the end of the nineteenth century among women students of the intelligentsia; they were less attached to their personal cause than to revolutionary action in general; they "went to the people" and used nihilistic methods against the Okhrana: in 1878 Vera Zasulich shot the police chief Trepov. During the Russo-Japanese War, women replaced men in many areas of work; their consciousness raised, the Russian Union for Women's rights demanded political equality of the sexes; in the first Duma, a parliamentary women's rights group was created, but it was powerless. Women workers' emancipation would come from the revolution. Already in 1905, they were actively participating in the mass political strikes that broke out in the country, and they mounted the barricades. On March 8, 1917, International Women's Day and a few days before the revolution, they massively demonstrated in the streets of St. Petersburg demanding bread, peace, and their husbands' return. They took part in the October insurrection; between 1918 and 1920, they played an important economic and even military role in the U.S.S.R.'s fight against the invaders. True to Marxist tradition, Lenin linked women's liberation to that of the workers; he gave them political and economic equality.

Article 122 of the 1936 constitution stipulates: "In the U.S.S.R., woman enjoys the same rights as man in all aspects of economic, official, cultural, public, and political life." And these principles were spelled out by the Communist International. It demands "social equality of man and woman before the law and in daily life. Radical transformation in conjugal rights and in the family code. Recognition of maternity as a social function. Entrusting society with the care and education of children and adolescents. Organization of a civil effort against ideology and traditions that make woman a slave." In the economic area, woman's conquests were stunning. She obtained equal wages with male workers, and she took on a highly active role in production; thereby gaining considerable political and social importance. The brochure recently published by the Association France-U.S.S.R. reports that in the 1939 general elections there were 457,000 women deputies in the regional, district, town, and village soviets; 1,480 in the socialist republics of higher soviets, and 227 seated in the Supreme Soviet of the U.S.S.R. Close to 10 million are members of unions. They constitute 40 percent of the population of U.S.S.R. workers and employees, and a great number of workers among the Stakhanovites are women. The role of Russian women in the last war is well-known; they provided an enormous labor force even in production branches where masculine professions are dominant: metallurgy and mining, timber rafting and railways, and so forth. They distinguished themselves as pilots and parachutists, and they formed partisan armies.

This participation of woman in public life has raised a difficult problem: her role in family life. For a long while, means were sought to free her from her domestic constraints: on November 16, 1942, the plenary assembly of the Comintern proclaimed, "The revolution is impotent as long as the notion of family and family relations subsists." Respect for free unions, liberalization of divorce, and legalization of abortion ensured woman's liberty relative to men; laws for maternity leave, child-care centers, kindergartens, and so on lightened the burdens of motherhood. From passionate and contradictory witness reports, it is difficult to discern what woman's concrete situation really was; what is sure is that today the demands of repopulation have given rise to a different family policy: the family has become the elementary social cell, and woman is both worker and housekeeper.[7] Sexual morality is at its strictest; since the law of June 1936, re-inforced by that of June 7, 1941, abortion has been banned and divorce almost suppressed; adultery is condemned by moral standards. Strictly subordinated to the state like all workers, strictly bound to the home, but with access to political life and the dignity that productive work gives, the Russian woman is in a singular situation that would be worth studying in its singularity; circumstances unfortunately prevent me from doing this.

The recent session of the United Nations Commission on the Status of Women demanded that equal rights for both sexes be recognized in all nations, and several motions were passed to make this legal status a con-crete reality. It would seem, then, that the match is won. The future can only bring greater and greater assimilation of women in a hitherto mascu-line society.

Several conclusions come to the fore when taking a look at this history as a whole. And first of all this one: women's entire history has been written by men. Just as in America there is no black problem but a white one,[8] just as "anti-Semitism is not a Jewish problem, it's our problem,"[9] so the problem of woman has always been a problem of men. Why they had moral pres-tige at the outset along with physical strength has been discussed; they cre-ated the values, customs, and religions; never did women attempt to vie for that empire. A few isolated women—Sappho, Christine de Pizan, Mary Wollstonecraft, Olympe de Gouges—protested against their harsh des-tiny; and there were some collective demonstrations: but Roman matrons in league against the Oppian Law or Anglo-Saxon suffragettes only man-aged to wield pressure because men were willing to submit to it. Men always held woman's lot in their hands; and they did not decide on it based on her interest; it is their own projects, fears, and needs that counted. When they revered the Mother Goddess, it is because Nature frightened them, and as soon as the bronze tool enabled them to assert themselves against Nature, they instituted patriarchy; henceforth it was the family-state con-flict that has defined woman's status; it is the attitude of the Christian before God, the world, and his own flesh that is reflected in the condition he

---

7. Olga Michakova, secretary of the Central Committee of the Communist Youth Organiza-tion, stated in 1944 in an interview: "Soviet women should try to make themselves as attractive as nature and good taste permit. After the war, they should dress like women and act femi-nine . . . Girls will be told to act and walk like girls, and that is why they will wear skirts that will probably be very tight, making them carry themselves gracefully."

8. Cf. Myrdal, *An American Dilemma*.

9. Jean-Paul Sartre, *Réflexions sur la question juive* (*Anti-Semite and Jew*).

assigned to her; what was called the *querelle des femmes* in the Middle Ages was a quarrel between clergy and laity about marriage and celibacy; it is the social regime founded on private property that brought about the married woman's wardship, and it is the technical revolution realized by men that enfranchised today's women. It is an evolution of the masculine ethic that led to the decrease in family size by birth control and partially freed woman from the servitude of motherhood. Feminism itself has never been an autonomous movement: it was partially an instrument in the hands of politicians and partially an epiphenomenon reflecting a deeper social drama. Never did women form a separate caste: and in reality they never sought to play a role in history as a sex. The doctrines that call for the advent of woman as flesh, life, immanence, or the Other are masculine ideologies that do not in any way express feminine claims. For the most part, women resign themselves to their lot without attempting any action; those who did try to change attempted to overcome their singularity and not to confine themselves in it triumphantly. When they intervened in world affairs, it was in concert with men and from a masculine point of view.

This intervention, in general, was secondary and occasional. The women who enjoyed a certain economic autonomy and took part in production were the oppressed classes, and as workers they were even more enslaved than male workers. In the ruling classes woman was a parasite and as such was subjugated to masculine laws: in both cases, it was almost impossible for her to act. Law and custom did not always coincide: and a balance was set up between them so that woman was never concretely free. In the ancient Roman Republic, economic conditions give the matron concrete powers: but she has no legal independence; the same is often true in peasant civilizations and among lower-middle-class tradesmen; mistress-servant inside the home, woman is socially a minor. Inversely, in periods when society fragments, woman becomes freer, but she loses her fief when she ceases to be man's vassal; she has nothing but a negative freedom that is expressed only in license and dissipation, as for example, during the Roman decadence, the Renaissance, the eighteenth century, and the Directoire. Either she finds work but is enslaved, or she is enfranchised but can do nothing else with herself. It is worth noting among other points that the married woman had her place in society but without benefiting from any rights, while the single woman, honest girl or prostitute, had all man's capacities; but until this century she was more or less excluded from social life. The opposition between law and custom produced this among other curious paradoxes: free love is not prohibited by law, but adultery is a crime; the girl that "falls," however, is often dishonored, while the wife's shocking behavior is treated indulgently: from the eighteenth century to today many young girls got married so that they could freely have lovers. This ingenious system kept the great mass of women under guardianship: it takes exceptional circumstances for a feminine personality to be able to affirm itself between these two series of constraints, abstract or concrete. Women who have accomplished works comparable to men's are those whom the force of social institutions had exalted beyond any sexual differentiation. Isabella the Catholic, Elizabeth of England, and Catherine of Russia were neither male nor female: they were sovereigns. It is remarkable that once socially abolished, their femininity no longer constituted inferiority: there were infinitely more queens with great reigns than kings. Religion undergoes the same transformation: Catherine of Siena and Saint Teresa are saintly souls, beyond any physiological condition; their lay life and their mystical life, their actions and their writings, rise to heights that few men ever attain. It is legitimate to think that if other women failed to mark the world deeply, it is because they were trapped by their conditions. They were only able to intervene in a negative or indirect way. Judith, Charlotte Corday, and Vera Zasulich assassinate; the Frondeuses conspire; during the Revolution and the Commune, women fight alongside men against the established order; intransigent refusal and revolt against a freedom without rights and power are permitted, whereas it is forbidden for a woman to participate in positive construction; at best she will manage to insinuate herself into masculine enterprises by indirect means. Aspasia, Mme de Maintenon, and the princesse des Ursins were precious advisers: but someone still had to consent to listen to them. Men tend to exaggerate the scope of this influence when trying to convince woman she has the greater role; but in fact feminine voices are silenced when concrete action begins; they might foment wars, not suggest battle tactics; they oriented politics only inasmuch as politics was limited to intrigue: the real reins of the world have never been in women's hands; they had no role either in technology or in economy, they neither made nor unmade states, they did not discover worlds. They did set off some events: but they were pretexts more than agents. Lucretia's suicide had no more than a symbolic value. Martyrdom remains allowed for the oppressed; during Christian persecutions and in the aftermath of social or national defeats, women played this role of witness; but a martyr has never changed the face of the world. Even feminine demonstrations and initiatives were only worth something if a masculine decision positively prolonged them. The American women united around Harriet Beecher Stowe aroused public opinion to fever pitch against slavery; but the real reasons for the Civil War were not sentimental.

The March 8, 1917, "woman's day" might have triggered the Russian Revolution: but it was nonetheless merely a signal. Most feminine heroines are extravagant: adventurers or eccentrics notable less for their actions than for their unique destinies; take Joan of Arc, Mme Roland, and Flora Tristan: if they are compared with Richelieu, Danton, or Lenin, it is clear their greatness is mainly subjective; they are exemplary figures more than historical agents. A great man springs from the mass and is carried by circumstances: the mass of women is at the fringes of history, and for each of them circumstances are an obstacle and not a springboard. To change the face of the world, one has first to be firmly anchored to it; but women firmly rooted in society are those subjugated by it; unless they are designated for action by divine right—and in this case they are shown to be as capable as men—the ambitious woman and the heroine are strange monsters. Only since women have begun to feel at home on this earth has a Rosa Luxemburg or a Mme Curie emerged. They brilliantly demonstrate that it is not women's inferiority that has determined their historical insignificance: it is their historical insignificance that has doomed them to inferiority.[10]

This fact is striking in the cultural field, the area in which they have been the most successful in asserting themselves. Their lot has been closely linked to literature and the arts; among the ancient Germans, the roles of prophetess and priestess fell to women; because they are marginal to the world, men will look to them when they strive, through culture, to bridge the limits of their universe and reach what is other. Courtly mysticism, humanist curiosity, and the taste for beauty that thrive in the Italian Renaissance, the preciousness of the seventeenth century, and the progressive ideal of the eighteenth century bring about an exaltation of femininity in diverse forms. Woman is thus the main pole of poetry and the substance of works of art; her leisure allows her to devote herself to the pleasures of the mind: inspiration, critic, writer's audience, she emulates the writer; she can often impose a type of sensitivity, an ethic that feeds men's hearts, which is how she intervenes in her own destiny: women's education is mainly a feminine conquest. And yet as important as this collective role played by intellectual women is, their individual contributions are, on the whole, of a lesser order. Woman holds a privileged place in the fields of the mind and

---

10. It is worth noting that out of one thousand statues in Paris (not counting the queens that compose the corbel of the Luxembourg and fulfill a purely architectural role) there are only ten raised to women. Three are devoted to Joan of Arc. The others are Mme de Ségur, George Sand, Sarah Bernhardt, Mme Boucicaut and the baronne de Hirsch, Maria Deraismes, and Rosa Bonheur.

art because she is not involved in action; but art and thinking derive their impetus in action. Being on the fringes of the world is not the best place for someone who intends to re-create it: here again, to go beyond the given, one must be deeply rooted in it. Personal accomplishments are almost impossible in human categories collectively kept in an inferior situation. "Where can one go in skirts?" asked Marie Bashkirtseff. And Stendhal: "All the geniuses who are born *women* are lost for the public good." If truth be told, one is not born, but becomes, a genius; and the feminine condition has, until now, rendered this becoming impossible.

Antifeminists draw two contradictory arguments from examining history: (1) women have never created anything grand; (2) woman's situation has never prevented great women personalities from blossoming. There is bad faith in both of these assertions; the successes of some few privileged women neither compensate for nor excuse the systematic degrading of the collective level; and the very fact that these successes are so rare and limited is proof of their unfavorable circumstances. As Christine de Pizan, Poulain de la Barre, Condorcet, John Stuart Mill, and Stendhal stated, women have never been given their chances in any area. This explains why many of them today demand a new status; and once again, their demand is not to be exalted in their femininity: they want transcendence to prevail over immanence in themselves as in all of humanity; they want abstract rights and concrete possibilities to be granted to them, without which freedom is merely mystification.[11]

This will is being fulfilled. But this is a period of transition; this world that has always belonged to men is still in their hands; patriarchal civilization's institutions and values are still, to a great extent, alive. Abstract rights are far from being wholly granted to women: in Switzerland, women still cannot vote; in France, the 1942 law upholds the husband's prerogatives in a weaker form. And abstract rights, as has just been said, have never been sufficient to guarantee woman a concrete hold on the world: there is not yet real equality today between the two sexes.

First, the burdens of marriage are still much heavier for woman than for man. We have seen that the constraints of pregnancy have been limited by the overt or clandestine use of birth control, but the practice is neither

---

11. Here too the antifeminists are equivocal. At times, holding abstract liberty to be nothing, they glorify the great concrete role the enslaved woman can play in this world: What more does she want? And other times, they underestimate the fact that negative license does not open any concrete possibilities, and they blame abstractly enfranchised women for not having proven themselves.

universally disseminated nor rigorously applied; as abortion is officially forbidden, many women either jeopardize their health by resorting to unregulated abortion methods or are overwhelmed by the number of their pregnancies. Child care, like housekeeping, is still almost exclusively the woman's burden. In France in particular, the antifeminist tradition is so tenacious that a man would think it demeaning to participate in chores previously reserved for women. The result is that woman has a harder time reconciling her family and work life. In cases where society demands this effort from her, her existence is much more difficult than her spouse's.

Take, for example, the lot of peasant women. In France they make up the majority of the women involved in productive labor, and they are generally married. The single woman most often remains a servant in the father's, brother's, or sister's household; she only becomes mistress of a home by accepting a husband's domination; depending on the region, customs and traditions impose various roles on her: the Norman peasant woman presides over the meal, while the Corsican woman does not sit at the same table as the men; but in any case, as she plays one of the most important roles in the domestic economy, she shares the man's responsibilities, his interests, and his property; she is respected, and it is often she who really governs: her situation is reminiscent of the place she held in ancient agricultural communities. She often has as much moral prestige as her husband, and sometimes even more; but her concrete condition is much harsher. The care of the garden, barnyard, sheepfold, and pigpen falls on her alone; she takes part in the heavy work: cleaning the cowshed, spreading the manure, sowing, plowing, hoeing, and hay making; she digs, weeds, harvests, picks grapes, and sometimes helps load and unload wagons of straw, hay, wood and sticks, litter, and so on. In addition, she prepares the meals and manages the household: washing, mending, and such. She assumes the heavy burdens of pregnancies and child care. She rises at dawn, feeds the barnyard and small animals, serves the first meal to the men, takes care of the children, and goes out to the fields or the woods or the kitchen garden; she draws water from the well, serves the second meal, washes the dishes, works in the fields again until dinner, and after the last meal occupies her evening by mending, cleaning, husking the corn, and so forth. As she has no time to take care of her health, even during her pregnancies, she loses her shape quickly and is prematurely withered and worn out, sapped by illnesses. She is denied the few occasional compensations man finds in his social life: he goes to the city on Sundays and fair days, meets other men, goes to the café, drinks, plays cards, hunts, and fishes. She stays on the farm and has no leisure. Only the rich peasant women helped by servants or dispensed from field work lead a pleasantly balanced life: they are socially honored and enjoy greater authority in the home without being crushed by labor. But most of the time rural work reduces woman to the condition of a beast of burden.

The woman shopkeeper, the small-business owner, have always been privileged; they are the only ones since the Middle Ages whose civil capacities have been recognized by the code; women grocers, hoteliers, or tobacconists and dairy women have positions equal to man's; single or widowed, they have a legal identity of their own; married, they possess the same autonomy as their husbands. They are fortunate in working and living in the same place, and the work is not generally too consuming.

The situation of the woman worker, employee, secretary, or saleswoman working outside the home is totally different. It is much more difficult to reconcile her job with managing the household (errands, preparation of meals, cleaning, and upkeep of her wardrobe take at least three and a half hours of work a day and six on Sunday; this adds a lot of time to factory or office hours). As for the learned professions, even if women lawyers, doctors, and teachers manage to have some help in their households, the home and children still entail responsibilities and cares that are a serious handicap for them. In America, ingenious technology has simplified housework; but the appearance and elegance demanded of the working woman impose another constraint on her; and she maintains responsibility for the house and children. In addition, the woman who seeks her independence through work has far fewer possibilities than her masculine competitors. Her salary is inferior to man's in many fields; her job is less specialized and hence doesn't pay as well as that of a skilled worker; and for the same job, the woman is paid less. Because she is new to the world of males, she has fewer chances of success than they. Men and women alike are loath to work under a woman's orders; they always give more confidence to a man; if being a woman is not a defect, it is at least a pecularity. If she wants to "get ahead," it is useful for a woman to make sure she has a man's support. Men are the ones who take the best places, who hold the most important jobs. It must be emphasized that in economic terms men and women constitute two castes.[12]

---

12. In America, great business fortunes often end up in women's hands: younger than their husbands, women outlive and inherit from them; but they are then older and rarely take the initiative of new investments; they act as usufructuaries rather than owners. It is men who *dispose* of the capital. In any case, these rich privileged women make up a small minority. In America more than in Europe, it is almost impossible for a woman to reach a top position as a lawyer or doctor.

What determines women's present situation is the stubborn survival of the most ancient traditions in the new emerging civilization. Hasty observers are wrong to think woman is not up to the possibilities offered her today or even to see only dangerous temptations in these possibilities. The truth is that her situation is tenuous, which makes it very difficult for her to adapt. Factories, offices, and universities are open to women, but marriage is still considered a more honorable career, exempting her from any other participation in collective life. As in primitive civilizations, the amorous act is a service she has the right to be paid for more or less directly. Everywhere but in the U.S.S.R.,[13] the modern woman is allowed to use her body as capital. Prostitution is tolerated,[14] seduction encouraged. And the married woman can legally make her husband support her; in addition, she is cloaked in much greater social dignity than the unmarried woman. Social customs are far from granting her sexual possibilities on a par with those of the single male, in particular, the unwed mother is an object of scandal, as motherhood is more or less forbidden to her. How could the Cinderella myth not retain its validity? Everything still encourages the girl to expect fortune and happiness from a "Prince Charming" instead of attempting the difficult and uncertain conquest alone. For example, she can hope to attain a higher caste through him, a miracle her whole life's work will not bring her. But such a hope is harmful because it divides her strength and interests;[15] this split is perhaps the most serious handicap for woman. Parents still raise their daughters for marriage rather than promoting their personal development; and the daughter sees so many advantages that she desires it herself; the result is that she is often less specialized, less solidly trained than her brothers, she is less totally committed to her profession; as such, she is doomed to remain inferior in it; and the vicious circle is knotted: this inferiority reinforces her desire to find a husband. Every benefit always has a burden; but if the burden is too heavy, the benefit is no more

13. At least according to official doctrine.

14. In Anglo-Saxon countries prostitution has never been controlled. Until 1900, American and English common law did not deem it a crime unless it was scandalous and disturbed the peace. Since then, there has been more or less repression, applied with varying degrees of harshness and of success in England and America, whose legislation on this point varies a great deal from one state to the other. In France after a long abolitionist campaign, the April 13, 1946, law ordered brothels to be closed and the fight against procuremat to be reinforced: "Considering that the existence of these brothels is incompatible with the essential principles of human dignity and the role granted to woman in modern society . . ." Prostitution nevertheless continues to be practiced. Negative and hypocritical measures are obviously not the way the situation can be modified.

15. Cf. Philip Wylie, *Generation of Vipers*.

than a servitude; for most workers today, work is a thankless task: for woman, the chore is not offset by a concrete conquest of her social dignity, freedom of behavior, and economic autonomy; it is understandable that many women workers and employees see no more than an obligation in the right to work from which marriage would deliver them. However, because she has become conscious of self and can emancipate herself from marriage through work, a woman no longer accepts her subjection docilely. What she would hope for is to reconcile family life and profession, something that does not require exhausting acrobatics. Even then, as long as the temptations of facility remain—from the economic inequality that favors certain individuals and the woman's right to sell herself to one of these privileged people—she needs to expend a greater moral effort than the male to choose the path of independence. It has not been well enough understood that temptation is also an obstacle, and even one of the most dangerous. It is amplified here by a mystification since there will be one winner out of the thousands in the lucky marriage lottery. Today's period invites, even obliges women to work; but it lures them with an idyllic and delightful paradise: it raises up the happy few far above those still riveted to this earthly world.

Men's economic privilege, their social value, the prestige of marriage, the usefulness of masculine support—all these encourage women to ardently want to please men. They are on the whole still in a state of serfdom. It follows that woman knows and chooses herself not as she exists for herself but as man defines her. She thus has to be described first as men dream of her since her being-for-men is one of the essential factors of her concrete condition.

PART THREE

MYTHS

History has shown that men have always held all the concrete powers; from patriarchy's earliest times they have deemed it useful to keep woman in a state of dependence; their codes were set up against her; she was thus concretely established as the Other. This condition served males' economic interests; but it also suited their ontological and moral ambitions. Once the subject attempts to assert himself, the Other, who limits and denies him, is nonetheless necessary for him: he attains himself only through the reality that he is not. That is why man's life is never plenitude and rest, it is lack and movement, it is combat. Facing himself, man encounters Nature; he has a hold on it, he tries to appropriate it for himself. But it cannot satisfy him. Either it realizes itself as a purely abstract opposition—it is an obstacle and remains foreign—or it passively submits to man's desire and allows itself to be assimilated by him; he possesses it only in consuming it, that is, in destroying it. In both cases, he remains alone; he is alone when touching a stone, alone when digesting a piece of fruit. The other is present only if the other is himself present to himself: that is, true alterity is a consciousness separated from my own and identical to it. It is the existence of other men that wrests each man from his immanence and enables him to accomplish the truth of his being, to accomplish himself as transcendence, as flight toward the object, as a project. But this foreign freedom, which confirms my freedom, also enters into conflict with it: this is the tragedy of the unhappy consciousness; each consciousness seeks to posit itself alone as sovereign subject. Each one tries to accomplish itself by reducing the other to slavery. But in work and fear the slave experiences himself as essential, and by a dialectical reversal the master appears the inessential one. The conflict can be overcome by the free recognition of each individual in the other, each one positing both itself and the other as object and as subject in a reciprocal movement. But friendship and generosity, which accomplish this recognition of freedoms concretely, are not easy virtues; they are undoubtedly man's highest accomplishment; this is where he is in his truth: but this truth is a struggle endlessly begun, endlessly abolished; it demands that man surpass himself at each instant. Put into other words, man attains an authentically moral attitude when he renounces *being* in order to assume his existence; through this conversion he also renounces all possession, because possession is a way of searching for being; but the conversion by which he attains true wisdom is never finished, it has to be made ceaselessly, it demands constant effort. So much so that, unable to accomplish himself in solitude, man is ceaselessly in jeopardy in his relations with his peers: his life is a difficult enterprise whose success is never assured.

But he does not like difficulty; he is afraid of danger. He has contradictory aspirations to both life and rest, existence and being; he knows very well that "a restless spirit" is the ransom for his development, that his distance from the object is the ransom for his being present to himself; but he dreams of restfulness in restlessness and of an opaque plenitude that his consciousness would nevertheless still inhabit. This embodied dream is, precisely, woman; she is the perfect intermediary between nature that is foreign to man and the peer who is too identical to him.[1] She pits neither the hostile silence of nature nor the hard demand of a reciprocal recognition against him; by a unique privilege she is a consciousness, and yet it seems possible to possess her in the flesh. Thanks to her, there is a way to escape the inexorable dialectic of the master and the slave that springs from the reciprocity of freedoms.

It has been pointed out that there were not at first free women whom the males then enslaved and that the sexual division has never founded a division into castes. Assimilating the woman to the slave is a mistake; among slaves there were women, but free women have always existed, that is, women invested with religious and social dignity: they accepted man's sovereignty, and he did not feel threatened by a revolt that could transform him in turn into an object. Woman thus emerged as the inessential who never returned to the essential, as the absolute Other, without reciprocity. All the creation myths express this conviction that is precious to the male, for example, the Genesis legend, which, through Christianity, has spanned Western civilization. Eve was not formed at the same time as man; she was not made either from a different substance or from the same clay that

---

1. "Woman is not the useless repetition of man but the enchanted space where the living alliance of man and nature occurs. If she disappeared, men would be alone, foreigners without passports in a glacial world. She is earth itself carried to life's summit, the earth become sensitive and joyful; and without her, for man, earth is mute and dead," wrote Michel Carrouges in "Les pouvoirs de la femme" (Woman's Powers), *Cahiers du Sud*, no. 292 (1948).

Adam was modeled from: she was drawn from the first male's flank. Even her birth was not autonomous; God did not spontaneously choose to create her for herself and to be directly worshipped in turn: he destined her for man; he gave her to Adam to save him from loneliness, her spouse is her origin and her finality; she is his complement in the inessential mode. Thus, she appears a privileged prey. She is nature raised to the transparency of consciousness; she is a naturally submissive consciousness. And therein lies the marvelous hope that man has often placed in woman: he hopes to accomplish himself as being through carnally possessing a being while making confirmed in his freedom by a docile freedom. No man would consent to being a woman, but all want there to be women. "Thank God for creating woman." "Nature is good because it gave men woman." In these and other similar phrases, man once more asserts arrogantly and naively that his presence in this world is an inevitable fact and a right, that of woman is a simple accident—but a fortunate one. Appearing as the Other, woman appears at the same time as a plenitude of being by opposition to the nothingness of existence that man experiences in itself; the Other, posited as object in the subject's eyes, is posited as in-itself, thus as being. Woman embodies positively the lack the existent carries in his heart, and man hopes to realize himself by finding himself through her.

But she has not represented for him the only incarnation of the Other, and she has not always had the same importance throughout history. In various periods, she has been eclipsed by other idols. When the city or the state devours the citizen, he is no longer in any position to deal with his personal destiny. Dedicated to the state, the Spartan woman has a higher station than that of other Greek women. But she is not transfigured by any masculine dream. The cult of the chief, be it Napoleon, Mussolini, or Hitler, excludes any other. In military dictatorships and totalitarian regimes, woman is no longer a privileged object. It is understandable that woman is divinized in a country that is rich and where the citizens are uncertain about what meaning to give to their lives: this is what is happening in America. In contrast, socialist ideologies, which call for the assimilation of all human beings, reject the notion that any human category be object or idol, now and for the future: in the authentically democratic society that Marx heralded, there is no place for the Other. Few men, however, correspond exactly to the soldier or the militant that they have chosen to be; as long as these men remain individuals, woman retains a singular value in their eyes. I have seen letters written by German soldiers to French prostitutes in which, in spite of Nazism, the tradition of sentimentality proved to be naively alive. Communist writers like Aragon in France and Vittorini in Italy give a front-row place in their works to woman as lover and mother. Perhaps the myth of woman will be phased out one day: the more women assert themselves as human beings, the more the marvelous quality of Other dies in them. But today it still exists in the hearts of all men.

Any myth implies a Subject who projects its hopes and fears of a transcendent heaven. Not positing themselves as Subject, women have not created the virile myth that would reflect their projects; they have neither religion nor poetry that belongs to them alone: they still dream through men's dreams. They worship the gods made by males. And males have shaped the great virile figures for their own exaltation: Hercules, Prometheus, Parsifal; in the destiny of these heroes, woman has merely a secondary role. Undoubtedly, there are stylized images of man as he is in his relations with woman: father, seducer, husband, the jealous one, the good son, the bad son; but men are the ones who have established them, and they have not attained the dignity of myth; they are barely more than clichés, while woman is exclusively defined in her relation to man. The asymmetry of the two categories, male and female, can be seen in the unilateral constitution of sexual myths. Woman is sometimes designated as "sex"; it is she who is the flesh, its delights and its dangers. That for woman it is man who is sexed and carnal is a truth that has never been proclaimed because there is no one to proclaim it. The representation of the world as the world itself is the work of men; they describe it from a point of view that is their own and that they confound with the absolute truth.

It is always difficult to describe a myth; it does not lend itself to being grasped or defined; it haunts consciousnesses without ever being posited opposite them as a fixed object. The object fluctuates so much and is so contradictory that its unity is not at first discerned: Delilah and Judith, Aspasia and Lucretia, Pandora and Athena, woman is both Eve and the Virgin Mary. She is an idol, a servant, source of life, power of darkness; she is the elementary silence of truth, she is artifice, gossip, and lies; she is the medicine woman and witch; she is man's prey; she is his downfall, she is everything he is not and wants to have, his negation and his raison d'être.

"To be a woman," says Kierkegaard, "is something so strange, so confused, and so complicated that no one predicate can express it, and the multiple predicates that might be used contradict each other in such a way that only a woman could put up with it."[2] This comes from being considered not positively, as she is for herself, but negatively, such as she appears to man. Because if there are other *Others* than the woman, she is still always defined as Other. And her ambiguity is that of the very idea of Other: it is

---

2. *Stages on Life's Way.*

that of the human condition as defined in its relation with the Other. It has already been said that the Other is Evil; but as it is necessary for the Good, it reverts to the Good; through the Other, I accede to the Whole, but it separates me from the Whole; it is the door to infinity and the measure of my finitude. And this is why woman embodies no set concept; through her the passage from hope to failure, hatred to love, good to bad, bad to good takes place ceaselessly. However she is considered, it is this ambivalence that is the most striking.

———

Man seeks the Other in woman as Nature and as his peer. But Nature inspires ambivalent feelings in man, as has been seen. He exploits it, but it crushes him; he is born from and he dies in it; it is the source of his being and the kingdom he bends to his will; it is a material envelope in which the soul is held prisoner, and it is the supreme reality; it is contingency and Idea, finitude and totality; it is that which opposes Spirit and himself. Both ally and enemy, it appears as the dark chaos from which life springs forth, as this very life, and as the beyond it reaches for: woman embodies nature as Mother, Spouse, and Idea; these figures are sometimes confounded and sometimes in opposition, and each has a double face.

Man sinks his roots in Nature; he was engendered, like animals and plants; he is well aware that he exists only inasmuch as he lives. But since the coming of patriarchy, life in man's eyes has taken on a dual aspect: it is consciousness, will, transcendence, it is intellect; and it is matter, passivity, immanence, it is flesh. Aeschylus, Aristotle, and Hippocrates proclaimed that on earth as on Mount Olympus it is the male principle that is the true creator: form, number, and movement come from him; Demeter makes corn multiply, but the origin of corn and its truth are in Zeus; woman's fertility is considered merely a passive virtue. She is earth and man seed; she is water, and he is fire. Creation has often been imagined as a marriage of fire and water; hot humidity gives birth to living beings; the Sun is the spouse of the Sea; Sun and Fire are male divinities; and the Sea is one of the most universally widespread maternal symbols. Inert, water submits to the flamboyant rays that fertilize it. Likewise, the still earth, furrowed by the laborer's toil, receives the seeds in its rows. But its role is necessary: it is the soil that nourishes the seed, shelters it, and provides its substance. Man thus continued to worship fertility goddesses, even once the Great Mother was dethroned;[3] he owes his harvests, herds, and prosperity to

---

3. "Of Gaea sing I, Mother firm of all, the eldest one, who feedeth life on earth, whichever walk on land or swim the seas, or fly," says a Homeric hymn. Aeschylus also glorifies the earth that "gives birth to all beings, nourishes them, and then receives the fertilized germ once again."

Cybele. He owes her his very life. He exalts water and fire equally. "Glory to the sea! Glory to its waves encircled by sacred fire! Glory to the wave! Glory to the fire! Glory to the strange adventure," wrote Goethe in *Faust, Part Two*. He venerated earth: "the Matron Clay," as Blake called it. An Indian prophet advised his disciples not to dig up the earth because "it is a sin to hurt or cut, to tear our common mother in agricultural works . . . Do I take a knife to drive into my mother's breast? . . . Do I mutilate her flesh so as to reach her bones? . . . How could I dare to cut my mother's hair?" In central India the Baidya also thought that it was a sin to "rip the breast of their earth mother with the plow." Inversely, Aeschylus says of Oedipus that he "dared to sow the sacred furrow where he was formed." Sophocles spoke of "paternal furrows" and of the "laborer, master of a remote field that he visited only once during the sowing." The beloved in an Egyptian song declares: "I am the earth!" In Islamic texts, woman is called "field . . . grapevine." In one of his hymns, Saint Francis of Assisi speaks of "our sister, the earth, our mother, who preserves and cares for us, who produces the most varied fruits with many-colored flowers and with grass." Michelet, taking mud baths in Acqui, exclaims: "Dear common mother! We are one. I come from you, I return to you!" And there are even periods of vitalistic romanticism that affirm the triumph of Life over Spirit: so the earth's and woman's magic fertility appear to be even more marvelous than the male's concerted works; so the man dreams of once again losing himself in maternal darkness to find the true sources of his being. The mother is the root driven into the depths of the cosmos that taps its vital juices; she is the fountain from which springs forth sweet water that is also mother's milk, a warm spring, a mud formed of earth and water, rich in regenerating forces.[4]

But man's revolt against his carnal condition is more general; he considers himself a fallen god: his curse is to have fallen from a luminous and orderly heaven into the chaotic obscurity of the mother's womb. He desires to see himself in this fire, this active and pure breath, and it is woman who imprisons him in the mud of the earth. He would like himself to be as necessary as pure Idea, as One, All, absolute Spirit; and he finds himself enclosed in a limited body, in a place and time he did not choose, to which he was not called, useless, awkward, absurd. His very being is carnal con-

---

4. "To the letter the woman is Isis, fertile nature. She is the river and the bed of the river, the root and the rose, the earth and the cherry tree, the vine and the grape" (M. Carrouges, "Woman's Powers").

tingence to which he is subjected in his isolation, in his unjustifiable gratuitousness. It also dooms him to death. This quivering gelatin that forms in the womb (the womb, secret and sealed like a tomb) is too reminiscent of the soft viscosity of carrion for him not to turn away from it with a shudder. Wherever life is in the process of being made—germination and fermentation—it provokes disgust because it is being made only when it is being unmade; the viscous glandular embryo opens the cycle that ends in the rotting of death. Horrified by death's gratuitousness, man is horrified at having been engendered; he would like to rescind his animal attachments; because of his birth, murderous Nature has a grip on him. For the primitives, childbirth is surrounded by strict taboos; in particular, the placenta must be carefully burned or thrown into the sea, because whoever might get hold of it would hold the newborn's fate in his hands; this envelope in which the fetus is formed is the sign of its dependence; in annihilating it, the individual is able to detach himself from the living magma and to realize himself as an autonomous being. The stain of childbirth falls back on the mother. Leviticus and all the ancient codes impose purification rites on the new mother; and often in the countryside the postpartum ceremony maintains that tradition. Everyone knows that young boys and girls and men feel a spontaneous embarrassment, one often camouflaged by sneering, at seeing a pregnant woman's stomach or the swollen breasts of the wet nurse. In Dupuytren's museums, the curious contemplate the wax embryos and the preserved fetuses with the morbid interest they would show in a defiled grave. Notwithstanding all the respect that society surrounds it with, the function of gestation inspires spontaneous repulsion. And while the little boy in early childhood remains sensually attached to the mother's flesh, when he grows up, when he is socialized and becomes aware of his individual existence, this flesh frightens him; he wants to ignore it and to see his mother as institution only; if he wants to think of her as pure and chaste, it is less from amorous jealousy than from the refusal to acknowledge her as a body. An adolescent boy becomes embarrassed, blushes if he meets his mother, sisters, or women in his family when he is out with his friends: their presence recalls the regions of immanence from which he wants to escape; she reveals the roots that he wants to pull himself away from. The boy's irritation when his mother kisses and caresses him has the same significance; he gives up his family, mother, and mother's breast. He would like to have emerged, like Athena, into the adult world, armed from head to toe, invulnerable.[5] Being conceived and born is

5. See our study on Montherlant, the epitome of this attitude, a little further on.

the curse weighing on his destiny, the blemish on his being. And it is the warning of his death. The cult of germination has always been associated with the cult of the dead. Mother Earth engulfs the bones of its children within it. Women—the Parcae and Moirai—weave human destiny; but they also cut the threads. In most folk representations, Death is woman, and women mourn the dead because death is their work.[6]

Thus, Mother Earth has a face of darkness: she is chaos, where everything comes from and must return to one day; she is Nothingness. The many aspects of the world that the day uncovers commingle in the night: night of spirit locked up in the generality and opacity of matter, night of sleep and nothing. At the heart of the sea, it is night: woman is the *Mare tenebrarum* dreaded by ancient navigators; it is night in the bowels of the earth. Man is threatened with being engulfed in this night, the reverse of fertility, and it horrifies him. He aspires to the sky, to light, to sunny heights, to the pure and crystal clear cold of blue; and underfoot is a moist, hot, and dark gulf ready to swallow him; many legends have the hero falling and forever lost in maternal darkness: a cave, an abyss, hell.

But once again ambivalence is at work here: while germination is always associated with death, death is also associated with fertility. Detested death is like a new birth, and so it is blessed. The dead hero like Osiris is resurrected every springtime, and he is regenerated by a new birth. Man's supreme hope, says Jung, "is that the dark waters of death become the waters of life, that death and its cold embrace are the mother's lap, just as the sea, while engulfing the sun, re-births in the depths."[7] The theme of the burial of the sun god within the sea and its dazzling reemergence is common to many mythologies. And man wants to live, but he also hopes for rest, sleep, for nothingness. He does not wish for immortality for himself, and thus he can learn to love death. "Inorganic matter is the mother's breast," Nietzsche wrote. "Being delivered from life means becoming real again, completing oneself. Anyone who understands that would consider returning to unfeeling dust as a holiday." Chaucer puts this prayer into the mouth of an old man who cannot die:

---

6. Demeter is the archetype of the *mater dolorosa*. But other goddesses—Ishtar and Artemis—are cruel. Kali is holding a blood-filled skull. "The heads of your newly killed sons hang from your neck like a necklace . . . Your figure is beautiful like rain clouds, your feet are soiled with blood," says a Hindu poem.

7. *Metamorphoses of the Libido.*

Thus restless I my wretched way must make
And on the ground, which is my mother's gate,
I knock with my staff early, aye, and late
And cry: "O my dear mother, let me in!"

Man wants to assert his individual existence and proudly rest on his "essential difference," but he also wants to break the barriers of the self and commingle with water, earth, night, Nothingness, with the Whole. Woman who condemns man to finitude also enables him to surpass his own limits: that is where the equivocal magic surrounding her comes from.

In all civilizations and still today, she inspires horror in man: the horror of his own carnal contingence that he projects on her. The girl who has not yet gone through puberty does not pose a threat; she is not the object of any taboo and has no sacred characteristics. In many primitive societies her sex even seems innocent: erotic games between boys and girls are allowed in childhood. Woman becomes impure the day she might be able to procreate. In primitive sociéties the strict taboos concerning girls on the day of their first period have often been described; even in Egypt, where the woman is treated with particular respect, she remains confined during her whole menstrual period.[8] She is often put on a rooftop or relegated to a shack on the outskirts of the town; she can be neither seen nor touched: what's more, she must not even touch herself with her own hand; for peoples that practice daily flea removal, she is given a stick with which she is able to scratch herself; she must not touch food with her fingers; sometimes she is strictly forbidden to eat; in other cases, her mother and sister are permitted to feed her with an instrument; but all objects that come in contact with her during this period must be burned. After this first test, the menstrual taboos are a little less strict, but they remain harsh. In particular, in Leviticus: "And if a woman have an issue, and her issue in her flesh be blood, she shall be put apart seven days: and whosoever toucheth her shall be unclean until the even. And every thing that she lieth upon in her separation shall be unclean: every thing also that she sitteth upon shall be unclean. And whosoever toucheth her bed shall wash his clothes, and bathe himself in water, and be unclean until the even." This text is perfectly sym-

---

8. The difference between mystical and mythical beliefs and individuals' lived convictions is apparent in the following fact: Lévi-Strauss points out that "young Winnebago Indians visit their mistresses and take advantage of the privacy of the prescribed isolation of these women during their menstrual period."

metrical with one concerning gonorrhea-provoked impurity in man. And the purifying sacrifice is identical in the two cases. Seven days after she has been purified of her flow, two turtledoves or two young pigeons have to be brought to the sacrificer, who offers them to the Eternal. Even in matriarchal societies, the virtues connected to menstruation are ambivalent. On the one hand, it brings social activities to a halt, destroys the vital force, withers flowers, causes fruit to fall; but it also has beneficial effects: menses are used in love philters, in remedies, and in particular in healing cuts and bruises. Still today, when some Indians go off to fight spectral monsters haunting their rivers, they place a fiber wad filled with menstrual blood on the bow of their boat: its emanations are harmful to their supernatural enemies. In some Greek cities, young girls pay homage to the temple of Astarte by wearing linens stained by their first menstrual blood. But since patriarchy, only harmful powers have been attributed to the bizarre liquor flowing from the feminine sex. Pliny in his *Natural History* says: "The menstruating woman spoils harvests, devastates gardens, kills seeds, makes fruit fall, kills bees; if she touches the wine, it turns to vinegar; milk sours . . ."

An old English poet expresses the same thought:

Oh! Menstruating woman, thou'rt a fiend
From whom all nature should be closely screened!

These beliefs have been vigorously perpetuated right up to today. In 1878, a member of the British Medical Association wrote in the *British Medical Journal:* "It is an indisputable fact that meat goes bad when touched by menstruating women." He said that he personally knew of two cases of hams spoiling in such circumstances. In the refineries of the North at the beginning of this century, women were prohibited by law from going into the factory when they were afflicted by what the Anglo-Saxons call the "curse" because the sugar turned black. And in Saigon, women are not employed in opium factories: because of their periods, the opium goes bad and becomes bitter. These beliefs survive in many areas of the French countryside. Any cook knows how impossible it is to make mayonnaise if she is indisposed or simply in the presence of another woman who is indisposed. In Anjou, recently, an old gardener who had stocked that year's cider harvest in the cellar wrote to the master of the house: "Don't let the young women of the household and their female guests go through the cellar on certain days of the month: they would prevent the cider from fermenting." When the cook heard about this letter, she shrugged her shoulders. "*That* never prevented cider from fermenting," she said, "it is only bad for bacon fat: it cannot be salted in the presence of an indisposed woman; it would rot."[9]

Putting this repulsion in the same category as that provoked by blood is most inadequate: more imbued with the mysterious mana that is both life and death than anything else, blood, of course, is in itself a sacred element. But menstrual blood's baleful powers are more particular. Menstrual blood embodies the essence of femininity, which is why its flow endangers woman herself, whose mana is thus materialized. During the Chaga's initiation rites, girls are urged to carefully conceal their menstrual blood. "Do not show it to your mother, for she would die! Do not show it to your age-mates, for there may be a wicked one among them, who will take away the cloth with which you have cleaned yourself, and you will be barren in your marriage. Do not show it to a bad woman, who will take the cloth to place it in the top of her hut . . . with the result that you cannot bear children. Do not throw the cloth on the path or in the bush. A wicked person might do evil things with it. Bury it in the ground. Protect the blood from the gaze of your father, brothers and sisters. It is a sin to let them see it."[10] For the Aleuts, if the father sees his daughter during her first menstruation, she could go blind or deaf. It is thought that during this period woman is possessed by a spirit and invested with a dangerous power. Some primitives believe that the flow is provoked by snakebite, as woman has suspicious affinities with snakes and lizards; it is supposed to be similar to crawling animals' venom. Leviticus compares it to gonorrhea; the bleeding feminine sex is not only a wound but a suspicious sore. And Vigny associates the notion of soiling with illness: "Woman, sick child, and impure twelve times." The result of interior alchemic troubles, the periodic hemorrhage woman suffers from is bizarrely aligned with the moon's cycle: the moon also has dangerous whims.[11] Woman is part of the formidable workings

---

9. A doctor from the Cher region pointed out to me that women in that situation are banned from going into the mushroom beds. The question as to whether there is any basis for these preconceived ideas is still discussed today. Dr. Binet's only fact supporting them is an observation by Schink (cited by Vignes). Schink supposedly saw flowers wilt in an indisposed servant's hands; yeast cakes made by this woman supposedly rose only three centimeters instead of the five they usually rose. In any case, these facts are pretty feeble and poorly established when considering the importance and universality of the obviously mystical beliefs they come from.

10. Quoted in Lévi-Strauss, *The Elementary Structures of Kinship*.

11. The moon is a source of fertility; it is seen as the "master of women"; it is often believed that the moon, in the form of a man or a snake, couples with women. The snake is an epiphany of the moon; it molts and regenerates, it is immortal, it is a power that distributes fertility and science; it watches over holy sources, the Tree of Life, the Fountain of Youth, and so on, but it is also the snake that takes immortality away from man. It is said that it couples with women. Persian and rabbinical traditions claim that menstruation is due to the first woman's intercourse with the snake.

that order the course of planets and the sun; she is prey to the cosmic forces that determine the destiny of stars and tides, while men are subjected to their worrisome radiation. But it is especially striking that menstrual blood's effects are linked to the ideas of cream going sour, mayonnaise that does not take, fermentation, and decomposition; it is also claimed that it is apt to cause fragile objects to break; to spring violin and harp strings; but above all it influences organic substances that are midway between matter and life; this is less because it is blood than because it emanates from genital organs; even without knowing its exact function, people understood it to be linked to the germination of life: ignorant of the existence of the ovary, the ancients saw in menstruation the complement of the sperm. In fact, it is not this blood that makes woman impure, but rather, this blood is a manifestation of her impurity; it appears when the woman can be fertile; when it disappears, she becomes sterile again; it pours forth from this womb where the fetus is made. The horror of feminine fertility that man experiences is expressed through it.

The strictest taboo of all concerning woman in her impure state is the prohibition of sexual intercourse with her. Leviticus condemns man to seven days of impurity if he transgresses this rule. The Laws of Manu are even harsher: "The wisdom, energy, strength, and vitality of a man coming near a woman stained by menstrual excretions perish definitively." Priests ordered fifty days of penance for men who had sexual relations during menstruation. Since the feminine principle is then considered as reaching its highest power, it is feared that it would triumph over the male principle in intimate contact. Less specifically, man shies away from finding the mother's feared essence in the woman he possesses; he works at dissociating these two aspects of femininity: that explains why incest is prohibited by exogamy or more modern forms and is a universal law; that explains why man distances himself from woman sexually when she is particularly destined for her reproductive role: during her period, when she is pregnant, or when she is nursing. Not only does the Oedipus complex—whose description, incidentally, has to be revised—not contradict this attitude: on the contrary, it even implies it. Man guards himself against woman to the extent that she is the confused source of the world and disorder become organic.

However, this representation of woman also allows the society that has been separated from the cosmos and the gods to remain in communication with them. She still assures the fertility of the fields for the bedouins and the Iroquois; in ancient Greece, she heard subterranean voices; she understood the language of the wind and the trees: she was the Pythia, Sibyl, and prophetess. The dead and the gods spoke through her mouth. Still today, she has these powers of divination: she is medium, palmist, card reader, clairvoyant, inspired; she hears voices and has visions. When men feel the need to delve into vegetable and animal life—like Antaeus, who touched earth to recoup his strength—they call upon woman. Throughout the Greek and Roman rationalist civilizations, chthonian cults subsisted. They could usually be found on the periphery of official religious life; they even ended up, as in Eleusis, taking the form of mysteries: they had the opposite meaning of sun cults, where man asserted his will for separation and spirituality; but they complemented them; man sought to overcome his solitude by ecstasy: that is the goal of mysteries, orgies, and bacchanals. In the world reconquered by males, the male god Dionysus usurped Ishtar's and Astarte's magic and wild virtues; but it was women who went wild over his image: the maenads, thyades, and bacchantes led men to religious drunkenness and sacred madness. The role of sacred prostitution is similar: both to unleash and to channel the powers of fertility. Even today, popular holidays are exemplified by outbreaks of eroticism; woman is not just an object of pleasure but a means of reaching this hubris in which the individual surpasses himself. "What a being possesses in the deepest part of himself, what is lost and tragic, the 'blinding wonder' can no longer be found anywhere but on a bed," wrote Georges Bataille.

In sexual release, man in his lover's embrace seeks to lose himself in the infinite mystery of the flesh. But it has already been seen that his normal sexuality, on the contrary, dissociates Mother from Wife. He finds the mysterious alchemies of life repugnant, while his own life is nourished and enchanted by the tasty fruits of the earth; he desires to appropriate them for himself; he covets Venus freshly emerging from the waters. Woman first discovers herself in patriarchy as wife since the supreme creator is male. Before being the mother of humankind, Eve is Adam's companion; she was given to man for him to possess and fertilize as he possesses and fertilizes the soil; and through her, he makes his kingdom out of all nature. Man does not merely seek in the sexual act subjective and ephemeral pleasure. He wants to conquer, take, and possess; to have a woman is to conquer her; he penetrates her as the plowshare in the furrows; he makes her his as he makes his the earth he is working: he plows, he plants, he sows: these images are as old as writing; from antiquity to today a thousand examples can be mentioned. "Woman is like the field and man like the seeds," say the Laws of Manu. In an André Masson drawing there is a man, shovel in hand, tilling the garden of a feminine sex.[12] Woman is her husband's prey, his property.

---

12. Rabelais called the male sex "the worker of nature." The religious and historical origin of the phallus-plowshare–woman-furrow association has already been pointed out.

Man's hesitation between fear and desire, between the terror of being possessed by uncontrollable forces and the will to overcome them, is grippingly reflected in the virginity myths. Dreaded or desired or even demanded by the male, virginity is the highest form of the feminine mystery; this aspect is simultaneously the most troubling and the most fascinating. Depending on whether man feels crushed by the powers encircling him or arrogantly believes he is able to make them his, he refuses or demands that his wife be delivered to him as a virgin. In the most primitive societies, where woman's power is exalted, it is fear that dominates; woman has to be deflowered the night before the wedding. Marco Polo asserted that for the Tibetans, "none of them wanted to take a virgin girl as wife." A rational explanation has sometimes been given for this refusal: man does not want a wife who has not yet aroused masculine desires. Al-Bakri, the Arab geographer, speaking of the Slavic peoples, notes that "if a man gets married and finds that his wife is a virgin, he says: 'If you were worth something, men would have loved you and one of them would have taken your virginity.'" He then chases her out and repudiates her. It is also claimed that some primitives refuse to marry a woman unless she has already given birth, thus proving her fertility. But the real reasons for the very widespread deflowering customs are mystical. Certain peoples imagine the presence of a serpent in the vagina that would bite the spouse during the breaking of the hymen; terrifying virtues are given to virginal blood, linked to menstrual blood, and capable of ruining the male's vigor. These images express the idea that the feminine principle is so powerful and threatening because it is intact.[13] Sometimes the deflowering issue is not raised; for example, Malinowski describes an indigenous population in which, because sexual games are allowed from childhood on, girls are never virgins. Sometimes, the mother, older sister, or some other matron systematically deflowers the girl and throughout her childhood widens the vaginal opening. Deflowering can also be carried out by women during puberty using a stick, a bone, or a stone, and this is not considered a surgical operation. In other tribes, the girl at puberty is subjected to savage initiation rites: men drag her out of the village and deflower her with instruments or by raping her. Giving over virgins to passersby is one of the most common rites; either these strangers are not thought to be sensitive to this mana dangerous only for the tribes' males, or it does not matter what evils befall them. Even more often, the priest, medicine man, boss, or head

---

13. The power in combat attributed to the virgin comes from this: the Valkyries and Joan of Arc, for example.

of the tribe deflowers the fiancée the night before the wedding; on the Malabar Coast, the Brahmans have to carry out this act, apparently without joy, for which they demand high wages. All holy objects are known to be dangerous for the outsider, but consecrated individuals can handle them without risk; that explains why priests and chiefs are able to tame the malefic forces against which the spouse has to protect himself. In Rome all that was left of these customs was a symbolic ceremony: the fiancée was seated on a stone Priapus phallus, with the double aim of increasing her fertility and absorbing the overpowerful and therefore harmful fluids within her. The husband defends himself in yet another way: he himself deflowers the virgin but during ceremonies that render him invulnerable at this critical juncture; for example, he does it in front of the whole village with a stick or bone. In Samoa, he uses his finger covered in a white cloth and distributes bloodstained shreds to the spectators. There is also the case of the man allowed to deflower his wife normally but he has to wait three days to ejaculate in her so that the generating seed is not soiled by hymen blood.

In a classic reversal in the area of sacred things, virginal blood in less primitive societies is a propitious symbol. There are still villages in France where the bloody sheet is displayed to parents and friends the morning after the wedding. In the patriarchal regime, man became woman's master; and the same characteristics that are frightening in animals or untamed elements become precious qualities for the owner who knows how to subdue them. Man took the ardor of the wild horse and the violence of lightning and waterfalls as the instruments of his prosperity. Therefore, he wants to annex woman to him with all her riches intact. The order of virtue imposed on the girl certainly obeys rational motives: like chastity for the wife, the fiancée's innocence is necessary to protect the father from incurring any risk of bequeathing his goods to a foreign child. But woman's virginity is demanded more imperiously when man considers the wife as his personal property. First of all, the idea of possession is always impossible to realize positively; the truth is that one never has anything or anyone; one attempts to accomplish it in a negative way; the surest way to assert that a good is mine is to prevent another from using it. And then nothing seems as desirable to man as what has never belonged to any other human: thus conquest is a unique and absolute event. Virgin land has always fascinated explorers; alpinists kill themselves every year attempting to assault an untouched mountain or even trying to open up a new trail; and the curious risk their lives to descend underground to the bottom of unprobed caves. An object that men have already mastered has become a tool; cut off from its natural bonds, it loses its deepest attributes; there is more promise in the wild water of torrents than in that of public fountains. A virgin body has the freshness of secret springs, the morning bloom of a closed corolla, the orient of the pearl the sun has never yet caressed. Cave, temple, sanctuary, or secret garden: like the child, man is fascinated by these shadowy and closed places never yet touched by animating consciousness, waiting to be lent a soul; it seems to him that he in fact created what he is the only one to grasp and penetrate. Moreover, every desire pursues the aim of consuming the desired object, entailing its destruction. By breaking the hymen, man possesses the feminine body more intimately than by a penetration that leaves it intact; in this irreversible operation, he unequivocally makes it a passive object, asserting his hold on it. This exactly expresses the meaning in the legend of the knight who hacks his way through thorny bushes to pick a rose never before inhaled; not only does he uncover it, but he breaks its stem, thereby conquering it. The image is so clear that in popular language, "taking a woman's flower" means destroying her virginity, giving the origin of the word "deflowering."

But virginity only has this sexual attraction when allied with youth; otherwise, its mystery reverts to disquiet. Many men today are sexually repulsed by older virgins; psychological reasons alone do not explain why "old maids" are regarded as bitter and mean matrons. The curse is in their very flesh, this flesh that is object for no subject, that no desire has made desirable, that has bloomed and wilted without finding a place in the world of men; turned away from her destination, the old maid becomes an eccentric object, as troubling as the incommunicable thinking of a madman. Of a forty-year-old, still beautiful, woman presumed to be a virgin, I heard a man say with great vulgarity: "It's full of cobwebs in there." It is true that deserted and unused cellars and attics are full of unsavory mystery; they fill up with ghosts; abandoned by humanity, houses become the dwellings of spirits. If feminine virginity has not been consecrated to a god, it is easily then thought to imply marriage with the devil. Virgins that men have not subjugated, old women who have escaped their power, are more easily looked upon as witches than other women; as woman's destiny is to be doomed to another, if she does not submit to a man's yoke, she is available for the devil's.

Exorcised by deflowering rites or on the contrary purified by her virginity, the wife could thus be desirable prey. Taking her gives the lover all the riches of life he desires to possess. She is all the fauna, all the earthly flora: gazelle, doe, lilies and roses, downy peaches, fragrant raspberries; she is precious stones, mother-of-pearl, agate, pearls, silk, the blue of the sky, the freshness of springs, air, flame, earth, and water. All the poets of East and West have metamorphosed woman's body into flowers, fruits, and birds. Here again, throughout antiquity, the Middle Ages, and the modern period, it would be necessary to quote a thick anthology. The Song of Songs is well-known, in which the male loved one says to the female loved one:

> *Thou hast doves' eyes . . .*
> *thy hair is as a flock of goats . . .*
> *Thy teeth are like a flock of sheep that are even shorn . . .*
> *thy temples are like a piece of a pomegranate . . .*
> *Thy two breasts are like two young roes that are twins . . .*
> *Honey and milk are under thy tongue.*

In *Arcanum 17*, André Breton took up this eternal song: "Melusina at the instant of her second scream: she sprang up off her globeless haunches, her belly is the whole August harvest, her torso bursts into fireworks from her arched back, modeled on a swallow's two wings, her breasts are two ermines caught in their own scream, blinding because they are lit by scorching coals of their howling mouth. And her arms are the soul of streams that sing and float perfumes."

Man finds shining stars and the moody moon, sunlight, and the darkness of caves on woman; wildflowers from hedgerows and the garden's proud rose are also woman. Nymphs, dryads, mermaids, water sprites, and fairies haunt the countryside, the woods, lakes, seas, and moors. This animism is profoundly anchored in men. For the sailor, the sea is a dangerous woman, perfidious and difficult to conquer but that he cherishes by dint of taming it. Proud, rebellious, virginal, and wicked, the mountain is woman for the mountain climber who wants to take it, even at risk of life. It is often said that these comparisons manifest sexual sublimation; rather, they express an affinity between woman and the elements as primal as sexuality itself. Man expects more from possessing woman than the satisfaction of an instinct; she is the special object through which he subjugates Nature. Other objects can also play this role. Sometimes it is on young boys' bodies that man seeks the sand of beaches, the velvet of nights, the fragrance of honeysuckle. But sexual penetration is not the only way to realize this carnal appropriation of the earth. In his novel *To a God Unknown*, Steinbeck shows a man who chooses a mossy rock as mediator between him and nature; in *The Cat*, Colette describes a young husband who settles his love on his favorite female cat because this gentle wild animal enables him to have a grasp on the sensual universe that his woman companion cannot give. The Other can be embodied in the sea and the mountain just as well as in the woman; they provide man with the same passive and unexpected resistance that allows him to accomplish himself; they are a refusal to conquer, a prey to possess. If the sea and the mountain are woman, it is because woman is also the sea and the mountain for the lover.[14]

But not just any woman can play the role of mediator between man and the world; man is not satisfied with finding sexual organs complementary to his own in his partner. She must embody the wondrous blossoming of life while concealing its mysterious disturbances at the same time. First of all, she has to have youth and health, for man cannot be enraptured in his embrace of a living thing unless he forgets that all life is inhabited by death. And he desires still more: that his beloved be beautiful. The ideal of feminine beauty is variable; but some requirements remain constant; one of them is that since woman is destined to be possessed, her body has to provide the inert and passive qualities of an object. Virile beauty is the body's adaptation to active functions such as strength, agility, flexibility, and the manifestation of a transcendence animating a flesh that must never collapse into itself. The only symmetry to be found in the feminine ideal is in Sparta, Fascist Italy, and Nazi Germany, societies that destined woman for the state and not for the individual and that considered her exclusively as mother, with no place for eroticism. But when woman is delivered to the male as his property, he claims that her flesh be presented in its pure facticity. Her body is grasped not as the emanation of a subjectivity but as a thing weighted in its immanence; this body must not radiate to the rest of

---

14. The sentence by Samivel, quoted by Bachelard in *Earth and Reveries of Will*, is telling: "I had ceased, little by little, to regard the mountains crouching in a circle at my feet as foes to vanquish, as females to trample underfoot, or trophies to provide myself and others proof of my own worth." The mountain/woman ambivalence comes across in the common idea of "foes to vanquish," "trophies," and "proof of my own worth."

This reciprocity can be seen, for example, in these two poems by Senghor:

> *Naked woman, dark woman*
> *Ripe fruit with firm flesh, dark raptures of black wine,*
> *Mouth that gives music to my mouth*
> *Savanna of clear horizons, savanna quivering to the fervent caress*
> *Of the East Wind . . .*

And:

> *Oho! Congo, lying on your bed of forests, queen of subdued Africa.*
> *May the mountain phalluses hold high your pavilion*
> *For you are woman by my head, by my tongue, You are woman by my belly.*

the world, it must not promise anything but itself: its desire has to be stopped. The most naive form of this requirement is the Hottentot ideal of the steatopygous Venus, as the buttocks are the part of the body with the fewest nerve endings, where the flesh appears as a given without purpose. The taste of people from the East for fleshy women is similar; they love the absurd luxury of this fatty proliferation that is not enlivened by any project, that has no other meaning than to be there.[15] Even in civilizations of a more subtle sensibility, where notions of form and harmony come into play, breasts and buttocks were prized objects because of the gratuitousness and contingency of their development. Customs and fashions were often applied to cut the feminine body from its transcendence: the Chinese woman with bound feet could barely walk, the Hollywood star's painted nails deprived her of her hands; high heels, corsets, hoops, farthingales, and crinolines were meant less to accentuate the woman's body's curves than to increase the body's powerlessness. Weighted down by fat or on the contrary so diaphanous that any effort is forbidden to it, paralyzed by uncomfortable clothes and rites of propriety, the body thus appeared to man as his thing. Makeup and jewels were also used for this petrification of the body and face. The function of dress and ornaments is highly complex; for some primitives, it had a sacred character; but its most usual role was to complete woman's metamorphosis into an idol. An equivocal idol: man wanted her erotic, for her beauty to be part of that of flowers and fruits; but she also had to be smooth, hard, eternal like a stone. The role of dress is both to link the body more closely to and to wrest it away from nature, to give a necessarily set artifice to palpitating life. Woman was turned into plant, panther, diamond, or mother-of-pearl by mingling flowers, furs, precious stones, shells, and feathers on her body; she perfumed herself so as to smell of roses and lilies: but feathers, silk, pearls, and perfumes also worked to hide the animal rawness from its flesh and odor. She painted her mouth and her cheeks to acquire a mask's immobile solidity; her gaze was imprisoned in the thickness of kohl and mascara, it was no longer anything but her eyes' shimmering ornamentation; braided, curled, or sculpted, her hair lost its troublesome vegetal mystery. In the embellished woman,

15. "Hottentot women, in whom steatopygia is neither as developed nor as consistent as in Bushman women, think this body type is aesthetically pleasing and starting in childhood massage their daughters' buttocks to develop them. Likewise, the artificial fattening of women, a real stuffing by two means, immobility and abundant ingestion of specific foods, especially milk, is found in various regions of Africa. It is still practiced by rich Arab and Jewish city dwellers in Algeria, Tunisia, and Morocco" (Luquet, "Vénus des cavernes," *Journal de Psychologie,* 1934).

Nature was present but captive, shaped by a human will in accordance with man's desire. Woman was even more desirable when nature was shown off to full advantage and more rigorously subjugated: the sophisticated woman has always been the ideal erotic object. And the taste for a more natural beauty is often a specious form of sophistication. Rémy de Gourmont wanted women's hair to be loose, free as the streams and prairie grass: but it is on Veronica Lake's hair that the waves of water and wheat could be caressed, not on a mop of hair totally left to nature. The younger and healthier a woman is and the more her new and glossy body seems destined for eternal freshness, the less useful is artifice; but the carnal weakness of this prey that man takes and its ominous deterioration always have to be hidden from him. It is also because he fears contingent destiny, because he dreams her immutable and necessary, that man looks for the idea's exactitude on woman's face, body, and legs. In primitive people, this idea is the perfection of the popular type: a thick-lipped race with a flat nose forged a thick-lipped Venus with a flat nose; later, the canons of a more complex aesthetics would be applied to women. But in any case, the more the traits and proportions of a woman seemed contrived, the more she delighted the heart of man because she seemed to escape the metamorphosis of natural things. The result is this strange paradox that by desiring to grasp nature, but transfigured, in woman, man destines her to artifice. She is not only physis but just as much anti-physis; and not only in the civilization of electric permanents, hair waxing, latex girdles, but also in the country of African lip-disk women, in China, and everywhere on earth. Swift denounced this mystification in his famous ode to Celia; he railed against the coquette's paraphernalia, pointing out with disgust her body's animal servitudes; he was doubly wrong to become indignant; because man wants woman at the same time to be animal and plant and that she hide behind a fabricated armature; he loves her emerging from the waves and from a high-fashion house, naked and dressed, naked beneath her clothes, exactly as he finds her in the human universe. The city dweller seeks animality in woman; but for the young peasant doing his military service, the brothel embodies the magic of the city. Woman is field and pasture but also Babylonia.

However, here is the first lie, the first betrayal of woman: of life itself, which, even clothed in the most attractive forms, is still inhabited by the ferments of old age and death. The very use man makes of her destroys her most precious qualities; weighed down by childbirth, she loses her sexual attraction; even sterile, the passage of time is enough to alter her charms. Disabled, ugly, or old, woman repels. She is said to be withered, faded, like a plant. Man's decrepitude is obviously also frightful; but normal man does not experience other men as flesh; he has only an abstract solidarity with these autonomous and foreign bodies. It is on woman's body, this body meant for him, that man significantly feels the flesh's deterioration. It is through the male's hostile eyes that Villon's "once beautiful courtesan" contemplates her body's degradation. Old and ugly women not only are objects without assets but also provoke hatred mixed with fear. They embody the disturbing figure of Mother, while the charms of the Wife have faded away.

But even the Wife was a dangerous prey. Demeter survives in Venus emerging from the waters, fresh foam, the blond harvest; appropriating woman for himself through the pleasure he derives from her, man awakens in her the suspicious powers of fertility; it is the same organ he penetrates that produces the child. This explains why man in all societies is protected against the feminine sex's threats by so many taboos. There is no reciprocity as woman has nothing to fear from the male; his sex is considered secular, profane. The phallus can be raised to the dignity of a god: there is no element of terror in worshipping it, and in daily life woman does not have to be defended against it mystically; it is simply propitious for her. It also has to be pointed out that in many matriarchies, sexuality is very free; but this is only during woman's childhood, in her early youth, when coitus is not linked to the idea of generation. Malinowski is surprised that young people who sleep together freely in the "house of the unmarried" show off their love lives so readily; the explanation is that an unmarried daughter is considered unable to bear a child and the sexual act is merely a quiet and ordinary pleasure. On the contrary, once married, her spouse cannot give her any public sign of affection, nor touch her, and any allusion to their intimate relations is sacrilegious; she then has to be part of the formidable essence of mother, and coitus becomes a sacred act. From then on it is surrounded by taboos and precautions. Intercourse is forbidden when cultivating the earth, sowing, and planting: in this case fertilizing forces necessary for the harvests' prosperity cannot be wasted in inter-individual relations; respect for powers associated with fertility enjoins such relations to be economized. But on most occasions, chastity protects the spouse's virility; it is demanded when man goes off fishing or hunting and above all when he is preparing for war; in the union with woman, the male principle weakens, and he has to avoid intercourse whenever he needs the totality of his forces. It has been wondered if the horror man feels for woman comes from that inspired by sexuality in general, or vice versa. We have seen that in Leviticus, in particular, wet dreams are considered a stain even though woman has nothing to do with them. And in our modern societies, masturbation is considered a danger and a sin; many children and young boys who indulge in it suffer terrible anxieties because of it. Society and parents above all make solitary pleasure a vice; but more than one young boy has been spontaneously frightened by his first ejaculations: blood or sperm, any flow of one's own substance seems worrying; it is one's life, one's mana, that is running out. However, even if subjectively man can go through erotic experiences where woman is not present, she is objectively involved in his sexuality: as Plato said in the myth of the androgynes, the male organism presupposes the woman's. He discovers woman in discovering his own sex, even if she is not given to him in flesh and blood, nor in image; and inversely, woman is fearsome inasmuch as she embodies sexuality. The immanent and transcendent aspects of living experience can never be separated: what I fear or desire is always an avatar of my own existence, but nothing comes to me except through what is not my self. The nonself is involved in wet dreams, in erection, and if not in the precise figure of woman, at least in Nature and Life: the individual feels possessed by a foreign magic. Likewise, his ambivalence toward women is seen in his attitude toward his own sex organ; he is proud, he laughs about it, he is embarrassed by it. The little boy defiantly compares his penis with his friends'; his first erection fills him with pride and frightens him at the same time. The adult man looks upon his sex organ as a symbol of transcendence and power; he is as proud of it as a muscle and at the same time as a magical grace: it is a freedom rich with the whole contingence of the given, a given freely desired; this is the contradictory aspect that enchants him; but he suspects the trap in it; this sex organ by which he claims to assert himself does not obey him; full of unassuaged desires, arising unexpectedly, sometimes relieving itself in dreams, it manifests a suspicious and capricious vitality. Man claims to make Spirit triumph over Life, activity over passivity; his consciousness keeps nature at a distance, his will shapes it, but in the figure of his sex organ he rediscovers life, nature, and passivity in himself. "The sexual parts are the real center of the will and the opposite pole is the brain," wrote Schopenhauer. What he called will is attachment to life, which is suffering and death, while the brain is thought that separates itself from life while representing it: sexual shame according to him is what we feel about our stupid carnal stubbornness. Even if the pessimism of his theories is rejected, he is right to see the expression of man's duality in the sex-brain opposition. As a subject he posits the world, and, remaining outside the universe he posits, he makes himself the lord of it; if he grasps himself as flesh, as sex, he is no longer autonomous consciousness, transparent freedom: he is engaged in the world, a limited and perishable object; and it is undoubtedly true that the generative act goes beyond the body's limits: but he constitutes them at the very same instant. The penis, father of generations, is symmetrical to the maternal womb; grown from a fattened germ in woman's womb, man is the bearer of germs himself, and by this seed that gives life, it is also his own life that is disavowed. "The birth of children is the death of parents," said Hegel. Ejaculation is the promise of death, it affirms the species over the individual; the existence of the sex organ and its activity negate the subject's proud singularity. The sex organ is a focus of scandal because of this contestation of spirit over life. Man exalts the phallus in that he grasps it as transcendence and activity, as a means of appropriation of the other; but he is ashamed when he sees in it only passive flesh through which he is the plaything of Life's obscure forces. This shame is often disguised as irony. The sex organ of others draws laughter easily; but because the erection looks like a planned move-ment and yet is undergone, it often looks ridiculous; and the simple men-tion of genital organs provokes glee. Malinowski says that for the wild people among whom he lived, just mentioning the word for these "shame-ful parts" made them laugh uncontrollably; many crude or saucy jokes are not much more than rudimentary puns on these words. For some primitive peoples, during the days devoted to weeding out gardens, women had the right to brutally rape any stranger that dared to come into the village; attacking him all together, they often left him half-dead: the tribesmen laughed at this exploit; by this rape, the victim was constituted as passive and dependent flesh; he was possessed by the women and through them by their husbands, while in normal coitus man wants to affirm himself as possessor.

But this is where he will experience the ambiguity of his carnal condi-tion most obviously. He takes pride in his sexuality only to the extent that it is a means of appropriation of the Other: and this dream of possession only ends in failure. In authentic possession, the other as such is abolished, it is consumed and destroyed: only the sultan of *The Thousand and One Nights* has the power to cut off his mistresses' heads when dawn withdraws them from his bed; woman survives man's embraces, and she is thus able to escape from him; as soon as he opens his arms, his prey once again becomes foreign to him; here she is new, intact, completely ready to be possessed by a new lover in just as ephemeral a way. One of the male's dreams is to "brand" woman so that she remains his forever; but even the most arrogant male knows only too well that he will never leave her anything more than memories, and the most passionate images are cold compared with real sensation. A whole literature has denounced this failure. It is made objec-tive in the woman, who is called fickle and treacherous because her body destines her to man in general and not to a particular man. Her betrayal is even more perfidious: it is she who turns the lover into a prey. Only a body can touch another body; the male masters the desired flesh only by becoming flesh himself; Eve is given to Adam for him to accomplish his transcendence in her, and she draws him into the night of immanence; the mother forges the obscure wrapping for her son from which he now wants to escape, while the mistress encloses him in this opaque clay through the vertigo of pleasure. He wanted to possess: but here he is, possessed himself. Odor, damp, fatigue, boredom: a whole literature describes this dreary passion of a consciousness become flesh. Desire often contains an element of disgust and returns to disgust when it is assuaged. "*Post coïtum homo animal triste.*"* "The flesh is sad." And yet man has not even found definitive reassurance in his lover's arms. Soon his desire is reborn; and often it is the desire not only for woman in general but for this specific woman. She wields a singularly troubling power. Because in his own body man does not feel the sexual need except as a general one similar to hunger or thirst without a particular object, the bond that links him to this specific feminine body is forged by the Other. The link is mysterious like the foul and fertile womb of his roots, a sort of passive force: it is magic. The hackneyed vocabulary of serialized novels where the woman is described as an enchantress or a mermaid who fascinates man and bewitches him reflects the oldest and most universal of myths. Woman is devoted to magic. Magic, said Alain, is the spirit lurking in things; an action is magic when it emanates from a passivity instead of being produced by an agent; men have always considered woman precisely as the immanence of the given; if she produces harvests and children, it is not because she wills it; she is not subject, transcendence, or creative power, but an object charged with fluids. In societies where man worships such mysteries, woman, because of these qualities, is associated with religion and venerated as a priestess; but when he struggles to make society triumph over nature, reason over life, will over inert fact, woman is regarded as a sorceress. The difference between the priest and the magician is well-known: the former dominates and directs the forces he has mastered in keeping with the gods and laws, for the good of the community, on behalf of all its members, while the magician operates outside society, against the gods and laws, according to his own passions. But woman is not fully integrated into the world of men; as other, she counters them; it is natural for her to use the strengths she possesses, not to spread the hold of transcendence across the community of men and into the future, but, being separate and opposed, to draw males into the solitude of separation, into the darkness of immanence. She is the mermaid

---

* Most likely: *Post coïtum omne animal triste.* ("All animals are sad after sex.")—TRANS.

whose songs dashed the sailors against the rocks; she is Circe, who turned her lovers into animals, the water sprite that attracted the fisherman to the depths of the pools. The man captivated by her spell loses his will, his project, his future; he is no longer a citizen but flesh, slave to his desires, he is crossed out of the community, enclosed in the instant, thrown passively from torture to pleasure; the perverse magician pits passion against duty, the present against the unity of time, she keeps the traveler far from home, she spreads forgetfulness. In attempting to appropriate the Other, man must remain himself; but with the failure of impossible possession, he tries to become this other with whom he fails to unite; so he alienates himself, he loses himself, he drinks the potion that turns him into a stranger to himself, he falls to the bottom of deadly and roiling waters. The Mother dooms her son to death in giving him life; the woman lover draws her lover into relinquishing life and giving himself up to the supreme sleep. This link between Love and Death was pathetically illuminated in the Tristan legend, but it has a more primary truth. Born of flesh, man accomplishes himself in love as flesh, and flesh is destined to the grave. The alliance between Woman and Death is thus confirmed; the great reaper is the inverted figure of corn-growing fertility. But it is also the frightening wife whose skeleton appears under deceitful and tender flesh.[16]

What man thus cherishes and detests first in woman, lover as well as mother, is the fixed image of her animal destiny, the life essential to her existence, but that condemns her to finitude and death. From the day of birth, man begins to die: this is the truth that the mother embodies. In procreating, he guarantees the species against himself: this is what he learns in his wife's arms; in arousal and in pleasure, even before engendering, he forgets his singular self. Should he try to differentiate them, he still finds in both one fact alone, that of his carnal condition. He wants to accomplish it: he venerates his mother; he desires his mistress. But at the same time, he rebels against them in disgust, in fear.

An important text where we will find a synthesis of almost all these myths is Jean-Richard Bloch's *La nuit kurde* (*A Night in Kurdistan*), in which he describes young Saad's embraces of a much older but still beautiful woman during the plundering of a city:

The night abolished the contours of things and feelings alike. He was no longer clasping a woman to him. He was at last nearing the end of an interminable voyage that had been pursued since the

---

16. For example, in Prévert's ballet *Le rendez-vous* and in Cocteau's *Le jeune homme et la mort* (*The Young Man and Death*), Death is represented as a beloved young girl.

beginning of the world. Little by little he dissolved into an immensity that cradled him round without shape or end. All women were confused into one giant land, folded upon him, suave as desire burning in summer . . .

He, meanwhile, recognised with a fearful admiration the power that is enclosed within woman, the long, stretched, satin thighs, the knees like two ivory hills. When he traced the polished arch of the back, from the waist to the shoulders, he seemed to be feeling the vault that supports the world. But the belly ceaselessly drew him, a tender and elastic ocean, whence all life is born, and whither it returns, asylum of asylums, with its tides, horizons, illimitable surfaces.

Then he was seized with a rage to pierce that delightful envelope, and at last win to the very source of all this beauty. A simultaneous urge wrapped them one within the other. The woman now only lived to be cleaved by the share, to open to him her vitals, to gorge herself with the humours of the beloved. Their ecstasy was murderous. They came together as if with stabbing daggers . . .

He, man, the isolated, the separated, the cut off, was going to gush forth from out of his own substance, he, the first, would come forth from his fleshly prison and at last go free, matter and soul, into the universal matrix. To him was reserved the unheard of happiness of overpassing the limits of the creature, of dissolving into the one exaltation object and subject, question and answer, of annexing to being all that is not being, and of embracing, in an unextinguishable river, the empire of the unattainable . . .

But each coming and going of the bow awoke, in the precious instrument it held at its mercy, vibrations more and more piercing. Suddenly, a last spasm unloosed him from the zenith, and cast him down again to earth, to the mire.

As the woman's desire is not quenched, she imprisons her lover between her legs, and he feels in spite of himself his desire returning: she is thus an enemy power who grabs his virility, and while possessing her again, he bites her throat so deeply that he kills her. The cycle from mother to woman-lover to death meanders to a complex close.

There are many possible attitudes here for man depending on which aspect of the carnal drama he stresses. If a man does not think life is unique, if he is not concerned with his singular destiny, if he does not fear death, he will joyously accept his animality. For Muslims, woman is reduced to a state of abjection because of the feudal structure of society that does not allow recourse to the state against the family and because of religion, expressing this civilization's warrior ideal, that has destined man to death and stripped woman of her magic: What would anyone on earth, ready to dive without any hesitation into the voluptuous orgies of the Muhammadan paradise, fear? Man can thus enjoy woman without worrying or having to defend himself against himself or her. *The Thousand and One Nights* looks on her as a source of creamy delights much like fruits, jams, rich desserts, and perfumed oils. This sensual benevolence can be found today among many Mediterranean peoples: replete, not seeking immortality, the man from the Midi grasps Nature in its luxurious aspect, relishes women; by tradition he scorns them sufficiently so as not to grasp them as individuals: between the enjoyment of their bodies and that of sand and water there is not much difference for him; he does not experience the horror of the flesh either in them or in himself. In *Conversations in Sicily*, Vittorini recounts, with quiet amazement, having discovered the naked body of woman at the age of seven. Greek and Roman rationalist thought confirms this spontaneous attitude. Greek optimist philosophy went beyond Pythagorean Manichaeism; the inferior is subordinate to the superior and as such is useful to him: these harmonious ideologies show no hostility whatsoever to the flesh. Turned toward the heaven of Ideas or in toward the City or State, the individual thinking himself as nous or as a citizen thinks he has overcome his animal condition: whether he gives himself up to voluptuousness or practices asceticism, a woman firmly integrated into male society is only of secondary importance. It is true that rationalism has never triumphed totally and erotic experience remains ambivalent in these civilizations: rites, mythologies, and literature are testimony to that. But femininity's attractions and dangers manifest themselves there only in attenuated form. Christianity is what drapes woman anew with frightening prestige: one of the fears the rending of the unhappy consciousness takes for man is fear of the other sex. The Christian is separated from himself; the division of body and soul, of life and spirit, is consumed: original sin turns the body into the soul's enemy; all carnal links appear bad.[17] Man can be saved by being redeemed by Christ and turning toward the celestial kingdom; but at the beginning, he is no

---

17. Until the end of the twelfth century theologians—except Saint Anselm—thought, according to Saint Augustine's doctrine, that original sin was implied in the law of generation itself. "Concupiscence is a vice . . . human flesh born from it is sinful flesh," wrote Saint Augustine. And Saint Thomas: "Since sin, the union of the sexes, when accompanied by concupiscence, transmits original sin to the child."

more than rottenness; his birth dooms him not only to death but to damnation; divine grace can open heaven to him, but all avatars of his natural existence are cursed. Evil is an absolute reality; and flesh is sin. Since woman never stopped being Other, of course, male and female are never reciprocally considered flesh: the flesh for the Christian male is the enemy Other and is not distinguished from woman. The temptations of the earth, sex, and the devil are incarnated in her. All the Church Fathers emphasize the fact that she led Adam to sin. Once again, Tertullian has to be quoted: "Woman! You are the devil's gateway. You have convinced the one the devil did not dare to confront directly. It is your fault that God's Son had to die. You should always dress in mourning and rags." All Christian literature endeavors to exacerbate man's disgust for woman. Tertullian defines her as "*Templum aedificatum super cloacam.*"* Saint Augustine points out in horror the proximity of the sexual and excretory organs: "*Inter faeces et urinam nascimur.*"† Christianity's repugnance for the feminine body is such that it consents to doom its God to an ignominious death but saves him the stain of birth: the Council of Ephesus in the Eastern Church and the Lateran Council in the West affirm the virgin birth of Christ. The first Church Fathers—Origen, Tertullian, and Jerome—thought that Mary had given birth in blood and filth like other women; but the opinions of Saint Ambrose and Saint Augustine prevail. The Virgin's womb remained closed. Since the Middle Ages, the fact of having a body was considered an ignominy for woman. Science itself was paralyzed for a long time by this disgust. Linnaeus, in his treatise on nature, dismissed the study of woman's genital organs as "abominable." Des Laurens, the French doctor, dared to ask how "this divine animal full of reason and judgment that is called man can be attracted by these obscene parts of the woman, tainted by humors and placed shamefully at the lowest part of the trunk." Many other influences come into play along with Christian thought; and even this has more than one side; but in the puritan world, for example, hatred of the flesh still obtains; it is expressed in *Light in August,* by Faulkner; the hero's first sexual experiences are highly traumatic. In all literature, a young man's first sexual intercourse is often upsetting to the point of inducing vomiting; and if, in truth, such a reaction is very rare, it is not by chance that it is so often described. In puritan Anglo-Saxon countries in particular, woman stirs up more or less avowed terror in most adolescents and many men. This is quite true in France. Michel Leiris wrote in *L'âge d'homme* (*Manhood*): "I have a tendency to consider the feminine organ as

---

* "A temple built over a sewer."—TRANS.
† "We are born between shit and piss."—TRANS.

a dirty thing or a wound, not less attractive though for that, but dangerous in itself, as everything that is bloody, viscous, and contaminated." The idea of venereal maladies expresses these frights; woman is feared not because she gives these illnesses; it is the illnesses that seem abominable because they come from woman: I have been told about young men who thought that too frequent sexual relations caused gonorrhea. People also readily think that sexual intercourse makes man lose his muscular strength and mental lucidity, consumes his phosphorus, and coarsens his sensitivity. The same dangers threaten in masturbation; and for moral reasons society considers it even more harmful than the normal sexual function. Legitimate marriage and the desire to have children guard against the evil spells of eroticism. I have already said that the Other is implied in all sexual acts; and its face is usually woman's. Man experiences his own flesh's passivity the most strongly in front of her. Woman is vampire, ghoul, eater, drinker; her sex organ feeds gluttonously on the male sex organ. Some psychoanalysts have tried to give these imaginings scientific foundations: the pleasure woman derives from coitus is supposed to come from the fact that she symbolically castrates the male and appropriates his sex organ. But it would seem that these theories themselves need to be psychoanalyzed and that the doctors who invented them have projected onto them ancestral terrors.[18]

The source of these terrors is that in the Other, beyond any annexation, alterity remains. In patriarchal societies, woman kept many of the disquieting virtues she held in primitive societies. That explains why she is never left to Nature, why she is surrounded by taboos, purified by rites, and placed under the control of priests; man is taught never to approach her in her original nudity, but through ceremonies and sacraments that wrest her from the earth and flesh and metamorphose her into a human creature: thus the magic she possesses is channeled as lightning has been since the invention of lightning rods and electric power plants. It is even possible to use her in the group's interests: this is another phase of the oscillatory movement defining man's relationship to his female. He loves her because she is his, he fears her because she remains other; but it is as the feared other that he seeks to make her most deeply his: this is what will lead him to raise her to the dignity of a person and to recognize her as his peer.

———

Feminine magic was profoundly domesticated in the patriarchal family. Woman gave society the opportunity to integrate cosmic forces into it. In his work *Mitra-Varuna*, Dumézil points out that in India as in Rome, virile

---

18. We demonstrated that the myth of the praying mantis has no biological basis.

power asserts itself in two ways: in Varuna and Romulus, and in the Gandharvas and the Luperci, it is aggression, abduction, disorder, and hubris; thus, woman is the being to be ravished and violated; if the ravished Sabine women are sterile, they are whipped with goatskin straps, compensating for violence with more violence. But on the contrary, Mitra, Numa, the Brahman women, and the Flamen wives represent reasonable law and order in the city: so the woman is bound to her husband by a ritualistic marriage, and she collaborates with him to ensure his domination over all female forces of nature; in Rome, the *flamen dialis* resigns from his position if his wife dies. In Egypt as well, Isis, having lost her supreme power as Mother Goddess, remains nonetheless generous, smiling, benevolent, and obedient, Osiris's magnificent spouse. But when woman is thus man's partner, his complement, his other half, she is necessarily endowed with a consciousness and a soul; he could not so deeply depend on a being who would not participate in the human essence. It has already been seen that the Laws of Manu promised a legal wife the same paradise as her spouse. The more the male becomes individualized and claims his individuality, the more he will recognize an individual and a freedom in his companion. The Oriental man who is unconcerned with his own destiny is satisfied with a female who is his pleasure object; but Western man's dream, once elevated to consciousness of the singularity of his being, is to be recognized by a foreign and docile freedom. The Greek man cannot find the peer he wants in a woman who was prisoner of the gynaeceum: so he confers his love on male companions, whose flesh, like his own, is endowed with a consciousness and a freedom, or else he gives his love to hetaeras, whose independence, culture, and spirit made them near equals. But when circumstances permit, the wife best satisfies man's demands. The Roman citizen recognizes a person in the matron; in Cornelia or in Arria, he possesses his double. Paradoxically, it was Christianity that was to proclaim the equality of man and woman on a certain level. Christianity detests the flesh in her; if she rejects the flesh, she is, like him, a creature of God, redeemed by the Savior: here she can take her place beside males, among those souls guaranteed celestial happiness. Men and women are God's servants, almost as asexual as the angels, who, together with the help of grace, reject earth's temptations. If she agrees to renounce her animality, woman, from the very fact that she incarnated sin, will also be the most radiant incarnation of the triumph of the elect who have conquered sin.[19] Of course, the divine Savior who brings about Redemption is male; but humanity must cooperate in its own salvation, and perversely it will be called upon to manifest its submissive goodwill in its most humili-

---

19. This explains the privileged place she holds, for example, in Claudel's work (see pp. 237–246).

ated figure. Christ is God; but it is a woman, the Virgin Mother, who reigns over all human creatures. Yet only marginal sects restore the great goddesses' ancient privileges to the woman. The Church expresses and serves a patriarchal civilization where it is befitting for woman to remain annexed to man. As his docile servant, she will also be a blessed saint. Thus the image of the most perfected woman, propitious to men, lies at the heart of the Middle Ages: the face of the Mother of Christ is encircled in glory. She is the inverse figure of the sinner Eve; she crushes the serpent under her foot; she is the mediator of salvation, as Eve was of damnation.

It is as Mother that the woman was held in awe; through motherhood she has to be transfigured and subjugated. Mary's virginity has above all a negative value: she by whom the flesh has been redeemed is not carnal; she has been neither touched nor possessed. Neither was the Asiatic Great Mother assumed to have a husband: she had engendered the world and reigned over it alone; she could be lascivious by impulse, but her greatness as Mother was not diminished by imposed wifely servitudes. Likewise, Mary never experienced the stain connected with sexuality. Related to the woman warrior Minerva, she is an ivory tower, a citadel, an impregnable fortress. Like most Christian saints, the priestesses of antiquity were virgins: the woman devoted to good should be devoted with the splendor of her strength intact; she must conserve the principle of her femininity in its unbroken wholeness. One rejects in Mary her character as wife in order to more fully exalt in her the Woman-Mother. But she will be glorified only by accepting the subservient role assigned to her. "I am the handmaiden of the Lord." For the first time in the history of humanity, the mother kneels before her son; she freely recognizes her inferiority. The supreme masculine victory is consummated in the cult of Mary: it is the rehabilitation of woman by the achievement of her defeat. Ishtar, Astarte, and Cybele were cruel, capricious, and lustful; they were powerful; the source of death as well as life, in giving birth to men, they made them their slaves. With Christianity, life and death now depended on God alone, so man, born of the maternal breast, escaped it forever, and the earth gets only his bones; his soul's destiny is played out in regions where the mother's powers are abolished; the sacrament of baptism makes ceremonies that burned or drowned the placenta insignificant. There is no longer any place on earth for magic: God alone is king. Nature is originally bad, but powerless when countered with grace. Motherhood as a natural phenomenon confers no power. If woman wishes to overcome the original stain in herself, her only alternative is to bow before God, whose will subordinates her to man. And by this submission she can assume a new role in masculine mythology. As a vassal, she will be honored, whereas she was beaten and trampled underfoot when she saw herself as dominator or as long as she did not explicitly abdicate. She loses none of her primitive attributes; but their meanings change; from calamitous they become auspicious; black magic turns to white magic. As a servant, woman is entitled to the most splendid apotheosis.

And since she was subjugated as Mother, she will, as Mother first, be cherished and respected. Of the two ancient faces of maternity, modern man recognizes only the benevolent one. Limited in time and space, possessing only one body and one finite life, man is but one individual in the middle of a foreign Nature and History. Limited like him, similarly inhabited by the spirit, woman belongs to Nature, she is traversed by the infinite current of Life, she thus appears as the mediator between the individual and the cosmos. When the mother image became reassuring and holy, it is understandable that the man turned to her with love. Lost in nature, he seeks escape, but separated from her, he aspires to return to her. Solidly settled in the family and society, in accord with laws and customs, the mother is the very incarnation of the Good: the nature in which she participates becomes Good; she is no longer the spirit's enemy; and though she remains mysterious, it is a smiling mystery, like Leonardo da Vinci's Madonnas. Man does not wish to be woman, but he longs to wrap himself in everything that is, including this woman he is not: in worshipping his mother, he tries to appropriate her riches so foreign to him. To recognize himself as his mother's son, he recognizes the mother in him, integrating femininity insofar as it is a connection to the earth, to life, and to the past. In Vittorini's *Conversations in Sicily*, that is what the hero goes to find from his mother: his native land, its scents and its fruits, his childhood, his ancestors' past, traditions, and the roots from which his individual existence separated him. It is this very rootedness that exalts man's pride in going beyond; he likes to admire himself breaking away from his mother's arms to leave for adventure, the future, and war; this departure would be less moving if there were no one to try to hold him back: it would look like an accident, not a hard-won victory. And he also likes to know that these arms are ready to welcome him back. After the tension of action, the hero likes to taste the restfulness of immanence again, by his mother's side: she is refuge, slumber; by her hand's caress he sinks into the bosom of nature, lets himself be lulled by the vast flow of life as peacefully as in the womb or in the tomb. And if tradition has him die calling on his mother, it is because under the maternal gaze death itself, like birth, is tamed, symmetrical with birth, indissolubly linked with his whole carnal life. The mother remains connected to death as in ancient Parcae mythology; it is she who buries the dead, who mourns. But her role is precisely to integrate death with life, with society, with the good. And so the cult of "heroic mothers" is systematically encouraged: if society persuades mothers to surrender their sons to death, then it thinks it can claim the right to assassinate them. Because of the mother's hold on her sons, it is useful for society to make her part of it: this is why the mother is showered with signs of respect, why she is endowed with all virtues, why a religion is created around her from which it is forbidden to stray under severe risk of sacrilege and blasphemy; she is made the guardian of morality; servant of man, servant of the powers that be, she fondly guides her children along fixed paths. The more resolutely optimistic the collectivity and the more docilely it accepts this loving authority, the more transfigured the mother will be. The American "Mom" has become the idol described by Philip Wylie in *Generation of Vipers*, because the official American ideology is the most stubbornly optimistic. To glorify the mother is to accept birth, life, and death in both their animal and their social forms and to proclaim the harmony of nature and society. Auguste Comte makes the woman the divinity of future Humanity because he dreams of achieving this synthesis. But this is also why all rebels assail the figure of the mother; in holding her up to ridicule, they reject the given claims supposedly imposed on them through the female guardian of morals and laws.[20]

---

20. One ought to quote Michel Leiris's poem "La mère" (The Mother) in its entirety. Here are some typical passages:

The mother in black, mauve, violet—robber of nights—that's the sorceress whose hidden industry brings you into the world, the one who rocks you, coddles you, coffins you, when she doesn't abandon her curled-up body—one last little toy—into your hands, that lay it nicely into the coffin . . .

The mother—blind statue, fate set up in the middle of the inviolate sanctuary—she's nature caressing you, the wind censing you, the whole world that penetrates you, lifts you sky-high (borne on multiple spires) and rots you . . .

The mother—young or old, beautiful or ugly, merciful or obstinate—it's the carica-ture, the monster jealous woman, the fallen Prototype—assuming the Idea (a wrinkled Pythia perched on the tripod of her austere capital letter)—is but a parody of quick, light, iridescent thoughts . . .

The mother—hip round or dry, breast atremble or firm—is the decline promised to all women right from the start, the progressive crumbling of the rock that sparkles beneath the menstrual flood, the slow burying—under the sand of the old desert—of the luxuriant caravan heaped with beauty.

The mother—angel of spying death, of the embracing universe, of the love time's wave throws back—she's the shell with its senseless graphics (a sure sign of poison) to toss into the deep pools, generator of circles for the oblivious waters.

The mother—somber puddle, eternally in mourning for everything and ourselves—she is the misty pestilence that shimmers and bursts, expanding its great bestial shadow (shame of flesh and milk) bubble by bubble, a stiff veil that a bolt of lightning as yet unborn ought to rend . . .

Will it ever occur to any of these innocent bitches to drag themselves barefoot through the centuries as pardon for this crime: having given birth to us? [Translated by Beverley Bie Brahic.—Trans.]

The aura of respect around the Mother and the taboos that surround her repress the hostile disgust that mingles spontaneously with the carnal tenderness she inspires. However, lurking below the surface, the latent horror of motherhood survives. In particular, it is interesting that in France since the Middle Ages, a secondary myth has been forged, freely expressing this repugnance: that of the Mother-in-Law. From fabliau to vaudeville, there are no taboos on man's ridicule of motherhood in general through his wife's mother. He hates the idea that the woman he loves was conceived: the mother-in-law is the clear image of the decrepitude that she doomed her daughter to by giving her life, and her obesity and her wrinkles forecast the obesity and wrinkles that the future so sadly prefigures for the young bride; at her mother's side she is no longer an individual but an example of a species; she is no longer the desired prey or the cherished companion, because her individual existence dissolves into universality. Her individuality is mockingly contested by generalities, her spirit's autonomy by her being rooted in the past and in the flesh: this is the derision man objectifies as a grotesque character; but through the rancor of his laughter, he knows that the fate of his wife is the same for all human beings; it is his own. In every country, legends and tales have also personified the cruel side of motherhood in the stepmother. She is the cruel mother who tries to kill Snow White. The ancient Kali with the necklace of severed heads lives on in the mean stepmother—Mme Fichini whipping Sophie throughout Mme de Ségur's books.

Yet behind the sainted Mother crowds the coterie of white witches who provide man with herbal juices and stars' rays: grandmothers, old women with kind eyes, good-hearted servants, sisters of charity, nurses with magical hands, the sort of mistress Verlaine dreamed of:

Sweet, pensive and dark and surprised at nothing
And who will at times kiss you on the forehead like a child.

They are ascribed the pure mystery of knotted vines, of freshwater; they dress and heal wounds; their wisdom is life's silent wisdom, they understand without words. In their presence man forgets his pride; he understands the sweetness of yielding and becoming a child, because between him and her there is no struggle for prestige: he could not resent the inhuman virtues of nature; and in their devotion, the wise initiates who care for him recognize they are his servants; he submits to their benevolent powers because he knows that while submitting to them, he remains their master. Sisters, childhood girlfriends, pure young girls, and all future mothers belong to this blessed troupe. And the wife herself, when her erotic magic fades, is regarded by many men less as a lover than as the mother of their children. Once the mother is sanctified and servile, she can safely be with a woman friend, she being also sanctified and submissive. To redeem the mother is to redeem the flesh, and thus carnal union and the wife.

Deprived of her magic weapons by nuptial rites, economically and socially dependent on her husband, the "good wife" is man's most precious treasure. She belongs to him so profoundly that she shares the same nature with him: "*Ubi tu Gaius, ego Gaia*"; she has his name and his gods, and she is his responsibility: he calls her his other half. He takes pride in his wife as in his home, his land, his flocks, and his wealth, and sometimes even more; through her he displays his power to the rest of the world: she is his yardstick and his earthly share. For Orientals, a wife should be fat: everyone sees that she is well fed and brings respect to her master.[21] A Muslim is all the more respected if he possesses a large number of flourishing wives. In bourgeois society, one of woman's assigned roles is *to represent:* her beauty, her charm, her intelligence, and her elegance are outward signs of her husband's fortune, as is the body of his car. If he is rich, he covers her with furs and jewels. If he is poorer, he boasts of her moral qualities and her housekeeping talents; most deprived, he feels he owns something earthly if he has a wife to serve him; the hero of *The Taming of the Shrew* summons all his neighbors to show them his authority in taming his wife. A sort of King Candaules resides in all men: he exhibits his wife because he believes she displays his own worth.

But woman does more than flatter man's social vanity; she allows him a more intimate pride; he delights in his domination over her; superimposed on the naturalistic images of the plowshare cutting furrows are more spiritual symbols concerning the wife as a person; the husband "forms" his wife not only erotically but also spiritually and intellectually; he educates her, impresses her, puts his imprint on her. One of the daydreams he enjoys is the impregnation of things by his will, shaping their form, penetrating their substance: the woman is par excellence the "clay in his hands" that passively lets itself be worked and shaped, resistant while yielding, permitting masculine activity to go on. A too-plastic material wears out by its softness; what is precious in woman is that something in her always escapes all embraces; so man is master of a reality that is all the more worthy of being mastered as it surpasses him. She awakens in him a being heretofore ignored whom he recognizes with pride as himself; in their safe marital

21. See note 15, p. 177.

orgies he discovers the splendor of his animality: he is the Male; and woman, correlatively, the female, but this word sometimes takes on the most flattering implications: the female who broods, who nurses, who licks her young, who defends them, and who risks her life to save them is an example for humans; with emotion, man demands this patience and devotion from his companion; again it is Nature, but imbued with all of the virtues useful to society, family, and the head of the family, virtues he knows how to keep locked in his home. A common desire of children and men is to uncover the secret hidden inside things; but in this, the matter can be deceptive: a doll ripped apart with her stomach outside has no more interiority; the interior of living things is more impenetrable; the female womb is the symbol of immanence, of depth; it delivers its secrets in part as when, for example, pleasure shows on a woman's face, but it also holds them in; man catches life's obscure palpitations in his house without the mystery being destroyed by possession. In the human world, woman transposes the female animal's functions: she maintains life, she reigns over the zones of immanence; she transports the warmth and the intimacy of the womb into the home; she watches over and enlivens the dwelling where the past is kept, where the future is presaged; she engenders the future generation, and she nourishes the children already born; thanks to her, the existence that man expends throughout the world by his work and his activity is re-centered by delving into her immanence: when he comes home at night, he is anchored to the earth; the wife assures the days' continuity; whatever risks he faces in the outside world, she guarantees the stability of his meals and sleep; she repairs whatever has been damaged or worn out by activity: she prepares the tired worker's food, she cares for him if he is ill, she mends and washes. And within the conjugal universe that she sets up and perpetuates, she brings in the whole vast world: she lights the fires, puts flowers in vases, and domesticates the emanations of sun, water, and earth. A bourgeois writer cited by Bebel summarizes this ideal in all seriousness as follows: "Man wants not only someone whose heart beats for him, but whose hand wipes his brow, who radiates peace, order, and tranquillity, a silent control over himself and those things he finds when he comes home every day; he wants someone who can spread over everything the indescribable perfume of woman who is the vivifying warmth of home life."

It is clear how spiritualized the figure of woman became with the birth of Christianity; the beauty, warmth, and intimacy that man wishes to grasp through her are no longer tangible qualities; instead of being the summation of the pleasurable quality of things, she becomes their soul; deeper than carnal mystery, her heart holds a secret and pure presence that reflects truth in the world. She is the soul of the house, the family, and the home, as well as larger groups: the town, province, or nation. Jung observes that cities have always been compared to the Mother because they hold their citizens in their bosoms: this is why Cybele was depicted crowned with towers; for the same reason the term "mother country" is used and not only because of the nourishing soil; rather, a more subtle reality found its symbol in the woman. In the Old Testament and in the Apocalypse, Jerusalem and Babylon are not only mothers: they are also wives. There are virgin cities and prostitute cities such as Babel and Tyre. France too has been called "the eldest daughter" of the Church; France and Italy are Latin sisters. Woman's function is not specified, but femininity is, in statues that represent France, Rome, and Germany and those on the Place de la Concorde that evoke Strasbourg and Lyon. This assimilation is not only allegoric: it is affectively practiced by many men.[22] Many a traveler would ask woman for the key to the countries he visits: when he holds an Italian or Spanish woman in his arms, he feels he possesses the fragrant essence of Italy or Spain. "When I come to a new city, the first thing I do is to visit a brothel," said a journalist. If a cinnamon hot chocolate can make Gide discover the whole of Spain, all the more reason kisses from exotic lips will bring to a lover a country with its flora and fauna, its traditions, and its culture. Woman is the summation neither of its political institutions nor of its economic resources; but she is the incarnation of carnal flesh and mystical mana. From Lamartine's *Graziella* to Loti's novels and Morand's short stories, the foreigner is seen as trying to appropriate the soul of a region through women. Mignon, Sylvie, Mireille, Colomba, and Carmen uncover the most intimate truth about Italy, Valois, Provence, Corsica, or Andalusia. When the Alsatian Frederique falls in love with Goethe, the Germans take it as a symbol of Germany's annexation; likewise, when Colette Baudoche refuses to marry a German, Barrès sees it as Alsace refusing Germany. He personifies Aigues-Mortes and a whole refined and frivolous civilization in the sole person of Berenice; she represents the sensibility of the writer himself. Man recognizes his own mysterious double in her, she who is the soul of nature, cities, and the universe; man's soul is Psyche, a woman.

---

22. It is allegoric in Claudel's shameful recent poem, where Indochina is called "That yellow girl"; it is affectionate, by contrast, in the verses of the black poet [Guy Tirolien]:

> *Soul of the black country where the elders sleep*
> *live and speak*
> *tonight*
> *in the uneasy strength along your hollow loins.*

Psyche has feminine traits in Edgar Allan Poe's "Ulalume":

Here once, through an alley Titanic,
Of cypress, I roamed with my Soul—
Of cypress, with Psyche, my Soul . . .
Thus I pacified Psyche and kissed her . . .
And I said—"What is written, sweet sister,
On the door of this legended tomb?"

And Mallarmé, at the theater, in a dialogue with "a soul, or else our idea" (that is, divinity present in man's spirit) called it "a most exquisite abnormal lady [*sic*]."[23]

Thing of harmony, ME, a dream,
Firm, flexible feminine, whose silences lead
To pure acts! . . .
Thing of mystery, ME. *

Such is Valéry's way of hailing her. The Christian world substituted less carnal presences for nymphs and fairies; but homes, landscapes, cities, and individuals themselves are still haunted by an impalpable femininity.

This truth buried in the night of things also shines in the heavens; perfect immanence, the Soul is at the same time the transcendent, the Idea. Not only cities and nations but also entities and abstract institutions are cloaked in feminine traits: the Church, the Synagogue, the Republic, and Humanity are women, as well as Peace, War, Liberty, the Revolution, Victory. Man feminizes the ideal that he posits before him as the essential Other, because woman is the tangible figure of alterity; this is why almost all the allegories in language and in iconography are women.[24] Soul and Idea, woman is also the mediator between them: she is the Grace that leads the Christian to God, she is Beatrice guiding Dante to the beyond, Laura beckoning Petrarch to the highest peaks of poetry. She appears in all doctrines assimilating Nature to Spirit as Harmony, Reason, and Truth. Gnostic sects made Wisdom a woman, Sophia; they attributed the world's redemption to her, and even its creation. So woman is no longer flesh, she is glorious

---

23. Jotted down at the theater.
* Translated by James Lawler.—TRANS.
24. Philology is rather mysterious on this question; all linguists recognize that the distribution of concrete words into gender is purely accidental. Yet in French most entities are feminine: beauty and loyalty, for example. And in German, most imported foreign words, *others*, are feminine: *die Bar*, for instance.

body; rather than trying to possess her, men venerate her for her untouched splendor; the pale dead of Edgar Allan Poe are as fluid as water, wind, or memory; for courtly love, for *les précieux*, and in all of the gallant tradition, woman is no longer an animal creature but rather an ethereal being, a breath, a radiance. Thus it is that the feminine Night's opacity is converted into transparence, and obscurity into purity, as in Novalis's texts:

> Thou, Night-inspiration, heavenly Slumber, didst come upon me—
> the region gently upheaved itself; over it hovered my unbound,
> newborn spirit. The mound became a cloud of dust—and through
> the cloud I saw the glorified face of my beloved.
>
> Dost thou also take a pleasure in us, dark Night? . . . Precious
> balm drips from thy hand out of its bundle of poppies. Thou
> upliftest the heavy-laden wings of the soul. Darkly and inexpress-
> ibly are we moved—joy-startled, I see a grave face that, tender and
> worshipful, inclines toward me, and, amid manifold entangled locks,
> reveals the youthful loveliness of the Mother . . . More heavenly
> than those glittering stars we hold the eternal eyes which the Night
> hath opened within us.

The downward attraction exercised by woman is inverted; she beckons man no longer earthward, but toward heaven.

> *The Eternal Feminine*
> *Leads us upward,*

proclaimed Goethe at the end of *Faust, Part Two.*

As the Virgin Mary is the most perfected image, the most widely venerated image of the regenerated woman devoted to the Good, it is interesting to see how she appears through literature and iconography. Here are passages from medieval litanies showing how fervent Christians addressed her:

> Most high Virgin, thou art the fertile Dew, the Fountain of Joy, the
> Channel of mercy, the Well of living waters that cools our passions.
>   Thou art the Breast from which God nurses orphans.
>   Thou art the Marrow, the Inside, the Core of all good.
>   Thou art the guileless Woman whose love never changes.
>   Thou art the Probatic Pool, the Remedy of lepers, the subtle
> Physician whose like is found neither in Salerno nor in Montpellier.

Thou art the Lady of healing hands, whose fingers so beautiful,
so white, so long, restore noses and mouths, give new eyes and ears.
Thou calmest passions, givest life to the paralyzed, givest strength to
the weak, risest the dead.

Most of the feminine attributes we have referred to are found in these
invocations. The Virgin is fertility, dew, and the source of life; many of the
images show her at the well, the spring, or the fountain; the expression
"Fountain of Life" was one of the most common; she was not a creator, but
she nourishes, she brings to the light of day what was hidden in the earth.
She is the deep reality hidden under the appearance of things: the Core, the
Marrow. Through her, passions are tempered; she is what is given to man
to satiate him. Wherever life is threatened, she saves and restores it: she
heals and strengthens. And because life emanates from God, she as the
intermediary between man and life is likewise the intermediary between
humanity and God. "The devil's gateway," said Tertullian. But transfigured, she is heaven's portal; paintings represent her opening the gate or the
window onto paradise or raising a ladder from earth to the heavens. More
straightforward, she becomes an advocate, pleading beside her Son for the
salvation of men: many tableaux of the Last Judgment have her baring her
breast in supplication to Christ in the name of her glorious motherhood.
She protects men's children in the folds of her cloak; her merciful love follows them through dangers over oceans and battlefields. She moves Divine
Justice in the name of charity: the "Virgins of the Scales" are seen, smiling,
tilting the balance where souls are weighed to the side of the Good.

This merciful and tender role is one of the most important of all those
granted to woman. Even integrated into society, the woman subtly exceeds
its boundaries because she possesses the insidious generosity of Life. This
distance between the males' intended constructions and nature's contingency seems troubling in some cases; but it becomes beneficial when the
woman, too docile to threaten men's work, limits herself to enriching and
softening their too sharp edges. Male gods represent Destiny; on the goddesses' side are found arbitrary benevolence and capricious favor. The
Christian God has the rigors of Justice; the Virgin has gentleness and charity. On earth, men are the defenders of laws, reason, and necessity; woman
knows the original contingency of man himself and of the necessity he
believes in; from this comes her supple generosity and the mysterious irony
that touches her lips. She gives birth in pain, she heals males' wounds, she
nurses the newborn and buries the dead; of man she knows all that offends
his pride and humiliates his will. While inclining before him and submitting flesh to spirit, she remains on the carnal borders of the spirit; and she

contests the sharpness of hard masculine architecture by softening the angles; she introduces free luxury and unforeseen grace. Her power over men comes from her tenderly recalling a modest consciousness of their authentic condition; it is the secret of her illusionless, painful, ironic, and loving wisdom. Even frivolity, whimsy, and ignorance are charming virtues in her because they thrive beneath and beyond the world where man chooses to live but where he does not want to feel confined. Confronted with arrested meaning and utilitarian instruments, she upholds the mystery of intact things; she brings the breath of poetry into city streets and plowed fields. Poetry attempts to capture that which exists above everyday prose: woman is an eminently poetic reality since man projects onto her everything he is not resolved to be. She incarnates the Dream; for man, the dream is the most intimate and the most foreign presence, what he does not want, what he does not do, which he aspires to but cannot attain; the mysterious Other who is profound immanence and far-off transcendence will lend him her traits. Thus it is that Aurélia visits Nerval in a dream and gives him the whole world in a dream. "She began to grow in a bright ray of light so that little by little the garden took on her form, and the flower beds and the trees became the rosettes and festoons of her dress; while her face and her arms impressed their shape upon the reddened clouds in the sky. I was losing sight of her as she was being transfigured, for she seemed to be vanishing into her own grandeur. 'Oh flee not from me!' I cried; 'for nature dies with you.' "

Being the very substance of man's poetic activities, woman is understandably his inspiration: the Muses are women. The Muse is the conduit between the creator and the natural springs he draws from. It is through woman's spirit deeply connected to nature that man will explore the depths of silence and the fertile night. The Muse creates nothing on her own; she is a wise sibyl making herself the docile servant of a master. Even in concrete and practical spheres, her counsel will be useful. Man wishes to attain the goals he sets without the help of his peers, and he would find another man's opinion inopportune; but he supposes that the woman speaks to him in the name of other values, in the name of a wisdom that he does not claim to have, more instinctive than his own, more immediately in accord with the real; these are the "intuitions" that Egeria uses to counsel and guide; he consults her without fear for his self-esteem as he consults the stars. This "intuition" even enters into business or politics: Apasia and Mme de Maintenon still have flourishing careers today.[25]

---

25. It goes without saying that they, of course, demonstrate intellectual qualities perfectly identical to those of men.

There is another function that man willingly entrusts to woman: being the purpose behind men's activities and the source of their decisions, she is also the judge of values. She is revealed as a privileged judge. Man dreams of an Other not only to possess her but also to be validated by her; to be validated by men who are his peers entails constant tension on his part: that is why he wants an outside view conferring absolute value on his life, on his undertakings, on himself. God's gaze is hidden, foreign, disquieting: even in periods of faith, only a few mystics felt its intensity. This divine role often devolved on the woman. Close to the man, dominated by him, she does not posit values that are foreign to him: and yet, as she is other, she remains exterior to the world of men and can thus grasp it objectively. It is she who will denounce the presence or absence of courage, of strength, and of beauty while confirming from the outside their universal value. Men are too busy in their cooperative or combative relations to be an audience for each other: they do not think about each other. Woman is removed from their activities and does not take part in their jousts and combats: her entire situation predestines her to play this role of onlooker. The chevalier jousts in tournaments for his lady; poets seek woman's approval. When Rastignac sets out to conquer Paris, he thinks first of *having* women, less about possessing their bodies than enjoying that reputation that only they are capable of creating for a man. Balzac projected the story of his own youth onto his young heroes: his education began with older mistresses; and the woman played the role of educator not only in *Le lys dans la vallée* (*The Lily in the Valley*); she was also assigned this role in *L'Education senti-mental* (*Sentimental Education*), in Stendhal's novels, and in numerous other coming-of-age novels. It has already been observed that the woman is both physis and anti-physis; she personifies Society as well as Nature; through her the civilization of a period and its culture is summed up, as can be seen in courtly poetry, in the *Decameron,* and in *L'Astrée;* she launches fashions, presides over salons, directs and reflects opinion. Fame and glory are women. "The crowd is woman," said Mallarmé. In the company of women the young man is initiated into the "world," and into this complex reality called life. She is one of the privileged prizes promised to heroes, adventurers, and individualists. In ancient times, Perseus saved Androm-eda, Orpheus went to rescue Eurydice from hades, and Troy fought to keep the beautiful Helen. Novels of chivalry recount barely any prowess other than delivering captive princesses. What would Prince Charming do if he did not wake up Sleeping Beauty, or lavish gifts on Donkey Skin? The myth of the king marrying a shepherdess flatters the man as much as the woman. The rich man needs to give, or else his useless wealth remains an abstract object: he needs someone to give to. The Cinderella myth, indulgently described by Philip Wylie in *Generation of Vipers*, thrives in prosperous countries; it is more powerful in America than anywhere else because men are more embarrassed by their wealth: How would they spend this money for which they work their whole lives if they did not dedicate it to a woman? Orson Welles, among others, personifies the imperialism of this kind of generosity in *Citizen Kane:* Kane chooses to smother an obscure singer with gifts and impose her on the public as a great opera singer all for his own affirmation of power; in France there are plenty of small-time Citizen Kanes. In another film, *The Razor's Edge*, when the hero returns from India having acquired absolute wisdom, the only use he finds for it is to rescue a prostitute. Clearly man wants woman's enslavement when fantasizing himself as a benefactor, liberator, or redeemer; if Sleeping Beauty is to be awakened, she must be sleeping; to have a captive princess, there must be ogres and dragons. And the greater man's taste for difficult undertakings, the greater his pleasure in granting woman independence. Conquering is more fascinating than rescuing or giving. The average Western male's ideal is a woman who freely submits to his domination, who does not accept his ideas without some discussion, but who yields to his reasoning, who intelligently resists but yields in the end. The tougher his pride, the more he relishes dangerous adventure; it is far better to tame Penthesilea than to marry a consenting Cinderella. The "warrior" loves danger and plays, says Nietzsche. "For that reason he wants woman, as the most dangerous plaything." The man who loves danger and play is not displeased to see woman change into an Amazon as long as he keeps the hope of subjugating her:[26] what he demands in his heart of hearts is that this struggle remain a game for him, while for woman it involves her very destiny: therein lies the true victory for man, liberator, or conqueror—that woman freely recognize him as her destiny.

Thus the expression "to have a woman" conceals a double meaning: the object's functions are not dissociated from those of the judge. The moment woman is viewed as a person, she can only be conquered with her consent; she must be won. Sleeping Beauty's smile fulfills Prince Charming: the captive princesses' tears of happiness and gratitude give meaning to the knights' prowess. On the other hand, her gaze is not a masculine,

---

26. American detective novels—or American-style ones—are a striking example. Peter Cheyney's heroes, for instance, are always grappling with an extremely dangerous woman, unmanageable for anyone but them: after a duel that unfolds all through the novel, she is finally overcome by Campion or Callaghan and falls into his arms.

abstract, severe one—it allows itself to be charmed. Thus heroism and poetry are modes of seduction: but in letting herself be seduced, the woman exalts heroism and poetry. She holds an even more essential privilege for the individualist: she appears to him not as the measure of universally recognized values but as the revelation of his particular merits and of his very being. A man is judged by his fellow men by what he does, objectively and according to general standards. But certain of his qualities, and among others his vital qualities, can only interest woman; his virility, charm, seduction, tenderness, and cruelty only pertain to her: if he sets a value on these most secret virtues, he has an absolute need of her; through her he will experience the miracle of appearing as an other, an other who is also his deepest self. Malraux admirably expresses what the individualist expects from the woman he loves in one of his texts. Kyo wonders:

> "We hear the voices of others with our ears, our own voices with our throats." Yes. "One hears his own life, too, with his throat, and those of others? . . . To others, I am what I have done." To May alone, he was not what he had done; to him alone, she was something altogether different from her biography. The embrace by which love holds beings together against solitude did not bring its relief to man; it brought relief only to the madman, to the incomparable monster, dear above all things, that every being is to himself and that he cherishes in his heart. Since his mother had died, May was the only being for whom he was not Kyo Gisors, but an intimate partner . . . Men are not my kind, they are those who look at me and judge me; my kind are those who love me and do not look at me, who love me in spite of everything, degradation, baseness, treason—me, and not what I have or shall do—who would love me as long as I would love myself—even to suicide.[27]

What makes Kyo's attitude human and moving is that it implies reciprocity and that he asks May to love him in his authenticity, not to send back an indulgent reflection of himself. For many men, this demand is diluted: instead of a truthful revelation, they seek a glowing image of admiration and gratitude, deified in the depths of a woman's two eyes. Woman has often been compared to water, in part because it is the mirror where the male Narcissus contemplates himself: he leans toward her, with

---

27. *La condition humaine* (*Man's Fate*).

good or bad faith. But in any case, what he wants from her is to be, outside of him, all that he cannot grasp in himself, because the interiority of the existent is only nothingness, and to reach himself, he must project himself onto an object. Woman is the supreme reward for him since she is his own apotheosis, a foreign form he can possess in the flesh. It is this "incomparable monster," himself, that he embraces when he holds in his arms this being who sums up the World and onto whom he has imposed his values and his laws. Uniting himself, then, with this other whom he makes his own, he hopes to reach himself. Treasure, prey, game, and risk, muse, guide, judge, mediator, mirror, the woman is the Other in which the subject surpasses himself without being limited, who opposes him without negating him; she is the Other who lets herself be annexed to him without ceasing to be the Other. And for this she is so necessary to man's joy and his triumph that if she did not exist, men would have had to invent her.

They did invent her.[28] But she also exists without their invention. This is why she is the failure of their dream at the same time as its incarnation. There is no image of woman that does not invoke the opposite figure as well: she is Life and Death, Nature and Artifice, Light and Night. Whatever the point of view, the same fluctuation is always found, because the inessential necessarily returns to the essential. In the figures of the Virgin Mother and of Beatrice lie Eve and Circe.

"Through woman," wrote Kierkegaard, "ideality enters into life and what would man be without her? Many a man has become a genius through a young girl, . . . but none has become a genius through the young girl he married . . .

"It is only by a negative relation to her that man is rendered productive in his ideal endeavors. Negative relations with woman can make us infinite . . . positive relations with woman make the man finite to a far greater extent."[29] This means that woman is necessary as long as she remains an Idea into which man projects his own transcendence; but she is detrimental as objective reality, existing for herself and limited to herself. In refusing to marry his fiancée, Kierkegaard believes he has established the only valid relation with woman. And he is right in the sense that the myth of woman posited as infinite Other immediately entails its opposite.

Because she is faux Infinite, Ideal without truth, she is revealed as finitude and mediocrity and thus as falsehood. That is how she appears in

---

28. "Man created woman—but what out of? Out of a rib of his God, of his 'ideal' " (Nietzsche, *Twilight of the Idols*).
29. *In Vino Veritas.*

Laforgue: throughout his work he expresses rancor against a mystification he blames on man as much as woman. Ophelia and Salome are nothing but "little women." Hamlet might think: "Thus would Ophelia have loved me as her 'possession' and because I was socially and morally superior to her girlish friends' possessions. And those little remarks about comfort and well-being that slipped out of her at lamp-lighting time!" Woman makes man dream, yet she is concerned with comfort and stews; one speaks to her about her soul, but she is only a body. And the lover, believing he is pursuing the Ideal, is the plaything of nature that uses all these mystifications for the ends of reproduction. She represents in reality the everydayness of life; she is foolishness, prudence, mediocrity, and ennui. Here is an example of how this is expressed, in a poem titled "Notre petite compagne" (Our Little Companion):

> I have the talent of every school
> I have souls for all tastes
> Pick the flower of my faces
> Drink my mouth and not my voice
> And do not look for more:
> Not even I can see clearly
> Our loves are not equal
> For me to hold out my hand
> You are merely naive males
> I am the eternal feminine!
> My fate loses itself in the Stars!
> I am the Great Isis!
> No one has lifted my veil
> Dream only of my oases . . .

Man succeeded in enslaving woman, but in doing so, he robbed her of what made possession desirable. Integrated into the family and society, woman's magic fades rather than transfigures itself; reduced to a servant's condition, she is no longer the wild prey incarnating all of nature's treasures. Since the birth of courtly love, it has been a commonplace that marriage kills love. Either too scorned, too respected, or too quotidian, the wife is no longer a sex object. Marriage rites were originally intended to protect man against woman; she becomes his property: but everything we possess in turn possesses us; marriage is a servitude for the man as well; he is thus caught in the trap laid by nature: to have desired a lovely young girl, the male must spend his whole life feeding a heavy matron, a dried-out old woman; the delicate jewel intended to embellish his existence becomes an odious burden: Xanthippe is one of those types of women that men have always referred to with the greatest horror.[30] But even when the woman is young, there is mystification in marriage because trying to socialize eroticism only succeeds in killing it. Eroticism implies a claim of the instant against time, of the individual against the collectivity; it affirms separation against communication; it rebels against all regulation; it contains a principle hostile to society. Social customs are never bent to fit the rigor of institutions and laws: love has forever asserted itself against them. In its sensual form it addresses young people and courtesans in Greece and Rome; both carnal and platonic, courtly love is always directed at another's wife. *Tristan* is the epic of adultery. The period around 1900 that re-creates the myth of the woman is one where adultery becomes the theme of all literature. Certain writers, like Bernstein, in the supreme defense of bourgeois institutions, struggle to reintegrate eroticism and love into marriage; but there is more truth in Porto-Riche's *Amoureuse* (*A Loving Wife*), which shows the incompatibility of these two types of values. Adultery can disappear only with marriage itself. For the aim of marriage is to immunize man against *his* own wife: but other women still have a dizzying effect on him; it is to them he will turn. Women are accomplices. For they rebel against an order that tries to deprive them of their weapons. So as to tear woman from nature, so as to subjugate her to man through ceremonies and contracts, she was elevated to the dignity of a human person; she was granted freedom. But freedom is precisely what escapes all servitude; and if it is bestowed on a being originally possessed by malevolent forces, it becomes dangerous. And all the more so as man stopped at half measures; he accepted woman into the masculine world only by making her a servant, in thwarting her transcendence; the freedom she was granted could only have a negative use; it only manifests itself in refusal. Woman became free only in becoming captive; she renounces this human privilege to recover her power as natural object. By day she treacherously plays her role of docile servant, but by night she changes into a kitten, a doe; she slips back into a siren's skin, or riding on her broomstick, she makes her satanic rounds. Sometimes she exercises her nocturnal magic on her own husband; but it is wiser to conceal her metamorphoses from her master; she chooses strangers as her prey; they have no rights over her, and she remains for them a plant, wellspring, star, or sorceress. So there she is, fated to infi-

---

30. As we have seen, it was the theme of many lamentations in Greece and during the Middle Ages.

delity: it is the only concrete form her freedom could assume. She is unfaithful over and above her own desires, her thoughts, or her consciousness; because she is seen as an object, she is given up to any subjectivity that chooses to take her; it is still not sure that locked in harems, hidden behind veils, she does not arouse desire in some person: to inspire desire in a stranger is already to fail her husband and society. But worse, she is often an accomplice in this fate; it is only through lies and adultery that she can prove that she is nobody's thing, that she refutes male claims on her. This is why man's jealousy is so quick to awaken, and in legends woman can be suspected without reason, condemned on the least suspicion, as were Geneviève de Brabant and Desdemona; even before any suspicion, Griselda is subjected to the worst trials; this tale would be absurd if the woman were not suspected beforehand; there is no case presented against her: it is up to her to prove her innocence. This is also why jealousy can be insatiable; it has already been shown that possession can never be positively realized; even if all others are forbidden to draw from the spring, no one possesses the thirst-quenching spring: the jealous one knows this well. In essence, woman is inconstant, just as water is fluid; and no human force can contradict a natural truth. Throughout all literature, in *The Thousand and One Nights* as in the *Decameron*, woman's ruses triumph over man's prudence. But it is more than simply individualistic will that makes him a jailer: society itself, in the form of father, brother, and husband, makes him responsible for the woman's behavior. Chastity is imposed upon her for economic and religious reasons, every citizen having to be authenticated as the son of his own father. But it is also very important to compel woman to conform exactly to the role society devolves on her. Man's double demand condemns woman to duplicity: he wants the woman to be his own and yet to remain foreign to him; he imagines her as servant and sorceress at the same time. But he admits publicly only to the former desire; the latter is a deceitful demand hidden in the depths of his heart and flesh; it goes against morality and society; it is evil like the Other, like rebel Nature, like the "bad woman." Man is not wholly devoted to the Good he constructs and attempts to impose; he maintains a shameful connivance with the Bad. But whenever the Bad imprudently dares to show its face openly, he goes to war against it. In the darkness of night, man invites woman to sin. But in the light of day, he rejects sin and her, the sinner. And women, sinners themselves in the mysteries of the bed, show all the more passion for the public worship of virtue. Just as in primitive society the male sex is secular and woman's is laden with religious and magic qualities, today's modern societies consider man's failings harmless peccadilloes; they are often lightly dismissed; even if he disobeys community laws, the man continues to belong to it; he is merely an *enfant terrible*, not a profound threat to the collective order. If, on the other hand, the woman deviates from society, she returns to Nature and the devil, she triggers uncontrollable and evil forces within the group. Fear has always been mixed with the blame for licentious behavior. If the husband cannot keep his wife virtuous, he shares her fault; his misfortune is, in society's eyes, a dishonor, and there are civilizations so strict that it is necessary to kill the criminal to dissociate him from her crime. In others, the complaisant husband will be punished by noisy demonstrations or led around naked on a donkey. And the community will take it upon itself to punish the guilty woman in his place: because she offended the group as a whole and not only her husband. These customs were particularly brutal in superstitious and mystical Spain, sensual and terrorized by the flesh. Calderón, Lorca, and Valle-Inclán made it the theme of many plays. In Lorca's *The House of Bernarda Alba* the village gossips want to punish the seduced young girl by burning her with live coal "in the place where she sinned." In Valle-Inclán's *Divine Words*, the adulteress appears as a witch who dances with the devil: her fault discovered, the whole village assembles to tear off her clothes and drown her. Many traditions reported that the sinner was stripped; then she was stoned, as told in the Gospel, and she was buried alive, drowned, or burned. The meaning of these tortures is that she was thus returned to Nature after being deprived of her social dignity; by her sin she had released bad natural emanations: the expiation was carried out as a kind of sacred orgy where the women stripped, beat, and massacred the guilty one, releasing in turn their mysterious but beneficial fluids since they were acting in accordance with society.

This savage severity fades as superstitions diminish and fear dissipates. But in the countryside, godless and homeless bohemian women are still regarded with suspicion. The woman who freely exercises her charms— adventuress, vamp, femme fatale—remains a disquieting type. In Hollywood films the Circe image survives as the bad woman. Women were burned as witches simply because they were beautiful. And in the prudish intimidation of provincial virtues, the old specter of dissolute women is perpetuated.

These very dangers make woman captivating game for an adventurous man. Disregarding his rights as a husband, refusing to uphold society's laws, he will try to conquer her in single combat. He tries to annex the woman, including her resistance; he pursues in her the same freedom through which she escapes him. In vain. Freedom cannot be carved up: the free woman will often be free at the expense of man. Sleeping Beauty might wake up with displeasure, she might not recognize her Prince Charming in the one who awakens her, she might not smile. This is precisely the case of Citizen Kane, whose protégée is seen to be oppressed and whose generosity is revealed to be a will for power and tyranny; the hero's wife listens to his exploits indifferently, the Muse yawns, listening to the verses of the poet who dreams of her. Out of boredom, the Amazon can refuse combat; and she can also emerge victorious. Roman women of the decadence, and many American women today, impose their whims or their law on men. Where is Cinderella? The man wanted to give, and here is the woman taking. No longer a game, it is a question of self-defense. From the moment the woman is free, her only destiny is one she freely creates for herself. So the relation between the two sexes is a relation of struggle. Having become a peer to man, she seems as formidable as when she faced him as foreign Nature. The female nurturer, devoted and patient, turns into an avid and devouring beast. The bad woman also sets her roots in the earth, in Life; but the earth is a grave, and life a bitter combat: so the myth of the industrious honeybee or mother hen is replaced by the devouring insect, the praying mantis, the spider; the woman is no longer the one who nurses her young but the one who eats the male; the egg is no longer the storehouse of abundance but a trap of inert matter drowning the mutilated spermatozoid; the womb, that warm, peaceful, and safe haven, becomes the rank octopus, the carnivorous plant, abyss of convulsive darkness; within it lives a serpent that insatiably swallows the male's strength. Such a dialectic turns the erotic object into female black magic, turns the female servant into a traitor, Cinderella into a witch, and changes all women into the enemy: here is the ransom man pays for having posited himself in bad faith as the sole essential.

But this enemy face is not woman's definitive form either. Instead, Manichaeism is introduced within the feminine kind. Pythagoras linked the good principle to man and the bad principle to woman; men have tried to overcome the bad by annexing woman; they have been partially successful; but just as Christianity, by introducing the ideas of redemption and salvation, gave its full sense to the word "damnation," the bad woman stands out in opposition to the sanctified woman. In the course of this *querelle des femmes*, which has endured from the Middle Ages to our times, some men only want to see the blessed woman they dream of, while others want the cursed woman who belies their dreams. But in fact, if man can find *everything* in woman, it is because she has both faces. In a carnal and living way, she represents all the values and anti-values that give life meaning. Here, clear-cut, we have the good and the Bad, in opposition to each other in the guise of devoted Mother and perfidious Lover; in the Old English ballad "Lord Randal," a young knight dies in his mother's arms, poisoned by his mistress. Richepin's *La glu* (The Leech) takes up the same theme, but with more pathos and bad taste. Angelic Michaela is contrasted with dark Carmen. The mother, the faithful fiancée, and the patient wife provide healing to the wounds inflicted on men's hearts by vamps and witches. Between these clearly fixed poles a multitude of ambiguous figures were yet to be defined, the pitiful, the detestable, sinners, victims, coquettes, the weak, the angelic, the devilish. A multitude of behaviors and feelings thereby solicit man and enrich him.

The very complexity of woman enchants him: here is a wonderful servant who can excite him at little expense. Is she angel or devil? Uncertainty makes her a sphinx. One of the most famous brothels of Paris was placed under its aegis. In the grand epoch of Femininity, in the time of corsets, of Paul Bourget, of Henry Bataille, and of the French cancan, the sphinx theme is all the rage in comedies, poems, and songs: "Who are you, where do you come from, strange sphinx?" And dreams and queries about the feminine mystery continue still. To preserve this mystery, men have long implored women not to give up their long dresses, petticoats, veils, long gloves, and high boots: whatever accentuates difference in the Other makes them more desirable, since it is the Other as such that man wants to possess. In his letters, Alain-Fournier reproaches English women for their boyish handshake: French women's modest reserve flusters him. Woman must remain secret, unknown, to be adored as a faraway princess; Fournier seems not to have been terribly deferential to the women who entered his life, but it is in a woman, whose main virtue was to seem inaccessible, that he incarnates all the wonder of childhood, of youth, the nostalgia for a lost paradise. In Yvonne de Galais he traced a white and gold image. But men cherish even feminine defects if they create mystery. "A woman must have her caprices," said a man authoritatively to a reasonable woman. Caprices are unpredictable; they lend woman the grace of undulating water; lying embellishes her with glittering reflections; coquetry, even perversity, is her intoxicating perfume. Deceitful, evasive, misunderstood, duplicitous, it is thus that she best lends herself to men's contradictory desires; she is Maya of the innumerable metamorphoses. It is a commonplace to represent the Sphinx as a young woman: virginity is one of the secrets that men—and all the more so if they are libertines—find the most disconcerting; a young girl's purity gives hope for all kinds of license, and no one knows what perversities are concealed beneath her innocence; still close to animal and plant, already compliant with social rites, she is neither child nor adult; her timid femininity does not inspire fear, but mild unrest. It is understandable that she is one of the privileged figures of the feminine mystery. But as the "real young lady" fades, worshipping her has become a bit outdated. On the other hand, the prostitute's character that Gantillon, in his triumphantly successful play, gave to Maya still has a great deal of prestige. She is one of the most flexible of feminine types, one that best allows the great game of vices and virtues. For the timorous puritan, she embodies evil, shame, disease, and damnation; she inspires horror and disgust; she belongs to no man, but gives herself to all of them and lives on the trade; therein she regains the fearsome independence of lewd primitive Goddess Mothers, and she embodies the Femininity that masculine society has not sanctified, that remains rife with malevolent powers; in the sexual act, the male cannot imagine that he possesses her, he is only given over to demons of the flesh, a humiliation, a stain particularly felt by Anglo-Saxons in whose eyes the flesh is more or less reviled. On the other hand, a man who is not frightened by the flesh will love the prostitute's generous and rudimentary affirmation; in her he will see exalted femininity that no morality has diminished; he will find in her body again those magic virtues that in the past made the woman kin to the stars and the sea: a Henry Miller, sleeping with a prostitute, feels he has dived into the very depths of life, death, the cosmos; he meets God in the moist shadows of the receptive vagina. Because she is on the margins of a hypocritically moral world, a sort of pariah, the "lost girl" can be regarded as the challenger of all official virtues; her indignity relates her to authentic saints; for the oppressed shall be exalted; Christ looked upon Mary Magdalene with favor; sin opens the gates of heaven more easily than hypocritical virtue. Thus Raskolnikov sacrificed, at Sonya's feet, the arrogant masculine pride that led him to crime; murder exacerbated this will for separation that is in all men: resigned, abandoned by all, a humble prostitute is best suited to receive his vow of abdication.[31] The words "lost girl" awaken disturbing echoes;

---

31. Marcel Schwob poetically renders this myth in *Le livre de Monelle* (*The Book of Monelle*):

I will speak to you of the Little Women of Pleasure that you may know of the beginning . . . For you see, these little women call out to you . . . they utter a cry of compassion, and they hold your hand in their emaciated hands. They only understand you when you are unhappy; they can cry with you and console you . . . None of them may stay long with you. They would be too sad and too ashamed to remain. When you no longer weep, you have no need of them. They teach you the lesson they have learned from you, then they flee. They come through the cold and the rain to kiss your brow, to brush their lips across your eyes, to drive from you the terror and the sadness that you know . . . You must not think of what they do in the shadows.

many men dream of losing themselves: it is not so easy, one does not easily attain Evil in a positive form; and even the demoniac is frightened by excessive crimes; the woman enables the celebration of the black masses, where Satan is evoked without exactly being invited; she is on the margin of the masculine world: acts that concern her are really without consequence; yet she is a human being, and through her, dark revolts against human laws can be carried out. From Musset to Georges Bataille, visiting "girls" was hideous and fascinating debauchery. Sade and Sacher-Masoch satisfied their haunting desires; their disciples, and most men who had to satisfy their "vices," commonly turned to prostitutes. Of all women, they were the ones who were the most subjected to the male, and yet the ones who best escaped him; this is what makes them likely to take on numerous meanings. There is, however, no feminine figure—virgin, mother, wife, sister, servant, lover, fierce virtue, smiling odalisque—capable of encapsulating the inconstant yearnings of men.

It is for psychology—specifically psychoanalysis—to discover why an individual is drawn more particularly to one aspect or another of the multifaceted Myth and why he incarnates it in any one particular form. But this myth is involved in all complexes, obsessions, and psychoses. In particular, many neuroses are rooted in the vertigo of prohibition: and this vertigo can only emerge if taboos have previously been established; external social pressure is not enough to explain its presence; in fact, social prohibitions are not simply conventions; they have—among other significations—an ontological meaning that each individual experiences in his own way. For example, it is interesting to examine the Oedipus complex; it is too often considered as being produced by a struggle between instinctive tendencies and social directives; but it is first of all an interior conflict within the subject himself. The infant's attachment to the mother's breast is first an attachment to Life in its immediate form, in its generality and its immanence; the rejection of weaning is the rejection of the abandonment to which the individual is condemned once he is separated from the Whole; from then on, and as he becomes more individualized and separated, the taste he retains for the mother's flesh now torn from his own can be termed "sexual"; his sensuality is thus mediated, it has become transcendence toward a foreign object. But the sooner and more decidedly the child assumes itself as subject, the more the carnal bond that challenges his autonomy will become problematic for him. So he shuns his mother's caresses; his mother's authority, the rights she has over him, even her very presence, inspire a kind of shame in him. Particularly he finds it embarrassing and obscene to be aware of her as flesh, and he avoids thinking of her body; in the horror that he feels toward his father or a second husband or a lover, there is less jealousy than scandal; to be reminded that his mother is a carnal being is to be reminded of his own birth, an event he repudiates with all his force; or at least he wishes to give it the majesty of a great cosmic phenomenon; he thinks that Nature, which invests all individuals but belongs to none, should be contained in his mother; he hates her to become prey, not—as it is often presumed—because he wants to possess her himself, but because he wants her to exist above all possession: she must not have the ordinary features of wife or mistress. When in adolescence, however, his sexuality becomes virile, his mother's body begins to disturb him; but it is because he grasps femininity in general in her; and often the desire aroused by the sight of her thigh or her breast disappears as soon as the young boy realizes that this flesh is maternal flesh. There are many cases of perversion, since adolescence, being the age of confusion, is the age of perversion where disgust leads to sacrilege, where temptation is born from the forbidden. But it must not be thought that the son naively wishes to sleep with his mother and that exterior prohibitions interfere and oppress him; on the contrary, desire is born because this prohibition is constituted within the heart of the individual himself. This censure is the most normal, the most general reaction. But there again, it does not arise from social regulation masking instinctive desires. Rather, respect is the sublimation of an original disgust; the young man refuses to regard his mother as carnal; he transfigures her, he associates her with one of the pure images of the sacred woman society offers. This is how he helps strengthen the image of the ideal Mother who will save the next generation. But this image has such force only because it emanates from an individual dialectic. And since every woman is inhabited by the general essence of Woman, thus Mother, it is certain that the attitude to the Mother will have repercussions in his relations with wife and mistress; but less simply than is often imagined. The adolescent who has concretely and sensually desired his mother may have desired woman in general in her: and the fervor of his temperament will be appeased with any woman, no matter who; he is not doomed to incestuous nostalgia.[32] On the other hand, a young man who has had a tender but platonic respect for his mother may in every case wish for woman to be part of maternal purity.

The importance of sexuality, and therefore ordinarily of woman, in both pathological and normal behavior is well-known. Other objects can also be feminized; because woman is certainly to a large extent man's

---

32. Stendhal is a striking example.

invention, he could also invent her in the male body: in homosexuality, sexual division is maintained. But ordinarily Woman is sought in feminine beings. Through her, through the best and the worst of her, man learns happiness, suffering, vice and virtue, lust, renunciation, devotion, and tyranny, and learns about himself; she is play and adventure, but also contest; she is the triumph of victory and, more bitter, of failure overcome; she is the giddiness of loss, the fascination of damnation, of death. There is a world of significations that exist only through woman; she is the substance of men's actions and feelings, the embodiment of all the values that seek their freedom. It is understandable that even if he were condemned to the cruelest disavowals, man would not want to relinquish a dream containing all other dreams.

Here, then, is why woman has a double and deceptive image: she is everything he craves and everything he does not attain. She is the wise mediator between auspicious Nature and man; and she is the temptation of Nature, untamed against all reason. She is the carnal embodiment of all moral values and their opposites, from good to bad; she is the stuff of action and its obstacle, man's grasp on the world and his failure; as such she is the source of all man's reflection on his existence and all expression he can give of it; however, she works to divert him from himself, to make him sink into silence and death. As his servant and companion, man expects her also to be his public and his judge, to confirm him in his being; but she opposes him with her indifference, even with her mockery and her laughter. He projects onto her what he desires and fears, what he loves and what he hates. And if it is difficult to say anything about her, it is because man seeks himself entirely in her and because she is All. But she is All in that which is inessential: she is wholly the *Other*. And as other she is also other than herself, other than what is expected of her. Being all, she is never exactly *this* that she should be; she is everlasting disappointment, the very disappointment of existence that never successfully attains or reconciles itself with the totality of existents.

In order to confirm this analysis of the feminine myth, as it is collectively presented, we will look at the singular and syncretic form it takes on in certain writers. The attitude to women seems typical in, among others, Montherlant, D. H. Lawrence, Claudel, Breton, and Stendhal.

I. MONTHERLANT OR THE BREAD OF DISGUST·

Montherlant belongs to the long male tradition of adopting the arrogant Manichaeism of Pythagoras. Following Nietzsche, he belives that the Eternal Feminine was exalted only during periods of weakness and that the hero has to rise up against the Magna Mater. As a specialist in heroism, he has undertaken the task of dislodging her. Woman is night, disorder, and immanence. "These convulsive shadows are nothing more than 'the feminine in its pure state,' " he writes about Mme Tolstoy.[1] The stupidity and baseness of men today, he thinks, give a positive image of feminine deficiencies: the feminine instinct, feminine intuition, and women's clairvoyance are spoken about, while their absence of logic, stubborn ignorance, and inability to grasp the real should be denounced; they are neither good observers nor psychologists; they neither know how to see things nor understand human beings; their mystery is a trap, their unfathomable treasures have the depth of nothingness; they have nothing to give man and can only harm him. For Montherlant the mother is the first major enemy; in *L'exil* (Exile), an early play of his, he depicts a mother who keeps her son from enlisting; in *Les Olympiques*, the teenager who wants to devote himself to sport is barred by his mother's fearful egotism; in *Les célibataires*

---

1. *Pitié pour les femmes* (*Pity for Women*).

(*The Bachelors*) and in *Les jeunes filles* (*The Girls*), the mother is vilified. Her crime is to want to keep her son locked up forever in her womb's depths; she mutilates him to make him her own and thus to fill up the sterile vacuum of her being; she is the worst educator; she cuts the child's wings; she pulls him back from the heights he aspires to; she turns him into a moron and diminishes him. These reproaches are not without some basis. But it is clear from the explicit criticisms that Montherlant addresses to woman-mother that what he hates in her is his own birth. He thinks he is God; he wants to be God: because he is male, because he is a "superior man," because he is Montherlant. A god is not engendered; his body, if he has one, is a will molded in hard and disciplined muscles, not in flesh mutely inhabited by life and death; this flesh that he repudiates is perishable, contingent, and vulnerable and is his mother's fault. "The only part of Achilles' body that was vulnerable was the part his mother had held."[2] Montherlant never wanted to assume the human condition; what he calls his pride is, from the beginning, a panicked flight from the risks contained in a freedom engaged in the world through flesh; he claims to affirm freedom but to refuse engagement; without ties, without roots, he dreams he is a subjectivity majestically withdrawn upon itself; the memory of his carnal origins disturbs this dream, and he resorts to a familiar process: instead of prevailing over it, he repudiates it.

For Montherlant, the woman lover is just as harmful as the mother; she prevents man from resurrecting the god in himself; woman's lot, he says, is life in its most immediate form, woman lives on feelings, she wallows in immanence; she has a mania for happiness: she wants to trap man in it; she does not experience the élan of her transcendence, she does not have the sense of grandeur; she loves her lover in his weakness and not in his strength, in his troubles and not in his joys; she would like him defenseless, so unhappy as to try to convince him of his misery regardless of any proof to the contrary. He surpasses and thus escapes her: she means to reduce him to her size to take him over. Because she needs him, she is not self-sufficient; she is a parasite. Through Dominique's eyes, Montherlant portrayed the promenading women of Ranelagh, women "hanging on their lovers' arms like beings without backbones, like big disguised slugs";[3] except for sportswomen, women are incomplete beings, doomed to slavery; soft and lacking muscle, they have no grasp on the world; thus they fiercely work to annex a lover or, even better, a husband. Montherlant, to

---

2. Ibid.
3. *Le songe* (*The Dream*).

my knowledge, did not use the praying mantis myth, but the content is there: for woman, to love is to devour; she pretends to give of herself, and she takes. He quotes Mme Tolstoy's cry: "I live through him, for him; I demand the same thing for myself," and he denounces the dangers of such a furious love; he finds a terrible truth in Ecclesiastes: A man who wants to hurt you is better than a woman who wants to help you. He invokes Lyautey's experience: "A man of mine who marries is reduced to half a man." He deems marriage to be even worse for a "superior man"; it is a ridiculous conformism to bourgeois values; could you imagine saying: "Mrs. Aeschylus," or "I'm having dinner at the Dantes' "? A great man's prestige is weakened; and even more, marriage shatters the hero's magnificent solitude; he "needs not to be distracted from his own self."[4] I have already said that Montherlant has chosen a freedom *without object;* that is, he prefers an illusion of autonomy to an authentic freedom engaged in the world; it is this availability that he means to use against woman; she is heavy, she is a burden. "It was a harsh symbol that a man could not walk straight because the woman he loved was on his arm."[5] "I was burning, she puts out the fire. I was walking on water, she takes my arm, I sink."[6] How does she have so much power since she is only lack, poverty, and negativity and her magic is illusory? Montherlant does not explain it. He simply and proudly says that "the lion rightly fears the mosquito."[7] But the answer is obvious: it is easy to believe one is sovereign when alone, to believe oneself strong when carefully refusing to bear any burden. Montherlant has chosen ease; he claims to worship difficult values: but he seeks to attain them easily. "The crowns we give ourselves are the only ones worth being worn," says the king in *Pasiphaé*. How easy. Montherlant overloaded his brow, draping it with purple, but an outsider's look was enough to show that his diadems were papier-mâché and that, like Hans Christian Andersen's emperor, he was naked. Walking on water in a dream was far less tiring than moving forward on earthly land in reality. And this is why Montherlant the lion avoided the feminine mosquito with terror: he is afraid to be tested by the real.[8]

---

4. *Pity for Women*.
5. *The Girls*.
6. Ibid.
7. Ibid.
8. Adler considered this process the classic origin of psychoses. The individual, divided between a "will for power" and an "inferiority complex," sets up the greatest distance possible between society and himself so as to avoid the test of reality. He knows it would undermine the claims he can maintain only if they are hidden by bad faith.

If Montherlant had really deflated the Eternal Feminine myth, he would have to be congratulated: women can be helped to assume themselves as human beings by denying the Woman. But he did not smash the idol, as has been shown: he converted it into a monster. He too believed in this obscure and irreducible essence: femininity; like Aristotle and Saint Thomas, he believed it was defined negatively; woman was woman through a lack of virility; that is the destiny any female individual has to undergo without being able to modify it. Whoever claims to escape it places herself on the lowest rung of the human ladder: she does not manage to become man, she gives up being woman; she is merely a pathetic caricature, a sham; that she might be a body and a consciousness does not provide her with any reality: Platonist when it suited him, Montherlant seems to believe that only the Ideas of femininity and virility possessed being; the individual who partakes of neither has only an appearance of existence. He irrevocably condemns these "vampires" who dare to posit themselves as autonomous subjects, dare to think and act. And he intends to prove through his depiction of Andrée Hacquebaut that any woman endeavoring to make herself a person would be changed into a grimacing marionette. Andrée is, of course, ugly, ungainly, badly dressed, and even dirty, with dubious nails and forearms: the little culture she is granted is enough to kill all her femininity; Costals assures us she is intelligent, but with every page devoted to her, Montherlant convinces us of her stupidity; Costals claims he feels sympathy for her; Montherlant renders her obnoxious. Through this clever equivocation, the idiocy of feminine intelligence is proven, and an original fall perverting all the virile qualities to which women aspire is established.

Montherlant is willing to make an exception for sportswomen; they can acquire a spirit, a soul, thanks to the autonomous exercise of their body; yet it was easy to bring them down from these heights; he delicately moves away from the thousand-meter winner to whom he devoted an enthusiastic hymn; knowing he could easily seduce her, he wanted to spare her this disgrace. Alban calls her to the top, but Dominique does not remain there; she falls in love with him: "She who had been all spirit and all soul sweated, gave off body odours, and out of breath, she cleared her throat."[9] Alban chases her away, indignant. If a woman kills the flesh in her through the discipline of sports, she can still be esteemed; but an autonomous existence molded in a woman's flesh is a repulsive scandal; feminine flesh is abhor-

---

9. *The Dream.*

rent the moment a consciousness inhabits it. What is suitable for woman is to be purely flesh. Montherlant approves the Oriental attitude: as an object·of pleasure, the weak sex has a place—modest, of course, but worthwhile—on earth; the pleasure it gives man justifies it, and that pleasure alone. The ideal woman is totally stupid and totally subjugated; she is always willing to welcome the man and never ask anything of him. Such was Douce, and Alban likes her when it is convenient: "Douce, admirably silly and always lusted after the sillier she is . . . useless outside of love and thus firmly but sweetly avoided."[10] Such is Rhadidja, the little Arab woman, a quiet beast of love who docilely accepts pleasure and money. This "feminine beast" met on a Spanish train can thus be imagined: "She looked so idiotic that I began to desire her."[11] The author explains: "What is irritating in women is their claim to reason; if they exaggerate their animality, they border on the superhuman."[12]

However, Montherlant is in no way an Oriental sultan; in the first place, he does not have the sensuality. He is far from delighting in "feminine beasts" without ulterior motives; they are "sick, nasty, never really clean";[13] Costals admits that young boys' hair smelled stronger and better than women's; Solange sometimes makes him feel sick, her "cloying, almost disgusting, smell, and this body without muscles, without nerves, like a white slug."[14] He dreams of more worthy embraces, between equals, where gentleness was born of vanquished strength . . . The Oriental relishes woman voluptuously, thereby bringing about carnal reciprocity between lovers: the ardent invocations of the Song of Songs, the tales of *The Thousand and One Nights*, and so much other Arab poetry attest to the glory of the beloved; naturally, there are bad women; but there are also delicious ones, and sensual man lets himself go into their arms confidently, without feeling humiliated. But Montherlant's hero is always on the defensive: "Take without being taken, the only acceptable formula between superior man and woman."[15] He speaks readily about the moment of desire, an aggressive moment, a virile one; he avoids the moment of pleasure; he might find that he risks discovering he also sweated, panted, "gave off body odours"; but no, who would dare breathe in his odor, feel his

10. Ibid.
11. *La petite infante de Castille* (The Little Infanta of Castile).
12. Ibid.
13. *The Girls*.
14. Ibid.
15. Ibid.

dampness? His defenseless flesh exists for no one, because there is no one opposite him: his is the only consciousness, a pure transparent and sovereign presence; and if pleasure exists for his own consciousness, he does not take it into account: it would have power over him. He speaks complacently of the pleasure he gave, never what he receives: receiving means dependence. "What I want from a woman is to give her pleasure";[16] the living warmth of voluptuousness would imply complicity: he accepts none whatsoever; he prefers the haughty solitude of domination. He seeks cerebral, not sensual, satisfactions in women.

And the first of these is an arrogance that aspires to express itself, but without running any risks. Facing the woman, "we have the same feeling as facing the horse or the bull: the same uncertainty and the same taste *for testing one's strength*."[17] Testing it against other men would be risky; they would be involved in the test; they would impose unpredictable rankings, they would return an outside verdict; with a bull or a horse, one remains one's own judge, which is infinitely safer. A woman also, if she is well chosen, remains alone opposite the man. "I don't love in equality, because I seek the child in the woman." This truism does not explain anything: Why does he seek the child and not the equal? Montherlant would be more sincere if he declared that he, Montherlant, does not have any equal; and more precisely that he does not want to have one: his fellow man frightens him. He admires the rigors of the Olympic Games that create hierarchies in which cheating is not possible; but he has not himself learned the lesson; in the rest of his work and life, his heroes, like him, steer clear of all confrontation: they deal with animals, landscapes, children, women-children, and never with equals. In love with the hard clarity of sports, Montherlant accepts as mistresses only those women from whom his fearful pride risks no judgment. He chooses them "passive and vegetal," infantile, stupid, and venal. He systematically avoids granting them a consciousness: if he finds traces of one, he balks, he leaves; there is never a question of setting up any intersubjective relationship with woman: she has to be a simple animated object in man's kingdom; she can never be envisaged as subject; her point of view can never be taken into account. Montherlant's hero has a supposedly arrogant morality, but it is merely convenient: he is only concerned with his relations with himself. He is attached to woman—or rather he attaches woman—not to take pleasure in her but to take pleasure in him-

16. Ibid.
17. *The Little Infanta of Castile.*

self: as she is absolutely inferior, woman's existence shows up the substantial, the essential, and the indestructible superiority of the male; risk-free.

So Douce's foolishness enables Alban to "reconstruct in some way the sensations of the *ancient demigod* marrying a fabulous Goose."[18] At Solange's first touch, Costals changes into a mighty lion: "They had barely sat down next to each other when he put his hand on the girl's thigh (on top of her dress), then placed it in the middle of her body *as a lion* holds his paw spread out on the piece of meat he has won."[19] This gesture made daily by so many men in the darkness of cinemas is for Costals the "primitive gesture of the *Lord*."[20] If, like him, they had the sense of grandeur, lovers and husbands who kiss their mistresses before taking them would experience these powerful metamorphoses at low cost. "He vaguely sniffed this woman's face, *like a lion* who, tearing at the meat he held between his paws, stops to lick it."[21] This carnivorous arrogance is not the only pleasure the male gets out of his female; she is his pretext for him to experience his heart freely, spuriously, and always without risk. One night, Costals takes such pleasure in suffering that, sated with the taste of his own pain, he joyfully attacks a chicken leg. Rarely can one indulge in such a whim. But there are other powerful or subtle joys. For example, condescension; Costals condescends to answer some women's letters, and he even sometimes does it with care; to an unimportant, enthusiastic peasant, he writes at the end of a pedantic dissertation, "I doubt that you can understand me, but that is better than if I *abase* myself to you."[22] He likes sometimes to shape a woman to his image: "I want you to be like an Arab scarf for me . . . I did not *raise* you up to me for you to be anything else but me."[23] It amuses him to manufacture some happy memories for Solange. But it is above all when he sleeps with a woman that he drunkenly feels his prodigality. Giver of joy, peace, heat, strength, and pleasure: these riches he doles out fill him with satisfaction. He owes nothing to his mistresses; to be absolutely sure of that, he often pays them; but even when intercourse is an equal exchange, the woman is obliged to him without reciprocity: she gives nothing, he takes. He thinks nothing of sending Solange to the bathroom the day he deflowers her; even if a woman is dearly cherished, it would be out of the question for a man to go out of his way for her; he is male by divine right,

---

18. *The Dream.*
19. *The Girls.*
20. Ibid.
21. Ibid.
22. Ibid.
23. Ibid.

she by divine right is doomed to the douche and bidet. Costals's pride is such a faithful copy of caddishness that it is hard to tell him apart from a boorish traveling salesman.

Woman's first duty is to yield to his generosity's demands; when he imagines Solange does not appreciate his caresses, Costals turns white with rage. He cherishes Rhadidja because her face lights up with joy when he enters her. So he takes pleasure in feeling like both a beast of prey and a magnificent prince. One may be perplexed, however, by where this fever to take and to satisfy comes from if the woman taken and satisfied is just a poor thing, some tasteless flesh faintly palpitating with an ersatz consciousness. How can Costals waste so much time with these futile creatures?

These contradictions show the scope of a pride that is nothing but vanity.

A more subtle delectation belonging to the strong, the generous, the master, is pity for the unfortunate race. Costals from time to time is moved to feel such fraternal gravity, so much sympathy in his heart for the humble, so much "pity for women." What can be more touching than the unexpected gentleness of tough beings? He brings back to life this noble postcard image when deigning to consider these sick animals that are women. He even likes to see sportswomen beaten, wounded, exhausted, and bruised; as for the others, he wants them as helpless as possible. Their monthly misery disgusts him, and yet Costals confides that "he had always preferred women on those days when he knew them to be affected."[24] He even yields to this pity sometimes; he goes so far as to make promises, if not to keep them: he promises to help Andrée, to marry Solange. When pity retreats from his soul, these promises die: Doesn't he have the right to change his mind? He makes the rules of the game that he plays with himself as the only partner.

Inferior and pitiful, that is not enough. Montherlant wants woman to be despicable. He sometimes claims that the conflict of desire and scorn is a pathetic tragedy: "Oh! To desire what one disdains: what a tragedy! . . . To have to attract and repel in virtually the same gesture, to light and quickly put out as one does with a match, such is the tragedy of our relations with women!"[25] In truth, the only tragedy is from the match's point of view, that is, a negligible point of view. For the match lighter, careful not to burn his fingers, it is too obvious that this exercise delights him. If his pleasure were not to "desire what he disdains," he would not systematically refuse to

24. Ibid.
25. *The Little Infanta of Castile.*

desire what he esteems: Alban would not repel Dominique; he would choose what he desires: after all, what is so despicable about a little Spanish dancer, young, pretty, passionate, and simple; is it that she is poor, from a low social class, and without culture? In Montherlant's eyes, these would seem to be defects. But above all he scorns her as a woman, by decree; he says in fact that it is not the feminine mystery that arouses males' dreams but these dreams that create mystery; but he also projects onto the object what his subjectivity demands: it is not because they are despicable that he disdains women but because he wants to disdain them that they seem abject to him. He feels that the lofty heights he is perched on are all the higher as the distance between them and her is great; that explains why his heroes choose such pathetic sweethearts: against Costals, the great writer, he pits an old provincial virgin tortured by sex and boredom, and a little far-right bourgeois, vacuous and calculating; this is measuring a superior individual with humble gauges: the result is that he comes across as very small to the reader through this awkward caution. But that does not matter as Costals thinks himself grand. The humblest weaknesses of woman are sufficient to feed his pride. A passage in *The Girls* is particularly telling. Before sleeping with Costals, Solange is preparing herself for the night. "She has to go to the toilet, and Costals remembers this mare he had, so proud, so delicate that she neither urinated nor defecated when he was riding her." Here can be seen the hatred of the flesh (Swift comes to mind: Celia shits), the desire to see woman as a domestic animal, the refusal to grant her any autonomy, even that of urinating; but Costals's annoyance shows above all that he has forgotten he too has a bladder and intestines; likewise, when he is disgusted by a woman bathed in sweat and body odor, he abolishes all his own secretions: he is a pure spirit served by muscles and a sex organ of steel. "Disdain is nobler than desire," Montherlant declares in *Aux fontaines du désir* (At the Fountains of Desire), and Alvaro: "My bread is disgust."[26] What an alibi scorn is when it wallows in itself! Because one contemplates and judges, one feels totally other than the other that one condemns, and one dismisses the defects one is accused of free of charge. With what headiness has Montherlant exhaled his scorn for human beings throughout his whole life! It is sufficient for him to denounce their foolishness to believe he is intelligent, to denounce their cowardice to believe himself brave. At the beginning of the Occupation, he indulged in an orgy of scorn for his vanquished fellow countrymen: he who is neither French nor vanquished; he is

26. *Le maître de Santiago* (*The Master of Santiago*).

above it all. Incidentally, all things considered, Montherlant, the accuser, did no more than the others to prevent the defeat; he did not even consent to being an officer; but he quickly and furiously resumed his accusations that take him well beyond himself.[27] He affects to be distressed by his disgust so as to feel it is more sincere and to take more delight in it. The truth is that he finds so many advantages in it that he systematically seeks to drag the woman into abjection. He amuses himself by tempting poor girls with money and jewels: he exults when they accept his malicious gifts. He plays a sadistic game with Andrée, for the pleasure not of making her suffer but of seeing her debase herself. He encourages Solange in infanticide; she welcomes this possibility, and Costals's senses are aroused: he takes this potential murderess in a ravishment of scorn.

The apologue of the caterpillars provides the key to this attitude: whatever his hidden intention, it is significant in itself.[28] Pissing on caterpillars, Montherlant takes pleasure in sparing some and exterminating others; he takes a laughing pity on those that are determined to live and generally lets them off; he is delighted by this game. Without the caterpillars, the urinary stream would have been just an excretion; it becomes an instrument of life and death; in front of the crawling insect, man relieves himself and experiences God's despotic solitude, without running the risk of reciprocity. Likewise, faced with female animals, the male, from the top of his pedestal, sometimes cruel, sometimes tender, sometimes fair, sometimes unpredictable, gives, takes back, satisfies, pities, or gets irritated; he defers to nothing but his own pleasure; he is sovereign, free, and unique. But these animals must not be anything but animals; they would be chosen on purpose, their weaknesses would be flattered; they would be treated as animals with such determination that they would end up accepting their condition. In similar fashion, the blacks' petty robberies and lies charmed the whites of Louisiana and Georgia, confirming the superiority of their own skin color; and if one of these Negroes persists in being honest, he is treated even worse. In similar fashion, the debasement of man was systematically practiced in the concentration camps: the ruling race found proof in this abjection that it was of superhuman essence.

This was no chance meeting. Montherlant is known to have admired Nazi ideology. He loved seeing the swastika and the sun wheel triumph in a celebration of the sun. "The victory of the sun wheel is not just a victory of the Sun, of paganism. It is the victory of the sun principle, which is that

---

27. *Le solstice de juin* (June Solstice).
28. Ibid.

everything changes . . . I see today the triumph of the principle I am imbued with, that I praised, that with a full consciousness I feel governs my life."[29] It is also known with what a relevant sense of grandeur he presented these Germans who "breathe the great style of strength" as an example to the French during the Occupation.[30] The same panicky taste for facility that makes him run when facing his equals brings him to his knees when facing the winners: kneeling to them is his way of identifying with them; so now he is a winner, which is what he always wanted, be it against a bull, caterpillars, or women, against life itself and freedom. It must be said that even before the victory, he was flattering the "totalitarian magicians."[31] Like them, he has always been a nihilist, he has always hated humanity. "People aren't even worth being led (and humanity does not have to have done something to you [for you] to detest it to this extent)";[32] like them, he thinks that certain beings—race, nation, or he, Montherlant, himself—are in possession of an absolute privilege that grants them full rights over others. His morality justifies and calls for war and persecution. To judge his attitude regarding women, we must scrutinize this ethic, because after all it is important to know *in the name of what* they are condemned.

Nazi mythology had a historical infrastructure: nihilism expressed German despair; the cult of the hero served positive aims for which millions of soldiers lost their lives. Montherlant's attitude has no positive counterweight, and it expresses nothing but his own existential choice. In fact, this hero chooses fear. There is a claim to sovereignty in every consciousness: but it can only be confirmed by risking itself; no superiority is ever given since man is nothing when reduced to his subjectivity; hierarchies can only be established among men's acts and works; merit must be ceaselessly won: Montherlant knows it himself. "One only has rights over what one is willing to risk." But he never wants to risk *himself* amid his peers. And because he does not dare confront humanity, he abolishes it. "Infuriating obstacle that of beings," says the king in *La reine morte* (The Dead Queen). They give the lie to the complacent "fairyland" the conceited creates around himself. They have to be negated. It is noteworthy that *none* of Montherlant's works depicts a conflict between man and man; coexistence is the great living drama: he eludes it. His hero always rises up alone facing animals, children, women, landscapes; he is prey to his own

29. Ibid.
30. Ibid.
31. *L'équinoxe de septembre* (September Equinox).
32. *At the Fountains of Desire.*

desires (like the queen of *Pasiphaé*) or his own demands (like the master of Santiago), but *no person* is ever beside him. Even Alban in *The Dream* does not have a friend: when Prinet was alive, he disdained him; he only exalts him over his dead body. Montherlant's works, like his life, recognize only *one* consciousness.

With this, all feeling disappears from this universe; there can be no intersubjective relation if there is only one subject. Love is derisory; but it is not in the name of friendship that it is worthy of scorn, because "friendship lacks guts."[33] And all human solidarity is haughtily rejected. The hero was not engendered; he is not limited by space and time: "I do not see any reasonable reason to be interested in exterior things that are of my time more than any others of any past year."[34] Nothing that happens to others counts for him: "In truth events never counted for me. I only liked them for the rays they made in me by going through me . . . Let them be what they want to be."[35] Action is impossible: "Having had passion, energy, and boldness and not being able to put them to any use through lack of faith in anything human!"[36] That means that any *transcendence* is forbidden. Montherlant recognizes that. Love and friendship are twaddle, scorn prevents action; he does not believe in art for art's sake, and he does not believe in God. All that is left is the immanence of pleasure. "My one ambition is to use my senses better than others,"[37] he writes in 1925. And again: "In fact, what do I want? To possess beings that please me in peace and poetry."[38] And in 1941: "But I who accuse, what have I done with these twenty years? They have been a dream filled with my pleasure. I have lived high and wide, drunk on what I love: what a mouth-to-mouth with life!"[39] So be it. But is it not precisely because she wallows in immanence that woman is trodden upon? What higher aims, what great designs does Montherlant set against the mother's or lover's possessive love? He also seeks "possession"; and as for the "mouth-to-mouth with life," many women can give that back in kind. He does partake of unusual pleasures: those that can be had from animals, boys, and preadolescent girls; he is indignant that a passionate mistress would not dream of putting her twelve-year-old daughter in

33. Ibid.
34. *La possession de soi-même* (The Possession of Oneself).
35. *June Solstice.*
36. *At the Fountains of Desire.*
37. Ibid.
38. Ibid.
39. *June Solstice.*

his bed: this indignation is not very solar. Can he not be aware that women's sensuality is no less tormented than men's? If that were the criterion for ranking the sexes, women would perhaps be first. Montherlant's inconsistencies are truly abominable. In the name of "alternation" he declares that since nothing is worth anything, everything is equal; he accepts everything, he wants to embrace everything, and it pleases him that mothers with children are frightened by his broad-mindedness; but he is the one who demanded an "inquisition" during the Occupation that would censure films and newspapers;[40] American girls' thighs disgust him, the bull's gleaming penis exalts him: to each his own; everyone re-creates his own "phantasm"; in the name of what values does this great orgiast spit with disgust on the orgies of others? Because they are not his own? So can all morality be reduced to being Montherlant?

He would obviously answer that pleasure is not everything: style matters. Pleasure should be the other side of renunciation; the voluptuary also has to feel he is made of the stuff of heroes and saints. But many women are expert in reconciling their pleasures with the high image they have of themselves. Why should we think that Montherlant's narcissistic dreams are worth more than theirs?

Because, in truth, this is a question of dreams. Because he denies them any objective content, the words Montherlant juggles with—"grandeur," "holiness," and "heroism"—are merely eye-catchers. Montherlant is afraid of risking his own superiority among men; to be intoxicated on this exalting wine, he retreats into the clouds: the Unique is obviously supreme. He closes himself up in a museum of mirages: mirrors reflect his own image infinitely, and he thinks that he can thus populate the earth; but he is no more than a reclusive prisoner of himself. He thinks he is free; but he alienates his liberty in the interests of his ego; he models the Montherlant statue on postcard-imagery standards. Alban repelling Dominique because he sees a fool in the mirror illustrates this enslavement: it is in the eyes of others that one is a fool. The arrogant Alban subjects his heart to this collective consciousness that he despises. Montherlant's liberty is an attitude, not a reality. Without an aim, action is impossible, so he consoles himself with gestures: it is mimicry. Women are convenient partners; they give him his lines, he takes the leading role, he crowns himself with laurels and

---

40. "We ask for a body that would have discretionary power to stop anything it deems to be harmful to the essence of French human values. Some sort of an inquisition in the name of French human values" (ibid.).

drapes himself in purple: but everything takes place on his private stage; thrown onto the public square, in real light, under a real sky, the actor no longer sees clearly, cannot stand, staggers, and falls. In a moment of lucidity, Costals cries out: "Deep down, these 'victories' over women are some farce!"[41] Yes. Montherlant's values and exploits are a sad farce. The noble deeds that intoxicate him are also merely gestures, never undertakings: he is touched by Peregrinus's suicide, Pasiphaé's boldness, and the elegance of the Japanese who shelters his opponent under his umbrella before taking his life in a duel. But he declares that "the adversary's specificity and the ideas he is supposedly representing are not all that important."[42] This declaration had a particular resonance in 1941. Every war is beautiful, he also says, whatever its aims; force is always admirable, whatever it serves. "Combat without faith is the formula we necessarily end up with to maintain the only acceptable idea of man: one where he is the hero and the sage."[43] But it is curious that Montherlant's noble indifference regarding all causes inclines him not toward resistance but toward national revolution, that his sovereign freedom chooses submission, and that he looks for the secret of heroic wisdom not in the Maquis but in the conquerors. This is not by chance either. The pseudo-sublime of *The Dead Queen* and *The Master of Santiago* is where these mystifications lead. In these plays that are all the more significant for their ambition, two imperious males sacrifice women guilty of simply being human beings to their hollow pride; they desire love and earthly happiness: as punishment, one loses her life and the other her soul. If once again one asks, what for? the author answers haughtily: for nothing. He does not want the king's reasons for killing Inès to be too imperious: the murder should be a banal political crime. "Why do I kill her? There is probably a reason, but I cannot see it," he says. The reason is that the solar principle triumphs over earthly banality; but this principle does not inform any aim: it calls for destruction, nothing more, as has already been seen. As for Alvaro, Montherlant says in a preface that he is interested in certain men of this period in "their clear-cut faith, their scorn for the outside reality, their taste for destruction, their passion for nothing." This is the passion to which the master of Santiago sacrifices his daughter. She will be arrayed in the beautiful shimmer of words mystical. Is it not boring to prefer happiness to mysticism? Sacrifices and renuncia-

---

41. *The Girls.*
42. *June Solstice.*
43. Ibid.

tions have meaning only in the light of an aim, a human aim; and aims that go beyond singular love or personal happiness can only exist in a world that recognizes the price of both love and happiness; the "shopgirl's morality" is more authentic than hollow phantasms because it is rooted in life and reality, where great aspirations can spring forth. Inès de Castro can easily be pictured in Buchenwald, with the king hurrying to the German embassy for reasons of state. Many shopgirls were worthy of a respect that we would not grant to Montherlant during the Occupation. The empty words he crams himself with are dangerous for their very hollowness: this super-human mysticism justifies all kinds of temporal devastations. The fact is that in the plays under discussion, this mystique is attested to by two mur-ders, one physical and the other moral; Alvaro does not have far to go to become a grand inquisitor: wild, solitary, unrecognizable; nor the king—misunderstood, rejected—to become a Himmler. They kill women, they kill Jews, they kill effeminate men and "Jewed" Christians, they kill every-thing they want or like to kill in the name of these lofty ideas. Only by negations can negative mysticisms be affirmed. True surpassing is a posi-tive step toward the future, toward humanity's future. The false hero, to convince himself he goes far and flies high, always looks back, at his feet; he despises, he accuses, he oppresses, he persecutes, he tortures, he mas-sacres. It is through the evil he does to his neighbor that he measures his superiority over him. Such are Montherlant's summits that he points out with an arrogant finger when he interrupts his "mouth-to-mouth with life."

"Like the donkey at an Arab waterwheel, I turn, I turn, blind and end-lessly retracing my steps. But I don't bring up freshwater." There is not much to add to this avowal that Montherlant signed in 1927. Freshwater never sprang forth. Maybe Montherlant should have lit Peregrinus's pyre: that would have been the most logical solution. He preferred to take refuge in his own cult. Instead of giving himself to this world, which he did not know how to nourish, he settled for seeing himself in it; and he organized his life in the interest of this mirage visible to his eyes alone. "Princes are at ease in all situations, even in defeat," he writes;[44] and because he delighted in defeat, he believes he is king. He learns from Nietzsche that "woman is the hero's amusement," and he thinks that it is enough to get pleasure from women to be anointed hero. The rest is the same. As Costals might say: "Deep down, what a farce!"

---

44. Ibid.

II. D. H. LAWRENCE OR PHALLIC PRIDE

Lawrence is the very antipode of Montherlant. His objective is not to define the special relations of woman and man but to situate them both in the truth of Life. This truth is neither representation nor will: it envelops the animality in which human beings have their roots. Lawrence passionately rejects the antithesis sex versus brain; he has a cosmic optimism radically opposed to Schopenhauer's pessimism, the will to live expressed in the phallus is joy: thought and action must derive their source from this, or else it would be an empty concept and a sterile mechanism. The sexual cycle alone is not sufficient, because it falls back into immanence: it is synonymous with death; but better this mutilated reality—sex and death— than an existence cut off from carnal humus. Unlike Antaeus, man needs more than to renew contact with the earth from time to time; his life as a male has to be wholly the expression of his virility, which posits and requires woman in its immediacy; she is thus neither diversion nor prey, she is not an object confronting a subject but a pole necessary for the existence of the pole of the opposite sign. Men who have misunderstood this truth—a Napoleon, for example—have missed their destiny as men: they are failures. It is by fulfilling his generality as intensely as possible, and not by affirming his singularity, that the individual can save himself: whether male or female, an individual should never seek the triumph of pride or the exaltation of his self in erotic relations; to use one's sex as a tool of one's will is the irreparable error; it is essential to break the barriers of the ego, transcend the very limits of consciousness, and renounce all personal sovereignty. Nothing could be more beautiful than that little statue of a woman giving birth: "A terrible face, void, peaked, abstracted almost into meaninglessness by the weight of sensation beneath."[45] This ecstasy is neither sacrifice nor abandon; there is no question of either sex letting itself be swallowed up by the other; neither the man nor the woman should be like a broken fragment of a couple; one's sex is not a wound; each one is a complete being, perfectly polarized; when one is assured in his virility, the other in her femininity, "each acknowledges the perfection of the polarized sex circuit";[46] the sexual act is without annexation, without surrender of either partner, the marvelous fulfillment of each other. When Ursula and Birkin finally found each other, they "would give each other this star-equilibrium

---

45. *Women in Love.*
46. Ibid.

which alone is freedom" . . . "For she was to him what he was to her, the immemorial magnificence of mystic, palpable, real otherness."[47] Attaining each other in the generous wrenching of passion, two lovers together attain the Other, the All. So it is for Paul and Clara in the moment of their love: she is for him "a strong, strange, wild life, that breathed with his in the darkness through this hour. It was all so much bigger than themselves, that he was hushed. They had met, and included in their meeting the thrust of the manifold grass stems, the cry of the peewit, the wheel of the stars."[48] Lady Chatterley and Mellors attain the same cosmic joys: blending into each other, they blend into the trees, the light, and the rain. Lawrence develops this doctrine extensively in *A Propos of "Lady Chatterley's Lover"*: "Marriage is no marriage that is not basically and permanently phallic, and that is not linked up with the sun and the earth, the moon and the fixed stars and the planets, in the rhythm of days, in the rhythm of months, in the rhythm of quarters, of years, of decades and of centuries. Marriage is no marriage that is not a correspondence of blood. For the blood is the substance of the soul." "The blood of man and the blood of woman are two eternally different streams, that can never be mingled." This is why these two streams encircle the whole of life in their meanderings. "The phallus is a column of blood, that fills the valley of blood of a woman. The great river of male blood touches to its depth the great river of female blood, yet neither breaks its bounds. It is the deepest of all communions . . . And it is one of the greatest mysteries." This communion is a miraculous enrichment; but it requires that claims to "personality" be abolished. When personalities seek to reach each other without surrendering themselves, as usually happens in modern civilization, their attempt is doomed to failure. There is a personal, blank, cold, nervous, poetic sexuality that dissolves each one's vital stream. Lovers treat each other like instruments, breeding hate between them: so it is with Lady Chatterley and Michaelis; they remain locked in their subjectivity; they can experience a fever analogous to that procured by alcohol or opium, but it is without object: they fail to discover the reality of the other; they attain nothing. Lawrence would have condemned Costals summarily. He depicted Gerald as one of those proud and egotistical males; and Gerald is in large part responsible for this hell he and Gundrun hurl themselves into.[49] Cerebral and willful, he delights in the empty assertion of his self and hardens himself against life: for the

---

47. Ibid.
48. *Sons and Lovers.*
49. *Women in Love.*

pleasure of mastering a spirited mare, he holds her firm against a fence where a train thunders past, bloodying her rebellious flanks and intoxicating himself with his power. This will to dominate debases the woman against whom it is directed; physically weak, she is thus transformed into a slave. Gerald leans over Pussum: "Her inchoate look of a violated slave, whose fulfilment lies in her further and further violation, made his nerves quiver . . . his was the only will, she was the passive substance of his will." Here is pitiful domination; if the woman is merely a passive substance, the male dominates nothing. He thinks he is taking, enriching himself: it is a delusion. Gerald embraces Gudrun tightly in his arms: "She was the rich, lovely substance of his being . . . So she was passed away and gone in him, and he was perfected." But as soon as he leaves her, he finds himself alone and empty; and the next day, she fails to appear at their rendezvous. If the woman is strong, the male claim arouses a symmetrical claim in her; fascinated and rebellious, she becomes masochistic and sadistic in turn. Gudrun is greatly disturbed when she sees Gerald press the frightened mare's flanks between his thighs; but she is also disturbed when Gerald's wet nurse tells her how in the past she "pinched his little bottom." Masculine arrogance provokes feminine resistance. While Ursula is won over and saved by Birkin's sexual purity, as Lady Chatterley was by the gamekeeper, Gerald drags Gudrun into a struggle with no way out. One night, unhappy, shattered by a death, he abandons himself in her arms. "She was the great bath of life, he worshipped her. Mother and substance of all life she was . . . But the miraculous, soft effluence of her breast suffused over him, over his seared, damaged brain, like a healing lymph, like a soft, soothing flow of life itself, perfect as if he were bathed in the womb again." That night he senses what communion with woman might be; but it is too late; his happiness is vitiated because Gudrun is not really present; she lets Gerald sleep on her shoulder, but she stays awake, impatient, apart. It is the punishment of the individual who is his own prey: alone he cannot end his solitude; in erecting barriers around his self, he erected those around the Other: he will never connect to it. In the end, Gerald dies, killed by Gudrun and by himself.

Thus it would seem at first that neither of the two sexes is privileged. Neither is subject. Woman is neither a prey nor a simple pretext. As Malraux notes, Lawrence thinks that it is not enough, unlike Hindus, for woman to be merely the occasion for a contact with the infinite, as would be a landscape: that would be another way of making her an object.[50] She is as

---

50. Preface to *L'amant de Lady Chatterley*.

real as the man; a real communion has to be reached. This is why Lawrence's heroes demand much more from their mistresses than the gift of their bodies: Paul does not want Myriam to give herself to him as a tender sacrifice; Birkin does not want Ursula to limit herself to seeking pleasure in his arms; cold or burning, the woman who remains closed within herself leaves the man to his solitude: he must reject her. Both have to give themselves to each other, body and soul. If this giving is accomplished, they have to remain forever faithful to each other. Lawrence believed in monogamous marriage. There is only a quest for variety if one is interested in the uniqueness of beings: but phallic marriage is founded on generality. When the virility-femininity circuit is established, desire for change is inconceivable: it is a perfect circuit, closed on itself and definitive.

Reciprocal gift, reciprocal fidelity: Is it really the reign of mutual recognition? Far from it. Lawrence passionately believes in male supremacy. The very expression "phallic marriage," the equivalence he establishes between the sexual and the phallic, is proof enough. Of the two bloodstreams that mysteriously marry, the phallic stream is favored. "The phallus is the connecting link between the two rivers, that establishes the two streams in a oneness." Thus man is not only one of the terms of the couple, but also their relationship; he is their surpassing: "The bridge to the future is the phallus." Lawrence wants to substitute the cult of the phallic for that of the Goddess Mother; when he wants to highlight the sexual nature of the cosmos, it is through man's virility rather than woman's womb. He almost never shows a man excited by a woman: but over and over he shows woman secretly overwhelmed by the vibrant, subtle, insinuating appeal of the male; his heroines are beautiful and healthy, but not sensuous, while his heroes are troubled wild animals. It is male animals that embody the troubling and powerful mystery of Life; women are subjugated by their spell: this one is affected by the fox, that one is taken with a stallion, Gudrun feverishly challenges a herd of young oxen; she is overwhelmed by the rebellious vigor of a rabbit. A social privilege is connected to this cosmic one. Because the phallic stream is impetuous and aggressive and bestrides the future—Lawrence does not make himself perfectly clear on this point—it is up to man to "carry forward the banner of life";[51] he reaches for goals, he incarnates transcendence; woman is absorbed by her sentiments, she is all interiority; she is doomed to immanence. Not only does man play the active role in sexual life, but it is through him that this life is

---

51. *Fantasia of the Unconscious.*

transcended; he is rooted in the sexual world, but he escapes from it; she remains locked up in it. Thought and action have their roots in the phallus; lacking the phallus, woman has no rights to either: she can play the man's role, and brilliantly at that, but it is a game without truth. "Woman is really polarised downwards, towards the centre of the earth. Her deep positivity is in the downward flow, the moon-pull. And man is polarised upwards, towards the sun and the day's activity."[52] For woman, "her deepest consciousness is in the loins and belly."[53] If she turns upward, the moment comes when everything collapses. In the domain of action, man must be the initiator, the positive; woman is the positive on the emotional level. Thus Lawrence goes back to the traditional bourgeois conception of Bonald, Auguste Comte, and Clément Vautel. Woman must subordinate her existence to that of man. "She's got to believe in you . . . , and in the deep purpose you stand for."[54] Then man will owe her tenderness and infinite gratitude. "Ah, how good it is to come home to your wife when she *believes* in you and submits to your purpose that is beyond her . . . You feel an unfathomable gratitude to the woman who loves you."[55] Lawrence adds that to merit this devotion, man must be authentically invested with a higher purpose; if his project is but a sham, the couple sinks into insignificant mystification; better still to enclose one's self in the feminine cycle—love and death—like Anna Karenina and Vronsky or Carmen and Don José, than to lie to each other like Pierre and Natasha. But subject to this reserve, Lawrence, like Proudhon and Rousseau, advocates monogamous marriage where woman derives the justification for her existence from her husband. Lawrence was just as vituperative as Montherlant concerning the woman who wants to reverse the roles. She should cease playing at the Magna Mater, claiming to be in possession of the truth of life; dominating and devouring, she mutilates the male, she forces him to fall back into immanence, and she leads him astray from his goals. Lawrence was far from disparaging motherhood: on the contrary; he rejoices in being flesh, he accepts his birth, he cherishes his mother; mothers appear in his work as magnificent examples of real femininity; they are pure renunciation, absolute generosity, and all their human warmth is devoted to their children; they accept them becoming men, they are proud of it. But the egotistical lover who tries to bring the man back to his childhood must be feared;

---

52. Ibid.
53. Ibid.
54. Ibid.
55. Ibid.

she cuts man down in his flight. "The moon, the planet of women, sways us back."[56] She speaks incessantly about love: but to love for her is to take, to fill the void she feels in herself; this love is close to hate; so it is that Hermione, who suffers from a horrible deficiency because she has never been able to give herself, wants to annex Birkin; she fails; she tries to kill him, and the voluptuous ecstasy she feels in striking him is identical to the egotistic spasm of pleasure.[57] Lawrence detests modern women, celluloid and rubber creatures who claim a consciousness. When the woman has become sexually conscious, "there she is, functioning away from her own head and her own consciousness of herself and her own automatic self-will."[58] He forbids her to have an autonomous sensuality; she is made to give, not to take. Putting words in Mellors's mouth, Lawrence cries out his horror of lesbians. But he also blames the woman who has a detached or aggressive attitude to the male; Paul feels wounded and irritated when Myriam caresses his loins, telling him: "You are so *fine*!" Gundrun, like Myriam, is at fault when she feels enchanted with her lover's beauty: this contemplation separates them, as much as the irony of icy women intellectuals who consider the penis pitiful or male gymnastics ridiculous; the intense quest for pleasure is no less blameworthy: there is an acute, solitary pleasure that also separates, and woman should not aim for it. Lawrence sketched many portraits of these independent, dominating women who have missed their feminine vocation. Ursula and Gudrun are of this type. At first Ursula is a dominator. "Man must render himself up to her. He must be quaffed to the dregs by her."[59] She will learn to overcome her will. But Gudrun is stubborn; cerebral, artistic, she fiercely envies men their independence and their potential for activity; she persists in keeping her individuality intact; she wants to live for herself; ironic and possessive, she will remain forever shut up in her subjectivity. The most significant figure is Myriam because she is the least sophisticated.[60] Gerald is partially responsible for Gudrun's failure; but vis-à-vis Paul, Myriam alone bears the full weight of her ill fate. She also would like to be a man, and she hates men; she does not accept herself in her generality; she wants to "distinguish herself"; because the great stream of life does not pass through her, she can be like a sorceress or a priestess, but never a bacchante; she is

---

56. Ibid.
57. *Women in Love*.
58. *Fantasia of the Unconscious*.
59. *Women in Love*.
60. *Sons and Lovers*.

moved by things only when she has re-created them in her soul, giving them a religious value: this fervor itself separates her from life; she is poetic, mystical, maladapted. "She was not clumsy, and yet none of her movements seemed quite THE movement . . . she put too much strength into the effort." She seeks interior joys, and reality frightens her; sexuality frightens her; when she sleeps with Paul, her heart stands aside in a kind of horror; she is always consciousness, never life: she is not a companion; she does not consent to meld with her lover; she wants to absorb him into herself. He is irritated by this will; he becomes violently angry when he sees her caressing flowers: she seems to want to tear their hearts out; he insults her: "You're always begging things to love you . . . as if you were a beggar for love . . . You don't want to love—your eternal and abnormal craving is to be loved. You aren't positive, you're negative. You absorb, absorb, as if you must fill yourself up with love, because you've got a shortage somewhere." Sexuality does not exist to fill a void; it must be the expression of a whole being. What women call love is their greed before the virile force they want to grab. Paul's mother lucidly thinks about Myriam: "She wants to absorb him. She wants to draw him out and absorb him till there is nothing left of him, even for himself. He will never be a man on his own feet—she will suck him up." The young girl is happy when her friend is ill because she can take care of him: she attempts to serve him, but it is a way of imposing her will on him. Because she lives apart from him, she excites in Paul "an intensity like madness. Which fascinated him, as drug taking might." But she is incapable of bringing him joy and peace; from the depth of her love, in her secret self "she had hated him because she loved him and he dominated her." And Paul distances himself from her. He seeks his balance with Clara; beautiful, lively, animal, she gives herself unreservedly; and the lovers reach moments of ecstasy that surpass them both; but Clara does not understand this revelation. She believes that she owes this joy to Paul himself, to his uniqueness, and she wants to appropriate him: she fails to keep him precisely because she wants him for herself. As soon as love is individualized, it changes into avid egotism, and the miracle of eroticism vanishes.

The woman must renounce personal love: neither Mellors nor Don Cipriano consents to saying words of love to his mistress. Teresa, the model wife, becomes indignant when Kate asks her if she loves Don Ramón.[61] "He is my life," she replies; the gift she concedes to him is something quite different from love. Woman must, like man, abdicate all pride

61. *The Plumed Serpent.*

and all will; if she embodies life for the man, he embodies it for her as well; Lady Chatterley only finds peace and joy because she recognizes this truth: "She would give up her own hard, bright female power. She was weary of it, stiffened with it. She would sink in the new bath of life, in the depths of her womb and her bowels, that sang the voiceless song of adoration": so she is called to the rapture of the bacchantes; blindly obeying her lover, not seeking herself in his arms, she forms with him a harmonious couple, in tune with the rain, the trees, and the spring flowers. Likewise, Ursula renounces her individuality in Birkin's hands, and they attain a "star-equilibrium." But it is *The Plumed Serpent* above all that reflects in its entirety Lawrence's ideal. For Don Cipriano is one of those men who "carry forward the banner of life"; he has a mission and is entirely given over to it to such an extent that virility in him is surpassed and exalted to the point of divinity: if he anoints himself god, it is not a mystification; every man who is fully man is a god; he thus deserves the absolute devotion of a woman. Imbued with Western prejudices, Kate at first refuses this dependence; she is attached to her personality and her limited existence; but little by little letting herself be penetrated by the great stream of life, she gives her body and soul to Cipriano. It is not a slave's surrender: before deciding to stay with him, she insists that he recognize his need for her; he recognizes it, since in fact woman is necessary for man; so she consents to never being anything other than his companion; she adopts his goals, his values, his universe. This submission expresses itself even in eroticism; Lawrence does not want the woman to be tense in the search for pleasure, separated from the male by the spasm that jolts her; he deliberately refuses to bring her to orgasm; Don Cipriano withdraws from Kate when he feels her close to this nervous pleasure; she renounces even this sexual autonomy. "Her strange seething feminine will and desire subsided in her and swept away, leaving her soft and powerfully potent, like the hot springs of water that gushed up so noiseless, so soft, yet so powerful, with a sort of secret potency."

We can see why Lawrence's novels are first and foremost "guidebooks for women." It is infinitely more difficult for the woman than for the man to submit to the cosmic order, because he submits in an autonomous fashion, whereas she needs the mediation of the male. When the Other takes on the form of a foreign consciousness and will, there is real surrender; on the contrary, an autonomous submission strangely resembles a sovereign decision. Lawrence's heroes are either condemned from the start or else from the start they hold the secret of wisdom;[62] their submission to the cosmos

---

62. With the exception of Paul in *Sons and Lovers*, who is the most vibrant of all. But that is the only novel that shows us a masculine learning experience.

was consummated so long ago and they derive such interior certitude from it that they seem as arrogant as a self-important individualist; there is a god who speaks through their mouths: Lawrence himself. But the woman must bow to their divinity. Even if the man is a phallus and not a brain, the virile individual keeps his privileges; woman is not evil, she is even good: but subordinated. Once again, it is the ideal of the "real woman" that Lawrence offers us, that is, of the woman who unhesitatingly assents to defining herself as the Other.

III. CLAUDEL OR THE HANDMAIDEN OF THE LORD

The originality of Claudel's Catholicism is of such an obstinate optimism that evil itself turns to good:

> *Evil itself*
> *Abides its own share of good which must not be wasted.*[63]

Adopting the point of view that can only be that of the Creator—since we assume the Creator to be all-powerful, omniscient, and benevolent—Claudel subscribes to creation entirely; without hell and sin, there could be no free will, no salvation; when he brought forth the world from nothing, God foresaw the Fall and the redemption. In the eyes of Jews and Christians, Eve's disobedience had put her daughters in a very bad position: we see how badly the Fathers of the Church have mistreated women. But here, on the contrary, she is justified if one accepts that she has served divine purposes. "Woman! that service she once by her disobedience rendered to God in the earthly Paradise; that deep agreement reached between her and him; that flesh she put at the disposal of redemption by way of the fault!"[64] There is no doubt she is the source of sin, and through her man lost paradise. But man's sins have been redeemed, and this world is blessed anew: "We have not left the paradise of delight in which God first put us!"[65]

"Every Land is the Promised Land."[66]

Nothing that has come from God's hands, nothing that is given, can be in itself bad: "We pray to God with the entirety of his work! Nothing he

---

63. *Partage de midi.* [*Break of Noon,* trans. Wallace Fowlie. All other Claudel translations in this section are by James Lawler.—TRANS.]

64. *Les aventures de Sophie* (The Adventures of Sophie).

65. *La cantate à trios voix* (Cantata for Three Voices).

66. *Conversations dans le Loir-et-Cher* (Conversations in the Loir-et-Cher).

made is in vain, nothing is alien to anything else."[67] And furthermore, there is nothing that is unnecessary. "All things that he has created commune together, all at one and the same time are necessary each to each."[68] Thus it is that woman has her place in the harmony of the universe; but it is not just an ordinary place; there is a "strange and, in Lucifer's eyes, scandalous passion that binds the Eternal to this momentary flower of Nothingness."[69]

Of course, woman can be destructive: In Lechy, Claudel incarnated the bad woman who drives man to his destruction;[70] in *Break of Noon*, Ysé ruins the life of those trapped by her love. But if there were not this risk of loss, there would not be salvation either. Woman "is the element of risk he deliberately introduced into the midst of his marvelous construction."[71] It is good that man should know the temptations of the flesh. "It is this enemy within us that gives our lives their dramatic element, their poignant salt. If our souls were not so brutally assailed, they would continue to sleep, yet here they leap up . . . This struggle is the apprenticeship of victory."[72] Man is summoned to become aware of his soul not only by the spiritual path but also by that of the flesh. "And what flesh speaks more forcefully to man than the flesh of a woman?"[73] Whatever wrenches him from sleep, from security, is useful: love in whatever form it presents has the virtue of appearing in "our small personal worlds, ordered by our conventional reasoning, as a deeply perturbing element."[74] Often woman is but a deceptive giver of illusions:

> I am the promise that cannot be kept, and my grace consists of that very thing. I am the sweetness of what is, with the regret for what is not. I am the truth that has the countenance of error, and he who loves me does not bother to disentangle each from each.[75]

But there is also usefulness in illusion; this is what the Guardian Angel announces to Doña Prouhèze:

---

67. *Le soulier de satin* (*The Satin Slipper*).
68. *L'annonce faite à Marie* (*The Tidings Brought to Mary*).
69. *The Adventures of Sophie*.
70. *L'échange* (*The Trade*).
71. *The Adventures of Sophie*.
72. *L'oiseau noir dans le soleil levant* (The Black Bird in the Rising Sun).
73. *The Satin Slipper*.
74. *Positions et propositions* (Positions and Propositions).
75. *La ville* (*The City*).

Even sin! Sin also serves.
So it was good for him to love me?
It was good for you to teach him desire.
Desire for an illusion? For a shadow that forever escapes him?
Desire is for what is, illusion is for what is not. Desire pursued to the
furthermost point of illusion
Is desire pursued to the furthermost point of what is not.[76]

By God's will, what Prouhèze was for Rodrigo is "a sword through his heart."[77]

But woman in God's hands is not only this blade, this burn; the riches of this world are not meant to be always refused: they are also nourishment; man must take them with him and make them his own. The loved one will embody for him all the recognizable beauty in the universe; she will be a chant of adoration on his lips.

"How lovely you are, Violaine, and how lovely is the world where you are."[78]

"Who is she who stands before me, gentler than the breeze, like the moon among the young foliage? . . . Here she is like the fresh honeybee unfolding its newborn wings, like a lanky doe, and like a flower that does not even know it is beautiful."[79]

"Let me breathe your scent like that of the earth, when it glows and is washed like an altar, and brings forth blue and yellow flowers.

"And let me breathe the summer's aroma that smells of grass and hay, and is like the autumn's fragrance."[80]

She is the sum of all nature: the rose and the lily, the star, the fruit, the bird, the wind, the moon, the sun, the fountain, "the peaceful tumult, in noon's light, of a great port."[81] And she is still more: a peer.

"Now, this time for me, that luminous point of night's living sands is something quite different from a star,

"Someone human like me . . ."[82]

"You will be alone no more, and I will be in you and with you, with you

---

76. *The Satin Slipper.*
77. Ibid.
78. *The Tidings Brought to Mary.*
79. *La jeune fille Violaine* (The Young Violaine).
80. *The City.*
81. *The Satin Slipper.*
82. Ibid.

forever, the devoted one. Someone yours forever who will never be absent, your wife."[83]

"Someone to listen to what I say and trust in me.

"A soft-voiced companion who takes us in her arms and attests she is a woman."[84]

Body and soul, in taking her into his heart, man finds his roots in this earth and accomplishes himself.

"I took this woman, and she is my measure and my earthly allotment."[85] She is a burden, and man is not made to be burdened.

"And the foolish man finds himself surprised by this absurd person, this great heavy and cumbersome thing.

"So many dresses, so much hair, what can he do?

"He is no longer able, he no longer wants to be rid of her."[86]

This burden is also a treasure. "I am a great treasure," says Violaine.

Reciprocally, woman achieves her earthly destiny by giving herself to man.

"For what is the use of being a woman, unless to be gathered?

"And being this rose, if not to be devoured? And of being born,

"Unless to belong to another and to be the prey of a powerful lion?"[87]

"What shall we do, who can only be a woman in his arms, and in his heart a cup of wine?"[88]

"But you my soul say: I have not been created in vain and he who is called to gather me is alive!"

"The heart that was waiting for me, ah! what joy for me to fill it."[89]

Of course this union of man and woman is to be consummated in the presence of God; it is holy and belongs in the eternal; it should be consented to by a deep movement of the will and *cannot* be broken by an individual caprice. "Love, the consent that two free people grant each other, seemed to God so great a thing that he made it a sacrament. In this as in all other matters the sacrament gives reality to that which was but the heart's supreme desire."[90] And further:

---

83. *The City.*
84. *Le pain dur (Crusts).*
85. *The City.*
86. *Break of Noon.*
87. *Cantata for Three Voices.*
88. Ibid.
89. Ibid.
90. *Positions and Propositions,* Volume 2.

"Marriage is not pleasure but the sacrifice of pleasure, it is the study made by two souls who forever, henceforth, and to end beyond themselves,

"Must be content with each other."[91]

It is not only joy that man and woman will bring to each other through this union; each will take possession of the other's being. "He it was who knew how to find that soul within my soul! . . . He it was who came to me and held out his hand. He was my calling! How can I describe it? He was my origin: it was he by whom and for whom I came into the world."[92]

"A whole part of myself which I thought did not exist because I was busy elsewhere and not thinking of it. Ah! My God, it exists, it does exist, terribly."[93]

And this being appears as justified, necessary for the one it completes. "It is in him that you were necessary," says Prouhèze's Angel. And Rodrigo:

"For what is it to die but to stop being necessary?

"When was she able to do without me? When shall I cease to be for her that without which she could not have been herself ?"[94]

"They say that no soul was made except in a life and in a mysterious relationship with other lives.

"But for us it is still more than that. For I exist as I speak; one single thing resonating between two people.

"When we were being fashioned, Orion, I think that a bit of your substance was left over and that I am made of what you lack."[95]

In the marvelous necessity of this union, paradise is regained, death conquered:

"At last the being who existed in paradise is here remade of a man and woman."[96]

"We will never manage to do away with death unless it be by one another.

"As purple mixed with orange gives pure red."[97]

Finally, in the form of another, each one attains the Other, that is God, in his plenitude.

"What we give one another is God in different guises."[98]

---

91. *The Satin Slipper.*
92. *L'histoire de Tobie et de Sara* (The History of Toby and Sara).
93. *Le père humilié* (*The Humiliation of the Father*).
94. *The Satin Slipper.*
95. *The Humiliation of the Father.*
96. *Feuilles de saints* (Leaves of Saints).
97. *The Satin Slipper.*
98. *Leaves of Saints.*

"Would your desire for heaven have been so great if you had not glimpsed it once in my eyes?"[99]

"Ah! Stop being a woman and let me at last see on your face the God you are powerless to hide."[100]

"The love of God calls in us on the same faculty as the love of his creatures, it calls on our feeling that we are not complete in ourselves and that the supreme God in which we are consummated is someone outside ourselves."[101]

Thus each finds in the other the meaning of his earthly life and also irrefutable proof of the insufficiency of this life:

"Since I cannot grant him heaven, at least I can tear him from the earth. I alone can give him need in the measure of his desire."[102]

"What I was asking from you, and what I wanted to give you, is not compatible with time, but with eternity."[103]

Yet woman's and man's roles are not exactly symmetrical. On the social level, man's primacy is evident. Claudel believes in hierarchies and, among others, the family's: the husband is the head. Anne Vercors rules over her home. Don Pelagio sees himself as the gardener entrusted with the care of this delicate plant, Doña Prouhèze; he gives her a mission she does not dream of refusing. The fact alone of being a male confers privilege. "Who am I, poor girl, to compare myself to the male of my race?" asks Sygne.[104] It is man who labors in the fields, who builds cathedrals, who fights with the sword, who explores the world, who acts, who undertakes. God's plans are accomplished on earth through him. Woman is merely an auxiliary. She is the one who stays in place, who waits, and, who, like Sygne, maintains: "I am she who remains and who am always there."

She defends the heritage of Coûfontaine, keeps his accounts in order while he is far away fighting for the cause. The woman brings the relief of hope to the fighter: "I bring irresistible hope."[105] And that of pity.

"I had pity on him. For where was he to turn, when he sought his mother, but to his own humiliated mother,

"In a spirit of confession and shame."[106]

---

99. Ibid.

100. *The Satin Slipper.*

101. *Positions and Propositions*, Volume 1.

102. *The Satin Slipper.*

103. *The Humiliation of the Father.*

104. *L'otage* (*The Hostage*).

105. *The City.*

106. *The Trade.*

And Tête d'Or, dying, murmurs:

"That is the wounded man's courage, the crippled man's support,

"The dying man's company . . ."

Claudel does not hold it against man that woman knows him in his weakest moments; on the contrary: he would find man's arrogance as displayed in Montherlant and Lawrence sacrilege. It is good that man knows he is carnal and lowly, that he forgets neither his origin nor his death, which is symmetrical to it. Every wife could say the same words as Marthe:

"It is true, it was not I who gave you life.

"But I am here to ask you for life once more. And a man's confusion in the presence of a woman comes from this very question

"Like conscience in the presence of a creditor."[107]

And yet this weakness has to yield to force. In marriage, the wife *gives herself* to the husband, who takes care of her: Lâla lies down on the ground before Coeuvre, who places his foot on her. The relation of woman to husband, of daughter to father, of sister to brother, is a relation of vassalage. In George's hands, Sygne takes the vow of the knight to his sovereign.

"You are the lord and I the poor sibyl who keeps the fire."[108]

"Let me take an oath like a new knight! O my lord! O my elder, let me swear in your hands

"After the fashion of a nun who makes her profession,

"O male of my race!"[109]

Fidelity and loyalty are the greatest of the female vassal's human virtues. Sweet, humble, resigned as a woman, she is, in the name of her race and her lineage, proud and invincible; such is the proud Sygne de Coûfontaine and Tête d'Or's princess, who carries on her shoulder the corpse of her assassinated father, who accepts the misery of a lonely and wild life, the suffering of a crucifixion, and who assists Tête d'Or in his agony before he dies at her side. Conciliator and mediator is thus how woman often appears: she is docile Esther accountable to Mordecai, Judith obeying the priests; she can overcome her weakness, her faintheartedness, and her modesty through loyalty to the cause that is hers since it is that of her masters; she draws strength from her devotion, which makes her a precious instrument.

So on the human level she is seen as drawing her greatness from her very subordination. But in God's eyes, she is a perfectly autonomous person. The fact that for man existence surpasses itself while for woman it

---

107. Ibid.
108. *The Hostage.*
109. Ibid.

maintains itself only establishes a difference between them on earth: in any case, transcendence is accomplished not on earth but in God. And woman has just as direct a connection with him as her companion does; perhaps hers is even more intimate and secret. It is through a man's voice—what is more, a priest's—that God speaks to Sygne; but Violaine hears his voice in the solitude of her heart, and Prouhèze only deals with the Guardian Angel. Claudel's most sublime figures are women: Sygne, Violaine, Prouhèze. This is partly because saintliness for him lies in renunciation. And woman is less involved in human projects; she has less personal will: made to give and not to take, she is closer to perfect devotion. It is through her that the earthly joys that are permissible and good will be surpassed, but their sacrifice is still better. Sygne accomplishes this for a definite reason: to save the pope. Prouhèze resigns herself to it first because she loves Rodrigo with a forbidden love:

"Would you then have wanted me to put an adulteress into your hands? . . . I would have been only a woman who soon dies on your heart and not that eternal star that you thirst for."[110]

But when this love could become legitimate, she makes no attempt to accomplish it in this world. For the Angel whispers to her:

"Prouhèze, my sister, luminous child of God whom I salute,

"Prouhèze whom the angels see and who does not know that he is watching, she it is whom you made so as to give her to him."[111]

She is human, she is woman, and she does not resign herself without revolt: "He will not know how I taste!"[112]

But she knows that her true marriage with Rodrigo is only consummated by her denial:

"When will there no longer be any way to escape, when he will be attached to me forever in an impossible marriage, when he will no longer find a way to wrench himself from the cry of my powerful flesh and that pitiless void, when I will have proved to him his nothingness and the nothingness of myself, when there will no longer be in his nothingness a secret that my secret cannot confirm.

"It is then that I shall give him to God, naked and torn, so that he may be filled in a blast of thunder, it is then that I will have a husband and clasp a god in my arms."[113]

---

110. *The Satin Slipper.*
111. Ibid.
112. Ibid.
113. Ibid.

Violaine's resolution is more mysterious and gratuitous still; for she chooses leprosy and blindness when a legitimate bond could have united her to the man she loves and who loves her.

"Jacques, perhaps

"We loved each other too much for it to be right for us to belong to each other, for it to be good to be each other's."[114]

But if women are so singularly devoted to saintly heroism, it is above all because Claudel still grasps them from a masculine perspective. To be certain, each of the sexes embodies the *Other* in the eyes of the complementary sex; but to his man's eyes it is, in spite of everything, the woman who is often regarded as an *absolute other*. There is a mystical surpassing insofar as "we know that in and of ourselves we are insufficient, hence the power of woman over us, like the power of Grace."[115] The "we" here represents only males and not the human species, and faced with their imperfection, woman is the appeal of infinity. In a way, there is a new principle of subordination here: by the communion of saints each individual is an instrument for all others; but woman is more precisely the instrument of salvation for man, without any reciprocity. *The Satin Slipper* is the epic of Rodrigo's salvation. The drama opens with a prayer his brother addresses to God on his behalf; it closes with the death of Rodrigo, whom Prouhèze has brought to saintliness. But, in another sense, the woman thereby gains the fullest autonomy: for her mission is interiorized in her, and in saving the man, or in serving as an example to him, she saves herself in solitude. Pierre de Craon prophesies Violaine's destiny to her, and he receives in his heart the wonderful fruits of her sacrifice; he will exalt her before mankind in the stones of cathedrals. But Violaine accomplishes it without help. In Claudel there is a mystique of woman akin to Dante's for Beatrice, to that of the Gnostics, and even to that of the Saint-Simonian tradition which called woman a regenerator. But because men and women are equally God's creatures, he also attributed an autonomous destiny to her. So that for him it is in becoming *other*—I am the Servant of the Lord—that woman realizes herself as subject; and it is in her for-itself that she appears as the Other.

There is a passage from *The Adventures of Sophie* that more or less sums up the whole Claudelian concept. God, we read, has entrusted to woman "this face which, however remote and deformed it may be, is a cer-

---

114. *The Young Violaine.*
115. *The Satin Slipper.*

tain image of his perfection. He has rendered her desirable. He has joined the end and the beginning. He has made her the keeper of his projects and capable of restoring to man that creative slumber in which even she was conceived. She is the foundation of destiny. She is the gift. She is the possibility of possession . . . She is the connection in this affectionate link that ever unites the Creator to his work. She understands him. She is the soul that sees and acts. She shares with Him in some way the patience and power of creation."

In a way, it seems that woman could not be more exalted. But deep down Claudel is only expressing in a poetic way a slightly modernized Catholic tradition. We have seen that the earthly vocation of woman does not cancel out any of her supernatural autonomy; on the contrary, in recognizing this, the Catholic feels authorized to maintain male prerogatives in this world. If the woman is venerated *in God*, she will be treated like a servant in this world: and further, the more total submission is demanded of her, the more surely will she move forward on the road to her salvation. Her lot, the lot the bourgeoisie has always assigned to her, is to devote herself to her children, her husband, her home, her realm, to country, and to church; man gives activity, woman her person; to sanctify this hierarchy in the name of divine will does not modify it in the least, but on the contrary attempts to fix it in the eternal.

IV. BRETON OR POETRY

In spite of the gulf separating Claudel's religious world and Breton's poetic universe, there is an analogy in the role they assign to women: she is an element that perturbs; she wrests man from the sleep of immanence; mouth, key, door, bridge, it is Beatrice initiating Dante into the beyond. "The love of man for woman, if we think for a moment about the palpable world, continues to fill the sky with gigantic and wild flowers. It is the most awful stumbling block for the mind that always feels the need to believe itself on safe ground." The love for an other, a woman, leads to the love of the Other. "It is at the height of elective love for a particular being that the floodgates of love for humanity open wide." But for Breton the beyond is not a foreign heaven: it is right here; it unveils itself if one knows how to lift the veils of everyday banality; eroticism, for one, dissipates the lure of false knowledge. "The sexual world, nowadays . . . has not stopped pitting its unbreakable core of night against our will to penetrate the universe." Colliding with the mystery is the only way of discovering it. Woman is enigma and poses enigmas; the addition of her multiple faces composes "the unique being in which we are granted the possibility of seeing the last metamorphosis of the Sphinx"; and that is why she is revelation. "You were the very image of secrecy," says Breton to a woman he loved. And a little farther: "That revelation you brought me: before I even knew what it consisted of, I knew it was a revelation." This means that woman is poetry. She plays that role in Gérard de Nerval as well: but in *Sylvie* and *Aurélia* she has the consistency of a memory or a phantom because the dream, more real than the real, does not exactly coincide with it; the coincidence is perfect for Breton: there is only one world; poetry is objectively present in things, and woman is unequivocally a being of flesh and bones. She can be found wide-awake and not in a half dream, in the middle of an ordinary day on a date like any other day on the calendar—April 5, April 12, October 4, May 29—in an ordinary setting: a café, a street corner. But she always stands out through some unusual feature. Nadja "carried her head high, unlike everyone else on the sidewalk . . . She was curiously made up . . . I had never seen such eyes." Breton approaches her. "She smiles, but quite mysteriously and somehow knowingly." In *L'amour fou* (*Mad Love*): "This young woman who just entered appeared to be swathed in mist—clothed in fire? . . . And I can certainly say that here, on the twenty-ninth of May 1934, this woman was *scandalously* beautiful."[116] The poet immediately admits she has a role to play in his destiny; at times this is a fleeting, secondary role, such as the child with Delilah's eyes in *Les vases communicants* (*Communicating Vessels*); even when tiny miracles emerge around her: the same day Breton has a rendezvous with this Delilah, he reads a good review written by a friend called Samson with whom he had not been in touch for a long time. Sometimes wonders occur; the unknown woman of May 29, Ondine, who had a swimming piece in her music-hall act, was presaged by a pun heard in a restaurant: "Ondine, one dines"; and her first long date with the poet had been described in great detail in a poem he wrote eleven years earlier. Nadja is the most extraordinary of these sorceresses: she predicts the future, and from her lips spring forth words and images her friend has in mind at the very same instant; her dreams and drawings are oracles: "I am the soul in limbo," she says; she went forward in life with "behavior, based as it was on the purest intuition alone and ceaselessly relying on miracle"; around her, objective chance spreads strange events; she is so marvelously liberated from appearances that she

---

116. Breton's italics.

scorns laws and reason: she ends up in an asylum. She is a "free genius, something like one of those spirits of the air which certain magical practices momentarily permit us to entertain but which we can never overcome." This prevents her from fulfilling her feminine role completely. Medium, prophetess, inspiration, she remains too close to the unreal creatures that visited Nerval; she opens the doors to the surreal world: but she is unable to give it because she could not give herself. Woman accomplishes herself and is really transformed in love; unique, accepting a unique destiny—and not floating rootless through the universe—so she is the sum of all. The moment her beauty reaches its highest point is at night, when "she is the perfect mirror in which everything that has been and everything that is destined to be is suffused adorably in what is going to be *this time*." For Breton "finding the place and the formula" is one with "possessing the truth within one soul and one body."* And this possession is only possible in reciprocal love, carnal love, of course. "The portrait of the woman one loves must be not only an image one smiles at but even more an oracle one questions"; but oracle only if this very woman is something other than an idea or an image; she must be the "keystone of the material world"; for the seer this is the same world as Poetry, and in this world he has to really possess Beatrice. "Reciprocal love alone is what conditions total magnetic attraction which nothing can affect, which makes flesh sun and splendid impression on the flesh, which makes spirit a forever-flowing stream, inalterable and alive whose water moves once and for all between marigold and wild thyme."

This indestructible love can only be unique. It is the paradox of Breton's attitude that from *Communicating Vessels* to *Arcanum 17,* he is determined to promise love both unique and eternal to different women. But according to him, it is social circumstances, thwarting the freedom of his choice, that lead man into erroneous choices; in fact, through these errors, he is really looking for *one* woman. And if he remembers the faces he has loved, he "will discover at the same time in all these women's faces one face only: the *last* face loved.[117] How many times, moreover, have I noticed that under extremely dissimilar appearances one exceptional trait was developing." He asks Ondine in *Mad Love:* "Are you at last this woman, is it only today you were to come?" But in *Arcanum 17:* "You know very well that

---

* Arthur Rimbaud, "Vagabonds," in *Illuminations,* and *"Adieu"* ("Farewell") in *Une saison en enfer* (*A Season in Hell*).—TRANS.
117. Breton's italics.

when I first laid eyes on you I recognized you without the slightest hesitation." In a completed, renewed world, the couple would be indissoluble, through an absolute and reciprocal gift: Since the beloved is all, how could there be any room for another? She is also this other; and all the more fully as she is more her self. "The unusual is inseparable from love. Because you are unique you can't help being for me always another, another you. Across the diversity of these inconceivable flowers over there, it is you over there changing whom I love in a red blouse, naked, in a gray blouse." And about a different but equally unique woman, Breton wrote: "Reciprocal love, such as I envisage it, is a system of mirrors which reflects for me, under the thousand angles that the unknown can take for me, the faithful image of the one I love, always more surprising in her divining of my own desire and more gilded with life."

This unique woman, both carnal and artificial, natural and human, casts the same spell as the equivocal objects loved by the surrealists: she is like the spoon-shoe, the table-magnifying glass, the sugar cube of marble that the poet discovers at the flea market or invents in a dream; she shares in the secret of familiar objects suddenly discovered in their truth, and the secret of plants and stones. She is all things:

> *My love whose hair is woodfire*
> *Her thoughts heat lightning*
> *Her hourglass waist . . .*
> *My love whose sex is*
> *Algae and sweets of yore . . .*
> *My love of savannah eyes.*

But she is Beauty, above and beyond every other thing. Beauty for Breton is not an idea one contemplates but a reality that reveals itself—and therefore exists—only through passion; only through woman does beauty exist in the world.

"And it is there—right in the depths of the human crucible, in this paradoxical region where the fusion of two beings who have really chosen each other renders to all things the lost colors of the times of ancient suns, where, however, loneliness rages also, in one of nature's fantasies which, around the Alaskan craters, demands that under the ashes there remain snow—it is there that years ago I asked that we look for a new beauty, a beauty 'envisaged exclusively to produce passion.' "

"Convulsive beauty will be veiled-erotic, fixed-explosive, magic-circumstantial, or it will not be."

It is from woman that everything that is derives meaning. "Love and love alone is precisely what the fusion of essence and existence realizes to the highest degree." It is accomplished for lovers and thus throughout the whole world. "The recreation, the perpetual recoloration of the world in a single being, such as they are accomplished through love, light up with a thousand rays the advance of the earth ahead." For all poets—or almost all—woman embodies nature; but for Breton, she not only expresses it: she delivers it. Because nature does not speak in a clear language, its mysteries have to be penetrated in order to grasp its truth, which is the same thing as its beauty: poetry is not simply the reflection of it but rather its key; and woman here cannot be differentiated from poetry. That is why she is the indispensable mediator without whom the whole earth would be silenced: "Nature is likely to light up and to fade out, to serve and not to serve me, only to the extent that I feel the rise and the fall of the fire of a hearth which is love, the only love, that for a single being . . . It was only lacking for a great iris of fire to emerge from me to give its value to what exists . . . I contemplate to the point of dizziness your hands opened above the fire of twigs which we just kindled and which is now raging, your enchanting hands, your transparent hands hovering over the fire of my life." Every woman loved is a natural wonder for Breton: "a tiny, unforgettable fern climbing the inside wall of an ancient well." "Something so blinding and serious that she could not but bring to mind . . . the great natural physical necessity while at the same time tenderly dreaming of the nonchalance of some tall flowers beginning to blossom." But inversely: every natural wonder merges with the beloved; he exalts her when he waxes emotional about a grotto, a flower, a mountain. Between the woman who warms his hands on a landing of Teide and Teide itself, all distance is abolished. The poet invokes both in one prayer: "Wonderful Teide, take my life! Mouth of the heavens and yet mouth of hell, I prefer you thus in your enigma, able to send natural beauty to the skies and to swallow up everything."

Beauty is even more than beauty; it fuses with "the deep night of knowledge"; it is truth and eternity, the absolute; woman does not deliver a temporal and contingent aspect of the world, she is the necessary essence of it, not a fixed essence as Plato imagined it, but a "fixed-explosive" one. "The only treasure I find in myself is the key that opens this limitless field since I have known you, this field made of the repetition of one plant, taller and taller, swinging in a wider and wider arc and leading me to death . . . Because one woman and one man, who until the end of time must be you and me, will drift in their turn without ever turning back as far as the path goes, in the optical glow, at the edges of life and of the oblivion of life . . . The greatest hope, I mean the one encompassing all the others, is that this be for all people, and that for all people this lasts, that the absolute gift of one being to another who cannot exist without his reciprocity be in the eyes of all the only natural and supernatural bridge spanning life."

Through the love she inspires and shares, woman is thus the only possible salvation for each man. In *Arcanum 17*, her mission spreads and takes shape: she has to save humanity. Breton has always been part of the Fourier tradition that, demanding rehabilitation of the flesh, exalts woman as erotic object; it is logical that he should come to the Saint-Simonian idea of the regenerating woman. In today's society, the male dominates to such an extent that it is an insult for someone like Gourmont to say of Rimbaud: "a girl's temperament." However, "the time has come to value the ideas of woman at the expense of those of man, whose bankruptcy is coming to pass fairly tumultuously today." "Yes, it is always the lost woman, she who sings in man's imagination, but after such trials for her and for him, it must also be the woman retrieved. And first of all, woman has to retrieve herself; she has to learn to recognize herself through the hells she is destined to by the more than problematic view that man, in general, carries of her."

The role she should fill is above all that of pacifier. "I've always been stupefied that she didn't make her voice heard, that she didn't think of taking every possible advantage, the immense advantage of the two irresistible and priceless inflexions given to her, one for talking to men during love, the other that commands all of a child's trust . . . What clout, what future would this great cry of warning and refusal from woman have had . . . When will we see a woman simply as woman perform quite a different *miracle* of extending her arms between those who are about to grapple to say: You are brothers." If woman today looks ill adapted or off balance, it is due to the treatment masculine tyranny has inflicted on her; but she maintains a miraculous power because her roots plunge deep into the wellspring of life whose secrets males have lost. "Melusina, half reclaimed by panic-stricken life, Melusina with lower joints of broken stones, aquatic plants or the down of a nest, she's the one I invoke, she's the only one I can see who could redeem this savage epoch. She's all of woman and yet woman as she exists today, woman deprived of her human base, prisoner of her mobile roots, if you will, but also through them in providential communication with nature's elemental forces. Woman deprived of her human base, legend has it, by the impatience and jealousy of man."

So today one has to be on woman's side; while waiting for her real worth to be restored to her, "Those of us in the arts must pronounce our-selves unequivocally against man and for woman." "The child-woman. Systematically art must prepare her advent into the empire of tangible things." Why child-woman? Breton explains: "I choose the child-woman not in order to oppose her to other women, but because it seems to me that in her and in her alone exists in a state of absolute transparency the *other* prism of vision."[118]

Insofar as woman is merely assimilated to a human being, she will be as unable as male human beings to save the doomed world; it is femininity as such that introduces this *other* element—the truth of life and poetry—into civilization, and that alone can free humanity.

As Breton's view is exclusively poetic, it is exclusively as poetry and thus as *Other* that woman is envisaged. If one were to ask about her own destiny, the response would be implied in the ideal of reciprocal love: her only vocation is love; this is in no way inferiority, since man's vocation is also love. However, one would like to know whether for her as well, love is the key to the world, the revelation of beauty; will she find this beauty in her lover? Or in her own image? Will she be capable of the poetic activity that makes poetry happen through a sentient being: or will she be limited to approving her male's work? She is poetry itself, in the immediate that is, for man; we are not told whether she is poetry for herself too. Breton does not speak of woman as subject. Nor does he ever evoke the image of the bad woman. In his work as a whole—in spite of a few manifestos and pam-phlets in which he vilifies the human herd—he focuses not on categorizing the world's superficial resistances but on revealing the secret truth: woman interests him only because she is a privileged "mouth." Deeply anchored in nature, very close to the earth, she also appears to be the key to the beyond. One finds in Breton the same esoteric naturalism as in the Gnostics who saw in Sophia the principle of redemption and even of creation, as in Dante choosing Beatrice for guide, or Petrarch illuminated by Laura's love. That is why the being most rooted in nature, the closest to the earth, is also the key to the beyond. Truth, Beauty, Poetry, she is All: once more all in the figure of the other, All except herself.

V. STENDHAL OR ROMANCING THE REAL

If now, leaving the present period, I return to Stendhal, it is because, leav-ing behind these carnivals where Woman is disguised as shrew, nymph,

118. Breton's italics.

morning star, or mermaid, I find it reassuring to approach a man who lives among flesh-and-blood women.

Stendhal loved women sensually from childhood; he projected the hopes of his adolescence onto them: he readily imagined himself saving a beautiful stranger and winning her love. Once he was in Paris, what he wanted the most ardently was a "charming wife; we will adore each other, she will know my soul." Grown old, he writes the initials of the women he loved the most in the dust. "I believe that dreaming was what I preferred above all," he admits. And his dreams are nourished by images of women; his memories of them enliven the countryside. "The line of rocks when approaching Arbois and coming from Dole by the main road was, I believe, a touching and clear image for me of Métilde's soul." Music, painting, architecture, everything he cherished, he cherished it with an unlucky lover's soul; while he is walking around Rome, a woman emerges at every turn of the page; by the regrets, desires, sadnesses, and joys women awakened in him, he came to know the nature of his own heart; it is women he wants as judges: he frequents their salons, he wants to shine; he owes them his greatest joys, his greatest pain, they were his main occupation; he prefers their love to any friendship, their friendship to that of men; women inspire his books, female figures populate them; he writes in great part for them. "I might be lucky enough to be read in 1900 by the souls I love, the Mme Rolands, the Mélanie Guilberts . . ." They were the very substance of his life. Where did this privilege come from?

This tender friend of women—and precisely because he loves them in their truth—does not believe in feminine mystery; there is no essence that defines woman once and for all; the idea of an eternal feminine seems pedantic and ridiculous to him. "Pedants have been repeating for two thousand years that women have quicker minds and men more solidity; that women have more subtlety in ideas and men more attention span. A Parisian passerby walking around the Versailles gardens once concluded that from everything he saw, the trees are born pruned." The differences that one notices between men and women reflect those of their situation. For example, how could women not be more romantic than their lovers? "A woman at her embroidery frame, insipid work that only involves her hands, dreams of her lover, who, galloping around the countryside with his troop, is put under arrest if he makes one false move." Likewise, women are accused of lacking common sense. "Women prefer emotions to reason; this is so simple: as they are not given responsibility for any family affair by virtue of our pedestrian customs, *reason is never useful to them* . . . Let your wife settle your affairs with the farmers on two of your lands, and I wager that the books are better kept than by you." If so few female geniuses are found in history, it is because society denies them any means of expression. "All the geniuses who are born *women* are lost for the public good; when chance offers them the means to prove themselves, watch them attain the most difficult skills."[119] The worst handicap they have to bear is the deadening education they are given; the oppressor always attempts to diminish those he oppresses; man intentionally refuses women their chances. "We allow their most brilliant qualities and the ones richest in happiness for themselves and for us to remain idle." At ten years of age, the girl is quicker, subtler than her brother; at twenty, the scamp is a quick-witted adult and the girl "a big awkward idiot, shy and afraid of a spider"; at fault is the training she has received. Women should be given exactly as much education as boys. Antifeminists object that cultured and intelligent women are monsters: the whole problem comes from the fact that they are still exceptional; if all women had equal access to culture as naturally as men, they would just as naturally take advantage of it. After having been mutilated, they are then subjected to laws against nature: married against their hearts, they are supposed to be faithful, and even divorce is reproached as wild behavior. A great number of them are destined to idleness when the fact is that there is no happiness without work. This condition scandalizes Stendhal, and therein he finds the source of all the faults blamed on women. They are neither angels nor demons nor sphinx: but human beings reduced to semi-slavery by idiotic customs.

It is precisely because they are oppressed that the best of them will avoid the faults that tarnish their oppressors; in themselves they are neither inferior nor superior to man: but by a curious reversal, their unfortunate situation works in their favor. It is well-known that Stendhal hates the spirit of seriousness:* money, honors, rank, and power are the saddest of idols to him; the immense majority of men alienate themselves in their pursuit; the pedant, the self-important man, the bourgeois, and the husband stifle in themselves any spark of life and truth; armed with preconceived ideas and learned feelings, obeying social routines, they are inhabited only by emptiness; a world populated with these creatures without a soul is a desert of boredom. There are unfortunately many women who stagnate in these dismal swamps; they are dolls with "narrow and Parisian ideas" or else self-righteous hypocrites; Stendhal experiences "a mortal disgust for decent women and the hypocrisy that is indispensable to them"; they bring to their

---

119. Stendhal's emphasis.

* *L'esprit de sérieux:* conventional thinking.—TRANS.

frivolous occupations the same seriousness that represses their husbands; stupid through education, envious, vain, talkative, mean through idleness, cold, emotionless, pretentious, harmful, they populate Paris and the provinces; they can be seen swarming about behind the noble figure of a Mme de Rênal or a Mme de Chasteller. The one Stendhal depicted with the most bitter care is undoubtedly Mme Grandet, the exact negative of a Mme Roland or a Métilde. Beautiful but expressionless, condescending and without charm, she intimidates by her "famous virtue" but does not know real modesty, which comes from the soul; full of admiration for self, imbued with her own personage, she only knows how to copy grandeur from the outside; deep down inside she is vulgar and inferior; "she has no character . . . she bores me," thinks M. Leuwen. "Perfectly reasonable, concerned by the success of her projects," she focuses all of her ambition on making her husband a minister; "her mind was arid"; careful and conformist, she always kept herself from love, she is incapable of a generous movement; when passion sets into this dry soul, it burns without illuminating her.

It is only necessary to reverse this image to discover what Stendhal asks of women: first, not to fall prey to the traps of seriousness; because the supposedly important things are out of their reach, women risk alienating themselves in them less than men; they have a better chance of preserving this natural side, this naïveté, this generosity that Stendhal places higher than any other merit; what he appreciates in them is what we would call today their authenticity: that is the common trait of all the women he loved or invented with love; all are free and true beings. For some, their freedom is strikingly visible: Angela Pietragrua, "sublime whore, Italian style, à la Lucrezia Borgia," and Mme Azur, "whore à la du Barry . . . one of the least doll-like French women that I have met," oppose social custom openly. Lamiel laughs at conventions, customs, and laws; Sanseverina throws herself ardently into the intrigue and does not stop at crime. Others rise above the vulgar through the vigor of their minds: like Menta or Mathilde de la Mole, who criticizes, denigrates, and scorns the society that surrounds her and wants to stand apart from it. For others, freedom takes a wholly negative form; what is remarkable in Mme de Chasteller is her indifference to everything secondary; subjected to her father's will and even his opinions, she still manages to contest bourgeois values by means of the indifference she is criticized for as childish, and that is the source of her carefree gaiety; Clélia Conti also stands apart by her reserve; balls and other traditional entertainments for girls leave her cold; she always seems distant "either out of scorn for what surrounds her or out of regret for

some missing chimera"; she judges the world, she takes offense at its indig-
nities. Mme de Rênal is the one whose soul's independence is the most
deeply hidden; she herself does not know she is not really resigned to her
lot; her extreme delicacy and acute sensitivity show her repugnance for her
milieu's vulgarity; she is without hypocrisy; she has kept a generous heart,
capable of violent emotions, and she has the taste for happiness; the fire that
smolders barely gives off any heat, but only a breath is needed for it to be
fully kindled. These women are, simply, *living;* they know the source of
real values is not in exterior things but in the heart; that is what makes the
charm of the world they inhabit: they chase away boredom merely by being
present with their dreams, desires, pleasures, emotions, and inventions.
Sanseverina, that "active soul," dreads boredom more than death. Stagnat-
ing in boredom "is preventing one from dying, she said, it is not living"; she
is "always totally involved in something, always active, always gay." Fool-
hardy, childish, or deep, gay or serious, reckless or secretive, they all refuse
the heavy sleep in which humanity sinks. And these women who have been
able to preserve their freedom, albeit unfulfilled, will rise up by passion to
heroism as soon as they meet an object worthy of them; their force of soul
and their energy attest to the fierce purity of total commitment.

But freedom alone would not be sufficient to endow them with so many
romantic attractions: a pure freedom inspires esteem but not emotion; what
is touching is their effort to accomplish themselves in spite of the obstacles
that beleaguer them; it creates even more pathos in women because the
struggle is more difficult. The victory over exterior constraints is sufficient
to enchant Stendhal; in *Chroniques italiennes* (*Three Italian Chronicles*) he
cloisters his heroines in remote convents, he locks them up in a jealous
spouse's palace: they have to invent a thousand tricks to meet their lovers;
secret doors, rope ladders, bloody chests, kidnappings, sequestrations, and
assassinations, the unleashing of passion and disobedience is served by an
ingenuity in which all the mind's resources are displayed; death and the
threat of tortures highlight even more the daringness of the deranged souls
he depicts. Even in his more mature work, Stendhal remains sympathetic to
this external expression of the romantic: it is the manifestation of the one
born from the heart; they cannot be distinguished from each other just as a
mouth cannot be separated from its smile. Clélia invents love anew by
inventing the alphabet that allows her to correspond with Fabrice; Sanseverina is described to us as "a soul always sincere who never acts with caution, who totally gives herself over to the impression of the moment"; it is
when she schemes, when she poisons the prince and floods Parma, that this
soul is revealed to us: she is no other than the sublime and mad escapade

that she has chosen to live. The ladder that Mathilde de la Mole leans against her window is much more than a prop: her proud recklessness, her penchant for the extraordinary, and her provocative courage take a tangible form. The qualities of these souls would not be revealed were they not surrounded by enemies: prison walls, a lord's will, and a family's harshness.

But the most difficult constraints to overcome are those that one finds in oneself: then the adventure of freedom is the most uncertain, the most poignant, and the most piquant. Clearly, the more often Stendhal's heroines are prisoners, the greater his sympathy for them. Yes, he enjoys whores—sublime or not—who have once and for all trampled on the conventions; but he cherishes Métilde more tenderly, restrained by her scruples and modesty. Lucien Leuwen is happy when near Mme d'Hocquincourt, that liberated person: but it is Mme de Chasteller, chaste, reserved, and hesitant, that he loves passionately; Fabrice admires the undivided soul of Sanseverina that stops at nothing; but he prefers Clélia, and it is the young girl who wins his heart. And Mme de Rênal, bound by her pride, her prejudices, and her ignorance, is perhaps the most astonishing of all the women Stendhal created. He readily places his heroines in the provinces, in a confined milieu, under the authority of a husband or a foolish father; it pleases him that they are uneducated and even full of false ideas. Mme de Rênal and Mme de Chasteller are both obstinately legitimist; the former is a timid mind and without experience, the latter is a brilliant intelligence, but she underestimates its worth; they are therefore not responsible for their errors, but they are the victims of them as much as of institutions and social customs; and it is from error that romance springs forth, as poetry is born from failure. A lucid mind that decides on its actions in full knowledge is approved or blamed coldly, whereas the courage and ruses of a generous heart seeking its way in the shadows are admired with fear, pity, irony, or love. It is because women are mystified that useless and charming qualities such as their modesty, pride, and extreme delicacy flourish; in one sense, these are defects: they lead to lies, susceptibilities, and anger, but they can be explained by the situation in which women are placed; it leads them to take pride in little things or at least in "things determined by feeling" because all the "supposedly important" objects are out of their reach; their modesty results from the dependence they suffer: because it is forbidden to them to show their worth in action, it is their very being that they put in question; it seems to them that the other's consciousness, and particularly that of their lover, reveals them in their truth: they are afraid, they try to escape it; in their evasions, their hesitations, their revolts, and even their lies, an authentic concern for worth is expressed; that is what makes them respectable; but it is expressed awkwardly, even with bad faith, and that makes them touching and even discreetly comic. When freedom is hoist by its own petard and cheats on itself, it is at the most deeply human and so in Stendhal's eyes at its most endearing. Stendhal's women are imbued with pathos when their hearts pose unexpected problems for them: no outside law, recipe, reasoning, or example can then guide them; they have to decide alone: this abandon is the extreme moment of freedom. Clélia is brought up with liberal ideas, she is lucid and reasonable: but learned opinions, whether right or wrong, are of no help in a moral conflict; Mme de Rênal loves Julien in spite of his morality, Clélia saves Fabrice in spite of herself: in both cases there is the same surpassing of all accepted values. This daring is what exalts Stendhal; but it is even more moving because it barely dares to declare itself: it is all the more natural, spontaneous, and authentic. In Mme de Rênal, boldness is hidden by innocence: because she does not know love, she does not recognize it and yields to it without resistance; one could say that having lived in darkness, she is defenseless against the violent light of passion; she welcomes it, blinded, even against God, against hell; when this fire goes out, she falls back in the shadows that husbands and priests govern; she does not trust her own judgment, but the evidence overwhelms her; as soon as she sees Julien again, she once more unburdens her soul to him; her remorse and the letter her confessor wrests from her show the distance this ardent and sincere soul had to span to tear herself away from the prison society enclosed her in and accede to the heaven of happiness. The conflict is more conscious for Clélia; she hesitates between loyalty to her father and pity inspired by love; she is searching for a rationale; the triumph of the values in which Stendhal believes is all the more striking to him in that this triumph is experienced as a defeat by the victims of a hypocritical civilization; and he delights in seeing them use ruses and bad faith to make the truth of passion and happiness prevail against the lies in which they believe: Clélia, promising the Madonna to no longer *see* Fabrice, and accepting his kisses and his embraces for two years, providing she closes her eyes, is both laughable and heartbreaking. Stendhal considers Mme de Chasteller's hesitations and Mathilde de la Mole's inconsistencies with the same tender irony; so many detours, changes of mind, scruples, victories, and hidden defeats in order to reach simple and legitimate ends is for him the most delightful of comedies; there is drollery in these dramas because the actress is both judge and party, because she is her own dupe, and because she burdens herself with complicated paths where a decree would suffice for the Gordian knot to be cut; but they nonetheless show the most respectable concern that could torture a noble soul: she wants to remain worthy of her own esteem; she places her own approbation higher than that of others, and thus she realizes herself as an absolute. These solitary debates without reverberation have more gravity than a ministerial crisis; when she wonders if she is going to respond to Lucien Leuwen's love or not, Mme de Chasteller decides for herself and the world: Can one have confidence in others? Can one trust one's own heart? What is the value of love and human vows? Is it mad or generous to believe and to love? These questions challenge the very meaning of life, that of each and every one. The so-called important man is futile, in fact, because he accepts ready-made justifications of his life, while a passionate and deep woman revises established values at each instant; she knows the constant tension of an unassisted freedom; thus she feels herself in constant danger: she can win or lose everything in a second. It is this risk, accepted with apprehension, that gives her story the color of a heroic adventure. And the stakes are the highest that can be: the very meaning of this existence of which everyone has a share, his only part. Mina de Vanghel's escapade can seem absurd in one sense; but she brings to it a whole ethic. "Was her life a false calculation? Her happiness lasted eight months. She had too ardent a soul to settle for the real life." Mathilde de la Mole is less sincere than Clélia or Mme de Chasteller; she orders her acts on the idea she has of herself rather than on the evidence of love and happiness: Is it more arrogant, grander to keep oneself than to lose oneself, to humiliate oneself before one's beloved than to resist him? She is alone with her doubts, and she risks this self-esteem that is more important to her than life itself. It is the ardent quest for the real reasons to live through the shadows of ignorance, prejudice, and mystifications, in the wavering and feverish light of passion, it is the infinite risk of happiness or death, of grandeur or shame that gives romantic glory to these women's destinies.

The woman is of course unaware of the seduction she radiates; self-contemplation and playacting are always inauthentic attitudes; by the mere fact of comparing herself to Mme Roland, Mme Grandet proves she does not resemble her; if Mathilde de la Mole continues to be endearing, it is because she gets confused in her playacting and is often prey to her heart just when she thinks she governs it; she moves us insofar as she is not ruled by her will. But the purest of heroines lack consciousness of themselves. Mme de Rênal is unaware of her grace just as Mme de Chasteller is of her intelligence. It is one of the deep joys of the lover with whom the author and the reader identify: he is the witness through whom these secret riches are revealed; the vivacity Mme De Rênal deploys out of everyone's sight, the "bright wit, changing and deep," unknown to Mme de Chasteller's milieu, he alone admires them; and even if others appreciate Sanseverina's wit, he is the one who penetrates the deepest into her soul. Faced with the woman, the man tastes the pleasure of contemplation; she intoxicates him like a landscape or a painting; she sings in his heart and lights up the sky. This revelation reveals him to himself: one cannot understand women's delicacy, their sensibilities, and their ardor without developing a delicate, sensitive, and ardent soul oneself; female feelings create a world of nuances and requirements whose discovery enriches the lover: when with Mme de Rênal, Julien becomes someone other than the ambitious man he had decided to be; he chooses himself anew. If the man has only a superficial desire for the woman, he will find seducing her amusing. But it is real love that will transfigure his life. "Love à la Werther opens the soul . . . to feeling and pleasure in the *beautiful* in whatever form it takes, even in a hair shirt. It makes happiness attainable even without wealth." "It is a new aim in life to which everything is connected and that changes the appearance of everything. Love-as-passion throws in man's eyes all of nature with its sublime aspects as if it were a novelty invented yesterday." Love shatters daily routine, chases away boredom, the boredom in which Stendhal sees such a deep evil because it is the absence of all the reasons for living or dying; the lover has an aim, and that is enough for each day to become an adventure: what a pleasure for Stendhal to spend three days hidden in Menta's cellar! Rope ladders and bloody chests represent this taste for the extraordinary in his novels. Love, that is woman, reveals the real ends of existence: beauty, happiness, the freshness of feelings and of the world. It tears man's soul out and thus gives him possession of it; the lover experiences the same tension, the same risks, as his mistress and feels himself more authentically than during a planned career. When Julien hesitates at the base of the ladder Mathilde has set up, he puts his whole destiny into question: in that very moment, he demonstrates his true worth. It is through women, under their influence, in reaction to their behavior, that Julien, Fabrice, and Lucien learn about the world and themselves. Test, reward, judge, or friend, the woman in Stendhal is really what Hegel was once tempted to make of her: that other consciousness that, in reciprocal recognition, gives to the other subject the same truth it receives from it. The happy couple that recognizes each other in love defies the universe and time; it is sufficient in itself, it realizes the absolute.

But this supposes that woman is not pure alterity: she is subject herself. Stendhal never describes his heroines as a function of his heroes: he provides them with their own destinies. He undertook something rarer and that no other novelist, I think, has ever done: he projected himself into a female character. He does not examine Lamiel as Marivaux does Marianne, or Richardson does Clarissa Harlowe: he shares her destiny as he had shared that of Julien. Precisely because of that, the character of Lamiel is singularly significant, if somewhat theoretical. Stendhal sets up all imaginable obstacles around the girl: she is a peasant, poor, ignorant, and brought up harshly by people imbued with every prejudice; but she eliminates from her path all the moral barriers the day she understands the scope of these little words: "It's stupid." Her mind's freedom enables her to take responsibility for all the movements of her curiosity, her ambition, her gaiety; faced with such a resolute heart, material obstacles cannot fail to decrease; her only problem will be to carve out a destiny worthy of her in a mediocre world. That destiny accomplishes itself in crime and death: but that is also Julien's lot. There is no place for great souls in society as it is: men and women are in the same boat.

It is remarkable that Stendhal is both so profoundly romantic and so decidedly feminist; feminists are usually rational minds that adopt a universal point of view in all things; but it is not only in the name of freedom in general but also in the name of individual happiness that Stendhal calls for women's emancipation. Love, he thinks, will have nothing to lose; on the contrary, it will be all the truer that woman, as the equal of man, will be able to understand him more completely. Undoubtedly, some of the qualities one enjoys in woman will disappear: but their value comes from the freedom that is expressed in them and that will show in other guises; and the romantic will not fade out of this world. Two separate beings, placed in different situations, confronting each other in their freedom, and seeking the justification of existence through each other, will always live an adventure full of risks and promises. Stendhal trusts the truth; as soon as one flees it, one dies a living death; but where it shines, so shine beauty, happiness, love, and a joy that carries in it its own justification. That is why he rejects the false poetry of myths as much as the mystifications of seriousness. Human reality is sufficient for him. Woman, according to him, is simply a human being: dreams could not invent anything more intoxicating.

VI

These examples show that the great collective myths are reflected in each singular writer: woman appears to us as *flesh*; male flesh is engendered by the maternal womb and re-created in the woman lover's embrace: thus, woman is akin to *nature*, she embodies it: animal, little vale of blood, rose in bloom, siren, curve of a hill, she gives humus, sap, tangible beauty, and the world's soul to man; she can hold the keys to *poetry;* she can be *mediator* between this world and the beyond: grace or Pythia, star or witch, she opens the door to the supernatural, the surreal; she is destined to *immanence;* and through her passivity she doles out peace and harmony: but should she refuse this role, she becomes praying mantis or ogress. In any case, she appears as the *privileged Other* through whom the subject accomplishes himself: one of the measures of man, his balance, his salvation, his adventure, and his happiness.

But these myths are orchestrated differently for each individual. The *Other* is singularly defined according to the singular way the *One* chooses to posit himself. All men assert themselves as freedom and transcendence: but they do not all give the same meaning to these words. For Montherlant transcendence is a state: he is the transcendent, he soars in the sky of heroes; the woman crouches on the ground, under his feet; he enjoys measuring the distance separating him from her; from time to time, he raises her to him, takes and then rejects her; never does he lower himself toward her sphere of viscous darkness. Lawrence situates transcendence in the phallus; the phallus is life and power only thanks to woman; immanence is thus good and necessary; the false hero who deigns not to touch the earth, far from being a demigod, fails to be a man; woman is not despicable, she is deep wealth, hot spring; but she must renounce all personal transcendence and settle for nourishing that of her male. Claudel demands the same devotion: woman is also for him the one who maintains life, while man prolongs the vital momentum by his activity; but for the Catholic everything that occurs on earth is steeped in vain immanence: the only transcendent is God; in God's eyes the active man and the woman who serves him are exactly equal; each one has to surpass his earthly condition: salvation in any case is an autonomous undertaking. For Breton sexual hierarchy is inverted; action and conscious thought in which the male situates his transcendence are for him a banal mystification that engenders war, stupidity, bureaucracy, and negation of the human; it is immanence, the pure opaque presence of the real, that is the truth; true transcendence would be accomplished by the return to immanence. His attitude is the exact opposite of Montherlant's: the latter likes war because women are banished from it, Breton venerates woman because she brings peace; one confuses mind and subjectivity, he rejects the given universe; the other thinks the mind is objectively present in the heart of the world; woman compromises Montherlant because she shatters his solitude; she is, for Breton, revelation because she wrests him from subjectivity. As for Stendhal, we saw that woman barely takes on a mythical value for him: he considers her as also being a transcendence; for this humanist, it is in their reciprocal relations that freedoms are accomplished; and it is sufficient that the *Other* is simply another for life to have, according to him, a little spice; he does not seek a stellar equilibrium, he does not nourish himself with the bread of disgust; he does not expect miracles; he wishes to concern himself not with the cosmos or poetry but with freedoms.

That is, he also experiences himself as a translucent freedom. The others—and this is one of the most important points—posit themselves as transcendences but feel they are prisoners of an opaque presence in their own hearts: they project onto woman this "unbreakable core of night." In Montherlant there is an Adlerian complex where heavy bad faith is born: these pretensions and fears are what he incarnates in woman; the disgust he feels for her is what he fears to feel for himself; he intends to trample in her the ever possible proof of his own insufficiency; he asks scorn to save him; woman is the ditch in which he throws all the monsters that inhabit him.[120] Lawrence's life shows us that he suffered from an analogous complex but more purely sexual: woman in his work has the value of a compensatory myth; through her is found an exalted virility of which the writer was not very sure; when he describes Kate at Don Cipriano's feet, he believes he has won a male triumph over Frieda; nor does he accept that his female companion challenges him: if she contested his aims, he would probably lose confidence in them; her role is to reassure him. He asks for peace, rest, and faith from her, just as Montherlant asks for the certitude of his superiority: they demand what they lack. Self-confidence is not lacking in Claudel: if he is shy, it is only the secret of God. Thus, there is no trace of the battle of the sexes. Man bravely takes on the weight of woman: she is the possibility of temptation or of salvation. For Breton it seems that man is only true through the mystery that inhabits him; it pleases him that Nadja sees that star he is going toward and that is like "a heartless flower"; his dreams, intuitions, and the spontaneous unfolding of his inner language: it is in these activities that are out of the control of will and reason that he recognizes himself: woman is the tangible figure of this veiled presence infinitely more essential than her conscious personality.

---

120. Stendhal judged in advance the cruelties with which Montherlant amuses himself: "In indifference, what should be done? Love-taste, but without the horrors. The horrors always come from a little soul that needs reassurance of its own merits."

As for Stendhal, he quietly coincides with himself; but he needs woman as she does him so that his dispersed existence is gathered in the unity of a figure and a destiny; it is as for-another that the human being reaches being; but another still has to lend him his consciousness: other men are too indifferent to their peers; only the woman in love opens her heart to her lover and shelters it in its entirety. Except for Claudel, who finds a perfect witness in God, all the writers we have considered expect, in Malraux's words, woman to cherish in them this "incomparable monster" known to themselves alone. In collaboration or combat, men come up against each other in their generality. Montherlant, for his peers, is a writer, Lawrence a doctrinaire, Breton a leader of a school, Stendhal a diplomat or a man of wit; it is women who reveal in one a magnificent and cruel prince, in another a disturbing animal, in still another a god or a sun or a being "black and cold . . . like a man struck by lightning, lying at the feet of the Sphinx,"[121] and in the other a seducer, a charmer, a lover.

For each of them, the ideal woman will be she who embodies the most exactly the *Other* able to reveal him to himself. Montherlant, the solar spirit, looks for pure animality in her; Lawrence, the phallic, demands that she sum up the female sex in its generality; Claudel defines her as a soul sister; Breton cherishes Melusina rooted in nature, he puts his hopes in the child-woman; Stendhal wants his mistress intelligent, cultivated, free of spirit and morals: an equal. But the only earthly destiny reserved to the woman equal, child-woman, soul sister, woman-sex, and female animal is always man. Regardless of the ego looking for itself through her, it can only attain itself if she consents to be his crucible. In any case, what is demanded of her is self-forgetting and love. Montherlant consents to be moved by the woman who enables him to measure his virile power; Lawrence addresses an ardent hymn to the woman who renounces herself for him; Claudel exalts the vassal, servant, and devoted woman who submits herself to God by submitting herself to the male; Breton puts his hopes in woman for humanity's salvation because she is capable of the most total love for her child and her lover; and even in Stendhal the heroines are more moving than the masculine heroes because they give themselves over to their passion with a more ardent violence; they help man to accomplish his destiny as Prouhèze contributes to Rodrigo's salvation; in Stendhal's novels, women often save their lovers from ruin, prison, or death. Feminine devotion is demanded as a duty by Montherlant and Lawrence; less arro-

---

121. *Nadja.*

gant, Claudel, Breton, and Stendhal admire it as a generous choice; they desire it without claiming to deserve it; but—except for the astonishing *Lamiel*—all their works show they expect from woman this altruism that Comte admired in and imposed on her, and which, according to him, also constituted both a flagrant inferiority and an equivocal superiority.

We could find many more examples: they would always lead to the same conclusions. In defining woman, each writer defines his general ethic and the singular idea he has of himself: it is also in her that he often registers the distance between his view of the world and his egotistical dreams. The absence or insignificance of the female element in a body of work in general is itself symptomatic; it has an extreme importance when it sums up in its totality all the aspects of the Other, as it does for Lawrence; it remains important if woman is grasped simply as another but the writer is interested in her life's individual adventure, which is Stendhal's case; it loses importance in a period like ours in which each individual's particular problems are of secondary import. However, woman as other still plays a role inasmuch as even to transcend himself, each man still needs to take consciousness of himself.

The myth of woman plays a significant role in literature; but what is its importance in everyday life? To what extent does it affect individual social customs and behavior? To reply to this question, we will need to specify the relation of this myth to reality.

There are different kinds of myths. This one, sublimating an immutable aspect of the human condition—that is, the "division" of humanity into two categories of individuals—is a static myth; it projects into a Platonic heaven a reality grasped through experience or conceptualized from experience; for fact, value, significance, notion, and empirical law, it substitutes a transcendent Idea, timeless, immutable, and necessary. This idea escapes all contention because it is situated beyond the given; it is endowed with an absolute truth. Thus, to the dispersed, contingent, and multiple existence of *women*, mythic thinking opposes the Eternal Feminine, unique and fixed; if the definition given is contradicted by the behavior of real flesh-and-blood women, it is women who are wrong: it is said not that Feminin-ity is an entity but that women are not feminine. Experiential denials cannot do anything against myth. Though in a way, its source is in experi-ence. It is thus true that woman is other than man, and this alterity is con-cretely felt in desire, embrace, and love; but the real relation is one of reciprocity; as such, it gives rise to authentic dramas: through eroticism, love, friendship, and their alternatives of disappointment, hatred, and rivalry, the relation is a struggle of consciousnesses, each of which wants to be essential, it is the recognition of freedoms that confirm each other, it is the undefined passage from enmity to complicity. To posit the Woman is to posit the absolute Other, without reciprocity, refusing, against experi-ence, that she could be a subject, a peer.

In concrete reality, women manifest themselves in many different ways; but each of the myths built around woman tries to summarize her as a whole; each is supposed to be unique; the consequence of this is a multiplicity of incompatible myths, and men are perplexed before the strange inconsistencies of the idea of Femininity; as every woman enters into many of these archetypes, each of which claims to incarnate its Truth alone, men also find the same old confusion before their companions as did the Sophists, who had difficulty understanding how a person could be light and dark at the same time. The transition to the absolute shows up in social representations: relations are quickly fixed in classes, and roles in types, just as, for the childlike mentality, relations are fixed in things. For example, patriarchal society, focused on preserving the patrimony, necessarily implies, in addition to individuals who hold and transmit goods, the existence of men and women who wrest them from their owners and circulate them; men—adventurers, crooks, thieves, speculators—are generally repudiated by the group; women using their sexual attraction can lure young people and even family men into dissipating their patrimony, all within the law; they appropriate men's fortunes or seize their inheritance; this role being considered bad, women who play it are called "bad women." But in other families—those of their fathers, brothers, husbands, or lovers—they can in fact seem like guardian angels; the courtesan who swindles rich financiers is a patroness of painters and writers. The ambiguity of personalities like Apasia and Mme de Pompadour is easy to understand as a concrete experience. But if woman is posited as the Praying Mantis, the Mandrake, or the Demon, then the mind reels to discover in her the Muse, the Goddess Mother, and Beatrice as well.

As group representation and social types are generally defined by pairs of opposite terms, ambivalence will appear to be an intrinsic property of the Eternal Feminine. The saintly mother has its correlation in the cruel stepmother, the angelic young girl has the perverse virgin: so Mother will be said sometimes to equal Life and sometimes Death, and every virgin is either a pure spirit or flesh possessed by the devil.

It is obviously not reality that dictates to society or individuals their choices between the two opposing principles of unification; in every period, in every case, society and individual decide according to their needs. Very often they project the values and institutions to which they adhere onto the myth they adopt. Thus paternalism that calls for woman to stay at home defines her as sentiment, interiority, and immanence; in fact, every existent is simultaneously immanence and transcendence; when he is offered no goal, or is prevented from reaching any goal, or denied the victory of it, his transcendence falls uselessly into the past, that is, it falls into immanence; this is the lot assigned to women in patriarchy; but this is in no way a vocation, any more than slavery is the slave's vocation. The development of this mythology is all too clear in Auguste Comte. To identify Woman with Altruism is to guarantee man absolute rights to her devotion; it is to impose on women a categorical must-be.

The myth must not be confused with the grasp of a signification; signification is immanent in the object; it is revealed to consciousness in a living experience, whereas the myth is a transcendent Idea that escapes any act of consciousness. When Michel Leiris in *L'âge d'homme* (*Manhood*) describes his vision of female organs, he provides significations and does not develop a myth. Wonder at the feminine body and disgust for menstrual blood are apprehensions of a concrete reality. There is nothing mythical in the experience of discovering the voluptuous qualities of feminine flesh, and expressing these qualities by comparisons to flowers or pebbles does not turn them into myth. But to say that Woman is Flesh, to say that Flesh is Night and Death, or that she is the splendor of the cosmos, is to leave terrestrial truth behind and spin off into an empty sky. After all, man is also flesh for woman; and woman is other than a carnal object; and for each person and in each experience the flesh is takes on singular significations. It is likewise perfectly true that woman—like man—is a being rooted in nature; she is more enslaved to the species than the male is, her animality is more manifest; but in her as in him, the given is taken on by existence; she also belongs to the human realm. Assimilating her with Nature is simply a prejudice.

Few myths have been more advantageous to the ruling master caste than this one: it justifies all its privileges and even authorizes taking advantage of them. Men do not have to care about alleviating the suffering and burdens that are physiologically women's lot since they are "intended by Nature"; they take this as a pretext to increase the misery of the woman's condition—for example, by denying woman the right to sexual pleasure, or making her work like a beast of burden.[1]

Of all these myths, none is more anchored in masculine hearts than the feminine "mystery." It has numerous advantages. And first it allows an easy explanation for anything that is inexplicable; the man who does not "understand" a woman is happy to replace his subjective deficiency with an objective resistance; instead of admitting his ignorance, he recognizes the

---

1. Cf. Balzac, *Physiology of Marriage:* "Do not trouble yourself in any way about her murmurings, her cries, her pains; nature has made her for your use, made her to bear all: the children, the worries, the blows, and the sorrows of man. But do not accuse us of harshness. In the codes of all the so-called civilised nations, man has written the laws which rule the destiny of woman beneath this blood inscription: *Vae victis!* Woe to the vanquished."

presence of a mystery exterior to himself: here is an excuse that flatters his laziness and vanity at the same time. An infatuated heart thus avoids many disappointments: if the loved one's behavior is capricious, her remarks stupid, the mystery serves as an excuse. And thanks to the mystery, this negative relation that seemed to Kierkegaard infinitely preferable to positive possession is perpetuated; faced with a living enigma, man remains alone: alone with his dreams, hopes, fears, love, vanity; this subjective game that can range from vice to mystical ecstasy is for many a more attractive experience than an authentic relation with a human being. Upon what bases does such a profitable illusion rest?

Surely, in a way, woman is mysterious, "mysterious like everyone," according to Maeterlinck. Each one is subject only for himself; each one can grasp only his own self in his immanence; from this point of view, the other is always mystery. In men's view, the opacity of the for-itself is more flagrant in the feminine other; they are unable to penetrate her unique experience by any effect of sympathy; they are condemned to ignorance about the quality of woman's sexual pleasure, the discomforts of menstruation, and the pains of childbirth. The truth is that mystery is reciprocal: as another, and as a masculine other, there is also a presence closed on itself and impenetrable to woman in the heart of every man; she is without knowledge of male eroticism. But according to a universal rule already mentioned, the categories in which men think the world are constituted from *their point of view as absolutes:* they fail to understand reciprocity here as everywhere. As she is mystery for man, woman is regarded as mystery in herself.

It is true that her situation especially disposes her to be seen in this image. Her physiological destiny is very complex; she herself endures it as a foreign story; her body is not for her a clear expression of herself; she feels alienated from it; the link that for every individual joins physiological to psychic life—in other words, the relation between the facticity of an individual and the freedom that assumes it—is the most difficult enigma brought about by the human condition: for woman, this enigma is posed in the most disturbing way.

But what is called mystery is not the subjective solitude of consciousness, or the secret of organic life. The word's true meaning is found at the level of communication: it cannot be reduced to pure silence, to obscurity, to absence; it implies an emerging presence that fails to appear. To say that woman is mystery is to say not that she is silent but that her language is not heard; she is there, but hidden beneath veils; she exists beyond these uncertain appearances. Who is she? An angel, a demon, an inspiration, an actress? One supposes that either there are answers impossible to uncover or none is adequate because a fundamental ambiguity affects the feminine being; in her heart she is indefinable for herself: a sphinx.

The fact is, deciding *who* she *is* would be quite awkward for her; the question has no answer; but it is not that the hidden truth is too fluctuating to be circumscribed: in this area there is no truth. An existent *is* nothing other than what he does; the possible does not exceed the real, essence does not precede existence: in his pure subjectivity, the human being *is nothing*. He is measured by his acts. It can be said that a peasant woman is a good or bad worker, that an actress has or does not have talent: but if a woman is considered in her immanent presence, absolutely nothing can be said about that, she is outside of the realm of qualification. Now, in amorous or conjugal relations and in all relations where woman is the vassal, the Other, she is grasped in her immanence. It is striking that the woman friend, colleague, or associate is without mystery; on the other hand, if the vassal is male and if, in front of an older and richer man or woman, a young man, for example, appears as the inessential object, he also is surrounded in mystery. And this uncovers for us an infrastructure of feminine mystery that is economic. A sentiment cannot *be* something, either. "In the domain of feeling, what is real is indistinguishable from what is imaginary," writes Gide. "And it is sufficient to imagine one loves, in order to love, so it is sufficient to say to oneself that when one loves one imagines one loves, in order to love a little less." There is no discriminating between the imaginary and the real except through behavior. As man holds a privileged place in this world, he is the one who is able actively to display his love; very often he keeps the woman, or at least he helps her out; in marrying her, he gives her social status; he gives her gifts; his economic and social independence permits his endeavors and innovations: separated from Mme de Villeparisis, M. de Norpois takes twenty-four-hour trips to be with her; very often he is busy and she is idle: he *gives* her the time he spends with her; she takes it: with pleasure, passion, or simply for entertainment? Does she accept these benefits out of love or out of one interest? Does she love husband or marriage? Of course, even the proof man gives is ambiguous: Is such a gift given out of love or pity? But while normally woman finds numerous advantages in commerce with man, commerce with woman is profitable to man only inasmuch as he loves her. Thus, the degree of his attachment to her can be roughly estimated by his general attitude, while woman barely has the means to sound out her own heart; according to her moods she will take different points of view about her own feelings, and as long as she submits to them passively, no interpretation will be truer than another. In the very rare cases where it is she who holds the economic and social privileges, the mystery is reversed: this proves that it is not linked to *this* sex rather than to the other but to a situation. For many women, the roads to transcendence are blocked: because they *do* nothing, they do not make themselves *be* anything; they wonder indefinitely what they *could have* become, which leads them to wonder what they *are:* it is a useless questioning; if man fails to find that secret essence, it is simply because it does not exist. Kept at the margins of the world, woman cannot be defined objectively through this world, and her mystery conceals nothing but emptiness.

Furthermore, like all oppressed people, woman deliberately dissimulates her objective image; slave, servant, indigent, all those who depend upon a master's whims have learned to present him with an immutable smile or an enigmatic impassivity; they carefully hide their real feelings and behavior. Woman is also taught from adolescence to lie to men, to outsmart, to sidestep them. She approaches them with artificial expressions; she is prudent, hypocritical, playacting.

But feminine Mystery as recognized by mythical thinking is a more profound reality. In fact, it is immediately implied in the mythology of the absolute Other. If one grants that the inessential consciousness is also a transparent subjectivity, capable of carrying out the cogito, one grants that it is truly sovereign and reverts to the essential; for all reciprocity to seem impossible, it is necessary that the Other be another for itself, that its very subjectivity be affected by alterity; this consciousness, which would be alienated as consciousness, in its pure immanent presence, would obviously be a Mystery; it would be a Mystery in itself because it would be it for itself; it would be absolute Mystery. It is thus that, beyond the secrecy their dissimulation creates, there is a mystery of the Black, of the Yellow, insofar as they are considered absolutely as the inessential Other. It must be noted that the American citizen who deeply confounds the average European is nonetheless not considered "mysterious": one more modestly claims not to understand him; likewise, woman does not always "understand" man, but there is no masculine mystery; the fact is that rich America and the male are on the side of the Master, and Mystery belongs to the slave.

Of course, one can only dream about the positive reality of the Mystery in the twilight of bad faith; like certain marginal hallucinations, it dissolves once one tries to pin it down. Literature always fails to depict "mysterious" women; they can only appear at the beginning of a novel as strange and enigmatic; but unless the story remains unfinished, they give up their secret in the end and become consistent and translucent characters.

The heroes in Peter Cheyney's books, for example, never cease to be amazed by women's unpredictable caprices; one can never guess how they will behave, they confound all calculations; in truth, as soon as the work-ings of their actions are exposed to the reader, they are seen as very simple mechanisms: this one is a spy or that one a thief; however clever the intrigue, there is always a key, and it could not be otherwise, even if the author had all the talent, all the imagination possible. Mystery is never more than a mirage; it vanishes as soon as one tries to approach it.

Thus we see that myths are explained in large part by the use man makes of them. The myth of the woman is a luxury. It can appear only if man escapes the imperious influence of his needs; the more relations are lived concretely, the less idealized they are. The fellah in ancient Egypt, the bedouin peasant, the medieval artisan, and the worker of today, in their work needs and their poverty, have relations with the particular woman who is their companion that are too basic for them to embellish her with an auspicious or fatal aura. Eras and social classes that had the leisure to day-dream were the ones who created the black-and-white statues of feminin-ity. But luxury also has its usefulness; these dreams were imperiously guided by interest. Yes, most myths have their roots in man's spontaneous attitude to his own existence and the world that invests it: but the move to surpass experience toward the transcendent Idea was deliberately effected by patriarchal society for the end of self-justification; through myths, this society imposed its laws and customs on individuals in an imagistic and sensible way; it is in a mythical form that the group imperative insinuated itself into each consciousness. By way of religions, traditions, language, tales, songs, and film, myths penetrate even into the existence of those most harshly subjected to material realities. Everyone can draw on myth to sub-limate his own modest experiences: betrayed by a woman he loves, one man calls her a slut; another is obsessed by his own virile impotence: this woman is a praying mantis; yet another takes pleasure in his wife's com-pany: here we have Harmony, Repose, Mother Earth. The taste for eternity at bargain prices and for a handy, pocket-sized absolute, seen in most men, is satisfied by myths. The least emotion, a small disagreement, become the reflection of a timeless Idea; this illusion comfortably flatters one's vanity.

The myth is one of those traps of false objectivity into which the spirit of seriousness falls headlong. It is once again a matter of replacing lived experience and the free judgments of experience it requires by a static idol. The myth of Woman substitutes for an authentic relationship with an autonomous existent the immobile contemplation of a mirage. "Mirage! Mirage! Kill them since we cannot seize them; or else reassure them, instruct them, help them give up their taste for jewelry, make them real equal companions, our intimate friends, associates in the here and now, dress them differently, cut their hair, tell them everything," cried Laforgue. Man would have nothing to lose, quite the contrary, if he stopped disguising woman as a symbol. Dreams, when collective and controlled—clichés—are so poor and monotonous compared to living reality: for the real dreamer, for the poet, living reality is a far more generous resource than a worn-out fantasy. The times when women were the most sincerely cherished were not courtly feudal ones, nor the gallant nineteenth century; they were the times—the eighteenth century, for example—when men regarded women as their peers; this is when women looked truly romantic: only read *Les liaisons dangereuses* (*Dangerous Liaisons*), *Le rouge et le noir* (*The Red and the Black*), or *A Farewell to Arms* to realize this. Laclos' heroines like Stendhal's and Hemingway's are without mystery: and they are no less engaging for it. To recognize a human being in a woman is not to impoverish man's experience: that experience would lose none of its diversity, its richness, or its intensity if it was taken on in its intersubjectivity; to reject myths is not to destroy all dramatic relations between the sexes, it is not to deny the significations authentically revealed to man through feminine reality; it is not to eliminate poetry, love, adventure, happiness, and dreams: it is only to ask that behavior, feelings, and passion be grounded in truth.[2]

"Woman is lost. Where are the women? Today's women are not women"; we have seen what these mysterious slogans mean. In the eyes of men—and of the legions of women who see through these eyes—it is not enough to have a woman's body or to take on the female function as lover and mother to be a "real woman"; it is possible for the subject to claim autonomy through sexuality and maternity; the "real woman" is one who accepts herself as Other. The duplicitous attitude of men today creates a painful split for women; they accept, for the most part, that woman be a peer, an equal; and yet they continue to oblige her to remain the inessential; for her, these two destinies are not reconcilable; she hesitates between them without being exactly suited to either, and that is the source of her lack of balance. For man, there is no hiatus between public and private life: the more he asserts his grasp on the world through action and work, the more virile he looks; human and vital characteristics are merged in him; but women's own successes are in contradiction with her femininity since the

---

2. Laforgue goes on to say about woman: "As she has been left in slavery, idleness, without arms other than her sex, she has overdeveloped it and has become the Feminine . . . we have permitted her to overdevelop; she is on the earth for us . . . Well, that is all wrong . . . we have played doll with the woman until now. This has gone on too long!"

"real woman" is required to make herself object, to be the Other. It is very possible that on this point even men's sensibility and sexuality are changing. A new aesthetic has already been born. Although the fashion for flat chests and narrow hips—the boyish woman—only lasted a short while, the opulent ideal of past centuries has nevertheless not returned. The feminine body is expected to be flesh, but discreetly so; it must be slim and not burdened with fat; toned, supple, robust, it has to suggest transcendence; it is preferred tanned, having been bared to a universal sun like a worker's torso, not white like a hothouse plant. Woman's clothes, in becoming more practical, have not made her look asexual: on the contrary, short skirts have shown off her legs and thighs more than before. There is no reason for work to deprive her of her erotic appeal. To see woman as both a social person and carnal prey can be disturbing: in a recent series of drawings by Peynet,[3] there is a young fiancé deserting his fiancée because he was seduced by the pretty mayoress about to celebrate the marriage; that a woman could hold a "man's office" and still be desirable has long been a subject of more or less dirty jokes; little by little, scandal and irony have lost their bite and a new form of eroticism seems to be coming about: perhaps it will produce new myths.

What is certain is that today it is very difficult for women to assume both their status of autonomous individual and their feminine destiny; here is the source of the awkwardness and discomfort that sometimes leads them to be considered "a lost sex." And without doubt it is more comfortable to endure blind bondage than to work for one's liberation; the dead, too, are better suited to the earth than the living. In any case, turning back is no more possible than desirable. What must be hoped is that men will assume, without reserve, the situation being created; only then can women experience it without being torn. Then will Laforgue's wish be fulfilled: "O young women, when will you be our brothers, our closest brothers without ulterior motives of exploitation? When will we give to each other a true handshake?" Then "Melusina, no longer under the burden of the fate unleashed on her by man alone, Melusina rescued," will find "her human base."[4] Then will she fully be a human being, "when woman's infinite servitude is broken, when she lives for herself and by herself, man—abominable until now—giving her her freedom."[5]

---

3. November 1948.

4. Breton, *Arcanum 17*.

5. Rimbaud, to Paul Demeny, May 15, 1871.

Lived Experience

What a curse to be a woman! And yet the very worst curse when one is a woman is, in fact, not to understand that it is one.

—KIERKEGAARD

Half victim, half accomplice, like everyone.

—J.-P. SARTRE

Introduction

Women of today are overthrowing the myth of femininity; they are beginning to affirm their independence concretely; but their success in living their human condition completely does not come easily. As they are brought up by women, in the heart of a feminine world, their normal destiny is marriage, which still subordinates them to man from a practical point of view; virile prestige is far from being eradicated: it still stands on solid economic and social bases. It is thus necessary to study woman's traditional destiny carefully. What I will try to describe is how woman is taught to assume her condition, how she experiences this, what universe she finds herself enclosed in, and what escape mechanisms are permitted her. Only then can we understand what problems women—heirs to a weighty past, striving to forge a new future—are faced with. When I use the word "woman" or "feminine," I obviously refer to no archetype, to no immutable essence; "in the present state of education and customs" must be understood to follow most of my affirmations. There is no question of expressing eternal truths here, but of describing the common ground from which all singular feminine existence stems.